AMERICAN

JUVENILE

JUSTICE

AMERICAN

JUVENILE

JUSTICE

Franklin E. Zimring

OXFORD
UNIVERSITY PRESS

2005

OXFORD
UNIVERSITY PRESS

Oxford University Press, Inc., publishes works that further
Oxford University's objective of excellence
in research, scholarship, and education.

Oxford   New York
Auckland   Cape Town   Dar es Salaam   Hong Kong   Karachi
Kuala Lumpur   Madrid   Melbourne   Mexico City   Nairobi
New Delhi   Shanghai   Taipei   Toronto

With offices in
Argentina   Austria   Brazil   Chile   Czech Republic   France   Greece
Guatemala   Hungary   Italy   Japan   Poland   Portugal   Singapore
South Korea   Switzerland   Thailand   Turkey   Ukraine   Vietnam

Copyright © 2005 by Oxford University Press, Inc.

Published by Oxford University Press, Inc.
198 Madison Avenue, New York, New York 10016

www.oup.com

Oxford is a registered trademark of Oxford University Press

Library of congress Cataloging-in-Publication Data
Zimring, Franklin E.
American juvenile justice / Franklin E. Zimring
p. cm.
ISBN-13 978-0-19-518116-6; 978-0-19-518117-3 (pbk.)
ISBN 0-19-518116-6; 0-19-518117-4 (pbk.)
1. Juvenile justice, Administration of—United States. 2. Juvenile
delinquency—Government policy—United States. 3. Juvenile
Courts—United States. I. Title.
HV9104.Z575   2005
364.36'0973—dc22   2005001816

9 8 7 6 5 4 3 2 1

Printed in the United States of America
on acid-free paper

To Michal avec amour

Acknowledgments

Writing a book on the installment plan is a process that requires both good luck and a variety of institutional and personal supports to complete. The major institutional support for the work that appears in these pages came first from the John D. and Catherine T. MacArthur Foundation and then from the Research Network on Adolescent Development and Juvenile Justice that the foundation created. Grants from the foundation supported my work on youth violence and juvenile court history, which produced four chapters in this book. The Research Network commissioned three further essays—on transfer to criminal court, penal proportionality for young offenders and minority overrepresentation in juvenile justice—that sustain this book's attempt to bridge the gap between legal theory and detailed policy analysis. Laurie Garduque of the MacArthur Foundation facilitated the foundation's support of my work. Laurence Steinberg, the head of the Research Network, was the architect of the edited volumes that were the first home of the policy essays. Jeffery Fagan of Columbia University coauthored chapter 7 and helped shape most of my recent research on juvenile violence.

Dedi Felman of Oxford University Press encouraged the project and made a multitude of helpful editorial suggestions that pushed the volume toward a general readership and away from the polysyllabic and opaque vocabulary of the wrong kind of academic.

Permission to reprint comes from Oxford University Press for chapters 8, 12, and 13; Northwestern University for chapter 6, which is reprinted by special permission of the *Journal of Criminal Law and Criminology*; Rutgers University Press for chapter 9, which was first published in *Early Parenthood and Coming of Age in the 1990s*, edited by Margaret Rosenheim and Mark Testa, © 1992; and the University of Chicago Press for chapters 4, 5, and 10, which are © 2000 and 2002 by the University of Chicago.

Anyone familiar with my disorderly lifestyle knows that the physical organization of this kind of effort came from the kindness of others. Dianne Christianson of the University of California, Irvine, helped launch this effort, and Toni Mendicino of the Earl Warren

Legal Institute at Boalt Hall kept the project and the manuscript together. Jamie Popper and Judith Randle provided research assistance as the final touches of this project were applied. My largest personal debt in the years when most of this work emerged is to Michal Crawford Zimring.

Contents

Introduction

The juvenile court of the twenty-first century displays a puzzling contrast between the wide popularity of its institutions and the lack of broadly accepted theoretical justifications for its separate functions. Invented in 1899 in Illinois, this American idea has achieved a worldwide popularity larger than any other Anglo-American innovation. There are juvenile courts throughout the world, and the American model is the basic structure emulated in a vast number of legal systems in both the developed and developing world.

But this most successful of American legal innovations has been without a formal jurisprudence since the U.S. Supreme Court issued its decision in *In re Gault* in 1967. The original theory of governmental beneficence and childhood dependence that *Gault* rejected almost four decades ago has not been replaced with any substantial framework of basic legal principles. For my entire professional life, the delinquency jurisdiction of juvenile justice has been a practice in search of a theory, an important challenge to theorists and practitioners to provide a sound legal theory for juvenile courts, and to apply such a theory consistently in confronting the large variety of policy problems that crop up in modern practice. What are the basic reasons for a separate court for young offenders? How should these principles produce policy on teenage pregnancy? On transfer to criminal courts? On gun access for minors? On punishment of 16-year-olds who kill?

For some time now, I have been writing a book on the installment plan on the relations between principle and practice in American juvenile justice. A cluster of essays on individual topics pursued over the last decade turns out also to be a larger project, a book about the theoretical foundations of a separate legal system for juvenile offenders. Here is that book!

This book is about four closely connected topics. The first is the emergence of adolescence as a distinctive legal and social phenomenon in the United States. Everything we debate about juvenile justice is a consequence of the special problems and ambitions of legal policy toward adolescent development. The first section of this book provides three short essays on adolescence as a legal concept and as a stage of development.

The second major topic is the general legal policy of juvenile courts toward adolescents who violate legal rules, the jurisprudence of delinquency in American juvenile courts. Part II contains two essays that attempt to summarize the legal theories and policy priorities of responding to delinquents. This is my version of the theoretical core of juvenile justice in America.

The third major concern of this book is the empirical reality of modern youth crime. Chapter 6 shows the distinctive importance of group involvement in adolescent crime. Chapter 7 (coauthored with Jeffrey Fagan) traces the increase and decrease in arrest rates during youth and adulthood for a variety of different offenses. Chapter 8 shows the uses and abuses of demographic projections in predicting levels of youth crime.

The fourth major concern is creating strategies of policy analysis for selecting appropriate legal rules. Part IV collects policy profiles of issues as diverse as transfer of juveniles to criminal court, teenage pregnancy, legal policy toward adolescent handgun ownership and use, penalties for young offenders who kill, and correcting the harms of minority overrepresentation in juvenile justice. The chapters in this section apply the general perspectives and statistical learning of the first parts of the book to different types of policy choice.

Drawing all of these essays into a single collection serves three purposes. First, it attempts to demonstrate the virtues of empirically informed legal theory as a way of evaluating juvenile justice policy. Second, this collection can be used as teaching materials for courses in juvenile justice that all too often lack any sustained legal theory content. Third, the cumulative impact of these essays approaches a systemic theory of juvenile justice, or at least comes as close to that as my style of thinking permits.

AMERICAN

JUVENILE

JUSTICE

Part I

ADOLESCENCE: SOCIAL FACTS AND LEGAL THEORY

At some point in Anglo-American legal history, it may have been reasonable to divide the legal status of persons merely into children and adults, and to withhold any recognition of legal autonomy until the age of adulthood was reached, but that time was long removed from the twentieth century. There are two reasons why modern legal systems must recognize a minor's autonomy long before he or she has finished growing up. The first reason is that the later stages of childhood now involve big, strong, and sophisticated young people for whom a wholly dependent legal status is plainly inappropriate. The second reason we must give adolescents the power to make some independent choices before they are fully mature is that the only way to learn how to be free is through the experience of making choices.

The three short chapters collected in this introductory part concern the historical development of and legal justification for adolescence as a period of development when kids begin to be given the power to make choices on their own. Chapter 1 shows how social developments during the twentieth century changed the location and content of the experience of adolescence. While children become better educated and somewhat more mobile at a young age, the period of expected education expanded from common school to high school. The 15- and 16-year-olds in high school were neither wholly dependent children requiring adult supervision in every detail of their lives nor fully autonomous adults.

Chapter 2 argues for the central importance of free choice in the process of growing up in a free society. The only way that young persons can learn to make their own decisions is to acquire experience in making choices. We thus must provide the young with some practice in free choice before they are fully mature. Chapter 3 shows how various legal strategies can cope with the fact that different kids grow up at different times.

Why begin a book on juvenile justice with materials on the content of modern adolescence? The relationship of privilege, maturity, and responsibility is central to modern arguments about the proper age for penal responsibility, as chapter 2 illustrates. Further, policy toward adolescence is central to every decision that concerns the delinquency jurisdiction of American juvenile courts.

ONE

Childhood and Public Law before the Revolution

When a comprehensive history of the United States in the 1970s is written, it will report that in 1974 Congress passed a law designed to persuade the states that 14- and 15-year-old boys and girls should not be detained in secure institutions that much resemble prisons because they disobey their parents or absent themselves from school.[1] Implementation of this legislation proved controversial.

That law, and many other recent reforms, cannot be comprehended without reference to the theories and institutions that preceded it. How did it come to pass that children who disobey their parents could be locked up in "state training schools"? What legal theory of adolescence could justify such an intervention? What kind of policy was being pursued? The theory was one of public responsibility for childhood care, custody, and discipline. The policy pursued was that the welfare of the children became the responsibility of the state. This theory of state responsibility was a liberal reform widely acclaimed and pursued with sincerity by a number of admirable figures.

This chapter will argue that recent changes in law were a delayed reaction to changes in the social meaning of adolescence throughout the twentieth century. I begin by describing briefly the institutions and mission of the child-saving movement at the turn of the century, passing next to the theory of youth that supported these reforms, the "jurisprudence of juvenility." Finally, I survey the changes in the social meanings of adolescence that forced the legal reforms of recent years.

Child Saving

The formal justification for the child protective reforms of the early twentieth century was a doctrine of *parens patriae,* a construction only loosely related to earlier common law doctrine.[2] This new theory, dominant for most of the twentieth century, rested on three postulates, as follows: (1) that childhood is a period of dependency and risk in which supervision is essential for survival; (2) that the family is of primary importance in the supervision of children, but the state should play a primary role in the education of children and intervene forcefully whenever the family setting fails to provide adequate nurture, moral training, or supervision; and (3) that when a child is at risk, the appropriate authority to decide what is in the child's best interest is a public official.

The institutions that gave expression to this theory included public schools, juvenile courts, public and private agencies of philanthropy, youth groups such as the Boy Scouts, and institutions for the housing and training of the young. Most of these institutions had historical antecedents, but the public optimism of the "progressive era" provided a mandate for expansion and change. Some form of public grade school education was common at the turn of the century, but fewer than 7 percent of all 17-year-olds graduated from high school in 1900.[3] Juvenile reformatories and child-oriented urban philanthropic outposts had an extensive nineteenth-century pedigree.

New legislation gave these institutions a twentieth-century mandate and a legitimating legal philosophy. Public institutions were to provide what boys and girls needed: training and control. The public common school was to provide basic training; soon, the public high school was enlisted as a supplement, and the age of compulsory education was increased. By 1940, 51 percent of all adolescents finished high school; by 1960, the percentage had increased to 63.[4]

The juvenile court was to pursue child welfare when children were at risk by using the agencies of state government to ensure that "the care, custody and discipline of the child shall approximate . . . that which should be given by its parents."[5] This most famous excerpt from the Juvenile Court Act of 1899 was the goal of the new state role in child rearing.

Public schools, public values, parents, and voluntary agencies would get the job done in most cases. When these institutions were insufficient to the task, the juvenile court would intervene.

This new court for children was granted jurisdiction in cases where minors were found to be neglected, dependent, or delinquent. If a child was at risk and it was the family's fault, that child was neglected. If the child was at risk and it was nobody's fault, he or she was dependent. If the child had committed a crime, or was in danger of leading an immoral life, or wasn't attending school, he or she was delinquent. The end result of this new legislation was quite simple: no matter what the cause, no matter who was at fault, state power could and should be invoked to save children. In theory, the particular label that justified state intervention had no relevance to the state's mission: the objective of the juvenile court was to provide assistance to all children within its jurisdiction. The degree of state intervention lay within the discretion of the judge. Wide discretion, broad jurisdictional categories, and informal processes were of central importance in furthering the purposes of the new legislation. The broader the definitions of delinquency, dependency, and neglect, the more kids would be eligible for aid. Since no children were to be punished, there was no need to distinguish between criminal and noncriminal acts in designating a child as "delinquent." And because the court was to be guided solely by the child's best interest, formal processes of fact finding were viewed as unnecessary.

This set of assumptions continued to inform the jurisprudence of juvenile courts through most of the 1900s. The basic nomenclature and jurisdictional rubrics of the original legislation remained almost intact during the first two-thirds of the twentieth century. Meanwhile, juvenile justice emerged as a major industry in every American state.[6]

The conceptions of family and youth that emerge from the expansive state role in child rearing deserve separate attention. The presumed governmental role in the supervision of children during the progressive era bears a striking resemblance to the allocation of power created during that period for other regulated industries. Families, like railroads, were free to pursue private motives only insofar as they adhered to public standards. For families, this meant standards of child welfare. Consumer interests, in this case those of children, were to be protected by administrative agencies operating within broad grants of discretionary power. But three instances where the analogy between railroad regulation and family regulation might break down also prove instructive.

First, the discretion of most regulatory agencies was far more structured and regularized than that exercised by teachers, principals, juvenile court judges, and probation officers. Except in the schools, there was little rule-making. There were very few rules of general applicability in the juvenile court; individualized justice meant individualized decisions.

Second, it was assumed that the state was taking power from the corporate world when it regulated railroads. The redistribution of power envisioned by the authors of family regulation was more complicated. In matters such as compulsory education, power was taken from both parent and child. Broad definitions of neglect were chiefly a reallocation from family decision-making to public standards. Regulation of adolescents "beyond control" came principally at the expense of the child, who could previously vote with his or her feet. State power to treat "ungovernable children" thus enhanced parental power: it added a powerful "or else" to the phrase "you had better behave."[7]

Third, in the case of education, the proper analogy is state enterprise rather than regulation. In the progressive view, family choice was to play a minimal role in primary education. The government's near monopoly of institutions of education was viewed as a positive— not merely necessary—aspect of child welfare. Thus, the ideology of public education was that of special-case socialism, at a time when socialism was a dirty word. And it was a rather authoritarian socialism at that, particularly with regard to the children it was to serve.[8]

The Jurisprudence of Juvenility

The image of the adolescent in public law was one of absolute dependency. This was the case, for "unemancipated" minors, in a great variety of settings. It is most obvious in the jurisprudence of the new court for children.

In Professor Robert Burt's phrase, the court was pursuing rights *for* children, intervening whether or not the particular minor wanted help, if that minor needed help.[9] In pursuing rights for children, the juvenile court was to do what was best for the child with or without his or her consent. To honor the rights of the child, by contrast, would have meant allowing a minor's will to prevail over the opinions of others in determining where his or her own best interests might lie.

In choosing between the child's will and his or her welfare, the philosophy of the juvenile court was unambiguous and consistent. The "minor" who was the subject of the juvenile court's concern was immature and thus in need of coercive guidance for his or her best interest. Delivering "care, custody and supervision," after all, requires a hell of a lot of power. The child's immaturity was viewed as outweighing both his or her will—and thus his or her responsibility—and crime control considerations in determining appropriate responses to young persons who violated the law, at least in theory.

The same image of immaturity and need for supervision justified the age-specific prohibitions and duties that were later to be labeled "status offenses." Minors could not drink, smoke, willfully absent themselves from school, or stay out late, since they were regarded as too young to exercise appropriate judgments in these matters. The young could not disobey their parents, educators, or the court, because such disobedience would put the child's welfare at risk. In the mindset of the original reformers, what was called "the right to custody" was the central factor in child welfare; the custodial agent was expected to subordinate the minor's wants to the minor's needs.

Much has been written about the motives of those who were responsible for this dependent image of youth, and about the institutions and constraints this philosophy justified. It has been noted that the values of the "child saving" movement were based on middle-class images of youth that "denied . . . [young people] the option of withdrawing from or changing the institutions that governed their lives."[10] And there is ample evidence that expansive state power was used to pursue punitive as well as protective agendas from the earliest days of juvenile courts and extended compulsory schooling. Child labor laws were early conceived of as ways to protect not only children but also adult jobs and wages.

But it is a flight of fancy to view the progressive era child-savers as part of an antiyouth cabal. Many of the key figures of child welfare and juvenile court movements were sincerely dedicated to youth welfare. It is difficult, even with the hindsight provided by history, to fault the motives of Jane Addams, a prominent advocate of the new court. And while his attitude toward youth might be called "middle class," Denver's Judge Ben Lindsey, the "Johnny Appleseed" of the juvenile court movement, was in reality a muckraking champion of the poor and the working class throughout the period he served as supersalesman for the children's court. Early in the century he became the eighth-most-admired man in America—a distinction as yet unequaled by any other member of the juvenile judiciary. He preached the virtues of community treatment, probation, and a juvenile court fueled by optimistic compassion.[11]

The Annual Report of Judge Lindsey's court contains compelling evidence of people caring about children. At least that is my reading of table 1.1.

Table 1.1. Loving the American Delinquent: "Facts and Figures" from the
Annual Report of the Denver Juvenile Court, 1903.

1903	Total
Number of reports from probationers received from school teachers during the year	2,275
Total reports received (each report represents a personal interview between the Judge of the Court and probationer)	3,139
Baths given probationers during the year	1,150
Positions secured during the year	252
Boys sent to the beet fields for the summer	77
Needy children relieved	175
Number of garments supplied (second hand)	175
Number of garments supplied (new)	220
Total garments supplied	395

Source: Report of the Denver Juvenile Court (1903).

Thus, evidence of early twentieth-century romantic and authoritarian images of youth should not be taken at face value by the historian or the law reformer. In fact, early reformers were not unmindful of the values of youth autonomy. Many of those who sought the establishment of juvenile courts, compulsory public education, and child labor laws did use the rhetoric of helplessness and dependency in arguing for an awakened public conscience and increased public investment in youth services. But many of the same reformer-professionals recognized the value of self-reliance in adolescents and of the exercise of independent judgment when dealing with kids.[12]

The darker side of this gap between rhetoric and reality concerned the treatment of 14-year-old armed robbers and twice-convicted burglars. Writing in 1909, Judge Julian Mack declared that the purpose of the juvenile court was "not so much to punish as to reform, not to degrade but to uplift, not to crush but to develop, not to make him a criminal but a worthy citizen.[13] But two years earlier, the annual report of Judge Mack's juvenile court reminded us:

> All right-minded people are willing to have boys and girls have chances to do the right thing, but after they persistently throw chances away the same people would have a right to insist that these young people be really controlled, even if it takes the criminal court process to do it.[14]

Judge Lindsey struck a more authentic chord in drafting legislation providing that "as far as practicable any delinquent child should be treated, not as a criminal, but as misdirected and misguided and needing aid, encouragement, and help and assistance."[15]

What Lindsey had in mind from the start was the protection of youth "as far as practicable." In the case of young burglars, we have spent decades, and will doubtless spend decades more, discussing just how far that is.

There is one further factor that is indispensable to understanding what I have called the jurisprudence of juvenility. The "boys and girls" who were the objects of public education and juvenile court control near the beginning of this century were younger than the current clientele of these institutions. Compulsory education spanned, at its inception, only the primary school years. High school graduation was a mark of distinction. The jurisdiction of Judge Lindsey's juvenile court ended at the sixteenth birthday, and the peak age for delinquency referral in Denver in 1903 was 12.[16]

By the time the revolution in juvenile justice was launched, we were living in a world where almost everyone went to high school, and the juvenile court's delinquency jurisdiction had been elevated in the majority of American states to the eighteenth birthday.

Just before the "Revolution"

The most amazing feature of the dependent legal theory of youth was not so much its early twentieth-century innocence as its capacity to persist unmolested in the face of rapid social and political change. What I have called the jurisprudence of juvenility was not merely a quaint feature of the early 1900s; it was the dominant legal conception of the teen years well into the 1960s. The social dimensions of adolescence changed dramatically through the first six decades of the twentieth century, but the legal image of growing up in the years just preceding adulthood remained static. Most of the distinctive features of modern adolescence developed without any major change in legal theory.

Consider the following short list of some social changes during this period of legal immobility.

High School and College

At the turn of the century, fewer than one out of twelve males would graduate from high school and less than 5 percent of the population between 18 and 22 attended college. By 1960, well over 60 percent of all American teenagers graduated from high school, more than half continued education at the college level, and 41 percent of the population between 18 and 21 were still pursuing some form of higher education by 1965.[17]

The social and economic impact of this shift cannot be overstated. In post-midcentury society, a high school diploma was a minimum condition for respectable entry into the work force. The high school "dropout" in metropolitan areas was marked with a social stigma only slightly less onerous than that associated with a criminal record. And high school was more than a credential; it was thousands of hours spent away from home or work in the age-segregated institution that spawned the "adolescent society."[18] The social demand for high school and college training also lengthened the period of economic dependency for those who in earlier years would have already entered the world of work.

Urbanization

In 1900, three-quarters of our population under 20 lived in rural areas, or towns under 25,000. The pace of urbanization was swift as the century progressed, as shown in figure 1.1.

Where kids grow up has a substantial impact on how they grow up and what kinds of adults they aspire to become. In the decades after 1920, dramatic migration occurred in the United States, as a predominantly rural and small-town populace shifted to cities and suburbs of metropolitan areas.

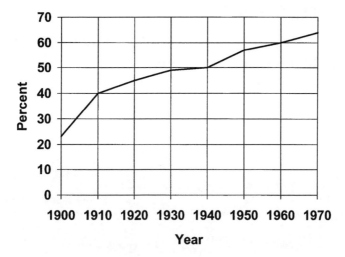

Figure 1.1. Percent of population under 20 living in urban areas, 1900–1975. *Source:* U.S. Bureau of the Census, *Decennial Census Reports,* from 1900 to 1970.

The "Family" Car and the "Family" Telephone

The telephone and the automobile were turn-of-the-century luxuries. By the late 1920s, both were transforming the character of American middle-class life, including the life patterns of the middle-class teenagers.[19] By 1960, the "average" American family couldn't be average without one or more telephones and one or more cars. Figure 1.2 tells the statistical story.

As the 1950s ended, there were four telephones and four cars for every 10 people in the United States, more than one per household. Well before this point, telephones and cars had become standard accessories to the American teen years, each important and together overpowering. The family telephone provides a means of leaving home while staying put, a method of reaching the outside world that favors communication outside the nuclear family to the detriment of communication within the family.

But the telephone had a relatively weak influence on adolescent development compared to that of the family car (or cars) and the teenage culture that revolved around access to the automobile. A car is not merely a means of leaving home; it *is* a mobile home for the kid lucky enough to have one, or to have a friend with one. And "four

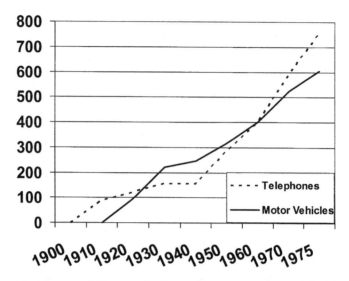

Figure 1.2. Motor vehicles and telephones per 1,000 people, 1900–1975. *Source:* For motor vehicles, U.S. Bureau of Highways, *Highway Statistics–1975* (Washington, DC: Government Printing Office, 1977) and U.S. Bureau of the Census, *Historical Statistics of the United States, Colonial Times to 1970* and *Statistical Abstract of the United States 1976* (Washington, DC: Government Printing Office). For telephones, U.S. Bureau of the Census, op. cit.

cars for every 10 people" suggests a nation with millions of lucky kids. The availability of cars rearranged adolescent life patterns in ways that had profound impact on parental control over teenage behavior. Consider, for one example, the consequences in metropolitan areas of shifting the arena of sexual experiment from the front parlor to the back seat of Dad's car!

For present purposes, it will not be necessary to discuss the additional impact of two world wars, radio, television, enormous growth in median family income, residential mobility, suburban development, the New Deal, the changing role of women, the baby boom, or the atomic age. By the mid-1950s, all of these and more had contributed to what sociologists were calling "the adolescent society." This was and is a social order in which kids look to other kids as much as to their parents for habits, values, and aspirations. It is a form of social organization in which 90 percent of urban high school boys interviewed in one study did not want to have the same kind of job that Dad held.[20]

And all of these changes took place before the legal changes that are the subject of this chapter. While the legal theory of youthful dependency stood still, the essential elements of modern adolescence fell into place: prolonged economic dependence, age segregation, and tremendous physical mobility. In the period after World War II, the terms "teenager" and "peer group" entered our language to stay. The mixture of power and dependence that is the essence of semi-autonomy had become a fixture of American society by midcentury. Family controls had weakened to the point where a whole generation of kids could run away from home without packing a suitcase.

How such momentous change could leave the essential legal conception of youth untouched is a puzzle I will not attempt to resolve. The central point of my argument from history is this: the legal changes I will study here were reactions to changes in social reality that had been in process for some time. Often there is a tendency to regard rapid legal changes as attempts by courts and legislatures to play leadership roles in reshaping the social order. In this instance, it is more accurate to view the 15 years after 1967 as a period in which the law attempted to catch up with the world, to fashion solutions for problems that had grown out of a half-century of social change.

But what's wrong with paternalism? Why shouldn't teachers be able to order kids to get haircuts? When all else fails, isn't it proper to lock up a 15-year-old who refuses to go to school? The following chapters attempt to provide a contemporary explanation of how we have come to appreciate the values of liberty and limits of bureaucratic paternalism.

Modern Adolescence as a Learner's Permit

Here are a few of the things we cannot learn to do well without practice: making decisions, making love, driving, flying, practicing law, parenting, taking risks, saying no, and—most important—choosing the path of our lives in a free society.

Being mature takes practice. To know this is to suppose still another justification for extending privileges in public law and family life to those who have not yet reached full maturity. We gamble when we extend choices to the not-yet-adult. If we win, the experience gained in decision-making becomes an integral part of a process of achieving adulthood. If we lose, harm can come to the adolescent and the community. But in positing contemporary adolescence as a "learner's permit" period of life, we can learn much about the dimensions of public policy that this kind of gambling requires.

Choice, Change, and Adolescent Liberty

In all societies, many of the skills of adulthood can best be achieved by adults training the young. In traditional societies, the skills, rituals, and roles are passed on from the adult to the child in family, clan, or tribal settings. If the skills and social meanings of adulthood are uniform and stable, the entire transition to adulthood can be programmed by an adult society in an orderly fashion.[1] The Amish farmer trains his children, and all is well, as long as the children remain on the farm. This is particularly the case when there is consensus about what types of adults individual children should become. If every boy wants to be "just like Dad" and every girl the spitting image of her mother, adult roles can be taught at low tuition, beginning at an early age. If nine out of ten kids don't wish to be "just like" their parents, life gets more complicated.

Today's high specialization and rapid change make training the young a more difficult and more specialized task.[2] The skills of one generation are generally not those that will be required of the next. But the larger society can provide more centralized training for social change, particularly if the nature of the change in adult roles can be anticipated. If parents are "inappropriate role models," other adults can be used to program the young for a very different future. This strategy was part of the agenda of the compulsory public high school movement during the Progressive era.[3] More recently, societies with less respect for individual liberty than ours have performed more radical experiments in training for change.[4]

But how do we train young people to be *free?* If the exercise of independent choice is an essential element of maturity, part of the process of becoming mature is learning to make independent decisions. This type of liberty cannot be taught; it can only be learned. And learning to make independent judgments is inevitably a risky process for the pupil and the larger society.

As in any gambling enterprise, we wish to maximize our gains and keep our losses small. The stakes are high.

And the calculus for determining" gains" and "losses" is somewhat more complicated than cursory inspection would suggest. In blackjack, an ideal "career" is never to lose a hand. In the game of learning to make free choices, winning every hand is poor preparation for the modern world, just as winning every hand is a terrible way to learn to play blackjack. We want adolescents to make mistakes, but we hope they make the right kinds of mistakes. An unsuccessful date may teach our child important lessons about his or her relations with the opposite sex at a far lower cost than an unsuccessful marriage.

An important part of cutting our losses during this period of development is minimizing the harm young persons do themselves, and keeping to a minimum the harm we inflict on them when they have abused opportunities in ways that harm the community. Above almost all else, we seek a legal policy that preserves the life chances for those who make serious mistakes, as well as preserving choices for their more fortunate (and more virtuous) contemporaries.

This learner's permit perspective is a splendid illustration of the limits of law as an instrument of social change. Nothing I have said has addressed the question of *when* our children should grow up. That is a question, hotly contested by theoreticians, which is in an important sense beyond the control of the state legislature. At present, we endure enormous social costs because so much "learning by experience" is centered in adolescence.[5] Some take this as evidence that youth is wasted on the young and learning experiences should be postponed.[6] Others preach that the best way of dispersing the process of learning by experience is to teach some of life's lessons earlier.[7] These two perspectives may in fact be consistent rather than contradictory. Some learning might occur earlier in a social universe that would also postpone certain more permanent decisions until later in life.

But one cannot legislate maturity. And our opportunities to control legally when children begin to "commit experience" are limited in the short run both by the mobility of kids and by the values of adult freedom and liberal Western democracy. Peer orientation, foolhardy attitudes toward risk, and the powerful combination of social immaturity and physical mobility make middle adolescence into a minefield. But the costs of attempting to defer learning periods beyond these years are also substantial, and the fact that many of the negative characteristics of adolescence are, in Arlene Skolnick's words, "merely social" makes them even less susceptible to legal control.[8]

To ask how old is old enough to date or to drive is, in this view, to ask the wrong questions. Instead, we must ask how old is old enough to learn to drive; to start a process, such as dating, that ends at competence if we're lucky; to invest, taking transitional risks, hoping that the result will be the right kind of adult.

This perspective provides general guidance on the goals pursued by legal policy toward youth, but no precise prescriptions for how these goals can be translated into effective programs or what price the general public should be willing to pay in the name of youth welfare. We want kids to participate in decisions about their education, but not at the price of sacrificing long-term opportunities to avoid short-term burdens. Work experience in younger years is a valuable preparation for later work, but unskilled labor should not be permitted to shut out educational experience that provides basic skills and the opportunity for later mobility. Part-time work at the local fast food emporium is valuable experience, but a lifetime behind the french-fry counter is too high a price to pay for teenage freedom of choice. Similarly, we want to give young law violators the chance to survive our legal system with their life opportunities still intact, but at what price and for how long? At the tactical level, the implications of a learner's permit perspective are distressingly inexact.

There is one issue, however, where this conception of adolescent development has decisive impact: the relationship between liberty and responsibility during the growing years. This can best be illustrated by analyzing the argument of Richard Kuh, objecting to a series of recommendations for sentencing young offenders:

> In its consideration of "youth crime" the task force construes the word "youth" very broadly. Were the term applied solely to those who I have heretofore regarded as juveniles—youngsters who have not reached puberty or those who have obtained it within three or four years—I would have no problems with such a lenient approach. But the task force has applied the term to individuals as old as twenty.[9]

Mr. Kuh wants to be lenient with youngsters for three or four years past puberty but no later. Why? Because of

> the fact that 18-year-olds today can vote and those between eighteen and twenty-one both typically are working or able to work or completing college, are sexually and physically mature (and mentally as close to being mature as they ever will be), and are in many cases married or the equivalent.[10]

The distinguished former district attorney of Manhattan is making one of two arguments. Either he is arguing that kids are fully mature by the time they reach their eighteenth birthday, or he is proposing that those given rights and privileges should, as a matter of quid pro quo, pay the full price when they violate the law. To see adolescence as a learner's permit is to reject both the evidence and the analysis he provides.

First the evidence. Are kids fully mature at 18 because they can vote, even if they don't vote? Is that why we passed the Twenty-sixth Amendment? Kids are "mentally as close to being mature as they will ever be." But doesn't it take more than an I.Q. to make decisions? Kids are married or "the equivalent." Eighteen-year-olds go to college and work, at least those lucky enough to find jobs or to finance an education. But, in my view, all of this is evidence that 18-year-olds are in the *process* of becoming adult. For that reason, using this kind of evidence to "prove" adulthood is like assuming a flight is over the moment the plane has left the ground. To impose full responsibility because adolescents have begun to make life choices is much like expecting every new bride to be an instant Betty Crocker. It isn't realistic and it isn't fair.

In Rights Begin Responsibilities?

But what about the quid pro quo argument: since they can vote, they should pay the full price for committing transgressions. At the outset, we must recall the special danger of this kind of argument when dealing with what should be called "least harm" reforms. We should never use the constitutional right to vaginal foam, extended only to protect immature kids from great harm, as the basis for making any kind of judgment about the penal responsibility of 14-year-olds.

Many adolescents are working or going to college or exercising their voting rights while they are in transition to full adulthood—while they are using their learner's permit. What sentence *is* appropriate for a 17-year-old burglar, if his 25-year-old brother would receive one year in prison for the same offense? Equal treatment for wrongdoing seems inappropriate to the transitional status of the learner.

Of course, no learning role is complete without, in some measure, learning responsibility for conduct. Thus, part of the initiation into the adult role is building toward adult responsibilities. Just as the learning theory of adolescence implies a transition toward adulthood, so, too, it also implies a progression toward adult levels of responsibility. The adolescent must be protected from the full burden of adult responsibilities, but pushed along by degrees toward the moral and legal accountability that we consider appropriate to adulthood.

Conclusion

Growing up in modern Western nations is a process of learning to choose freely the path of our lives. But the only way to learn free choice is to experience firsthand making choices and living with the consequences of those choices. This learning period is concentrated in modern adolescence, a period of time when privileges are gradually extended. It is inevitable that young people with less experience in making decisions will make more mistakes as a result. These are the necessary hazards of growing up in a free society.

The empirical studies in Part III of this book will show that the youth crimes that fill the dockets of America's juvenile courts are not spread evenly over the years of childhood but are clustered in the years after puberty. So one defining feature of modern juvenile justice is to fashion policy toward the harmful mistakes of those who the system hopes are growing through and will grow out of law violating. So the major focus of juvenile courts is dealing with the misdeeds of youth in a learner's permit transition to adulthood. What responses are consistent with both the need to condemn wrongdoing and the interest in facilitating the opportunity to grow up normally? Just as the development of the juvenile court was linked to the emergence of modern adolescence, any rational theory for dealing with delinquent youth must learn from the general principles of legal policy toward adolescent development.

THREE

The Problem of Individual Variation

A further problem haunts any jurisprudence of adolescence, one we can grapple with but never really solve. We observe it whenever we walk into an eighth-grade gym class. We confront it whenever we talk at length with a group of college freshmen. We see it in our children's lives and the lives of their friends. This is the problem of individual variation. Human beings simply don't all grow up the same way. Competencies are acquired at different levels and in different orders. Kids vary enormously.

Because this is so, a perfect fit between the realities of adolescent development and the law's response to growing up would give each individual child his or her own personal statute book, designed to respond to individual developmental events with precisely timed changes in legal status. This, of course, will never happen. Instead, we must choose among or mix three strategies: age-grading, individual competence testing, and decentralized discretion.

Age-grading is the tidiest, most "legal" response to the problem of individual variation. It should therefore come as no surprise that it "solves" the problem of individual variation by ignoring it. Nobody is old enough to vote at 17, and everybody is on his or her eighteenth birthday. Twelve-year-olds who read the *Political Science Quarterly* can't vote, but 19-year-olds who read *Mad* magazine are enfranchised.

In sharp contrast, a pure "competence" approach would attempt to design a test of political literacy, struggle toward a rough sense of what should be a passing score, and make anybody, at any age, pass the test once as a precondition to the franchise. Smart kids could vote at 10, and some of their classmates never. Competent drivers of *any* age could get their licenses. Of course, there are problems. Do we really know how to test political competence? Do we really know how to set a passing score? Even if we could define appropriate levels of minimal competence, what is to prevent our egalitarian sympathies from pushing the passing score well below true competence? Finally, what about the stigma of not passing the test? How does the older brother feel when he flunks the test his sister passes? What about those people who will never vote?

If objective standards are difficult to create, discretion provides an alternative approach to individual variation. Since every kid is unique, have another human being examine the individual and make a decision. Since there are millions of kids, this discretion will be decentralized. This is the least "legal" solution to the problem. It is a government of people, not laws. In its pure form, it carries unacceptable dangers of abuse.

But elements of discretion, when mixed with other mechanisms, are indispensable to a decently operating legal system. The tyranny of unguided discretion is why we have retreated from the lawlessness of the original juvenile court. The necessity of discretion is the mother of a number of legal inventions: the presumption of family liberty, the "emancipated" minor, the "special cases" exceptions to minimum ages for marriage.[1] The cost of living in a world of rules without exceptions is very high.[2]

Sometimes three wrongs can make a right. Each of the coping strategies I have described is imperfect. But systems that mix these three strategies—age-grading, competency testing, and discretion—may be less imperfect. Consider the case of driving, a privilege that is usually rationed by a system that uses all three strategies.

The age-grading is straightforward. My child has to be 15 and a half or 16 before he can get a learner's permit and 16 before he gets his license.[3] But age alone is not enough. He also has to pass a competency test. If the testing system is not corrupt, the public interest in avoiding incompetent drivers will keep the standards for driving from falling too low. But the Department of Motor Vehicles can only test driving ability, not personal judgment or the willingness to abide by the law. During adolescence, this kind of drivers' testing deals with a fraction of what it takes to be a safe driver. Age-grading and discretion will thus be necessary supplements if the system of allocating drivers' licenses protects kids and the public.

The discretions in the current system are many. Parental consent is frequently a legal necessity and almost always an economic precondition to teenage driving.[4] Legal requirements of liability insurance permit insurance companies as well as parents to discourage driving by setting high-risk rates.[5] The fact that human beings grade driving tests is yet another loophole, unless you truly believe that a 55-year-old widow new to driving and a 16-year-old boy will be held to identical skill standards on parallel parking by the person administering the test.

But why couldn't the system work just as well without age-grading? Pass the test, get Mom and Dad's permission, buy insurance, and drive at any age. My first problem with such a system is the added burden it would put on parents of the 14- and 15-year-old kids who would turn up the heat on Mom and Dad the minute the law was changed. Age-grading in law, in theory, usurps parental authority; in practice, millions of parents bless it as the good reason they need to postpone what they believe should be postponed. Age limits help strong parents avoid saying no and protect weak parents from saying yes.

The fact that we live in a world with weak as well as strong parents suggests another reason why minimum ages make social and legal sense—the "leakage" problem. If I'm weak-willed and my son passes the test, your daughter may be riding in the front seat of the car. Because this is so, the minimum age for driving has yet another public purpose: it protects other peoples' children from the consequences of inappropriate parental discretion. This is not a small matter. Data on traffic deaths provide two convincing demonstrations that the hazards of driving are socially spread among adolescents. The first evidence concerns the downward spread of driving risks. For males, the peak age group of traffic fatality is 20 through 24. For females (with lower risks), the highest risk age group is 15 through 19.[6] These data, and the high proportion of girls who die as passengers, suggest that risks generated by older drivers are a major threat to younger passengers. Nor are girls the only group at risk. Of the 4,010 boys between 15 and 19 killed in traffic accidents during 1976, 1,630 (41 percent of the total) died as passengers.[7] And not even the strongest parent can guard against the possibility of his or her child riding in a friend's car without fantastic curtailment of the child's freedom of movement. What economists call the "externalities" of weak parental discretion in making decisions about adolescent driving are substantial indeed!

There are other ways in which youth welfare is served by waiting in line until a specific birthday for the privilege of driving. Imagine the status symbol that a driver's license would become in a world without age-grading. All 14-year-olds would envy the lucky few. The children of strong parents would look up to the children of the weak. And since we can't judge judgment, more of our kids would drive, and more of our kids would die.

Further, many of our children would suffer a fate, to them, worse than death—the stigma of not driving when other kids their age are driving. They would resent the unequal treatment of 14-year-olds because *they* believe that age is important. If anything, 16 is too young to drive. If anything, further downward extensions of driving would make things worse for kids, family, and society.

Permit me one more excursion before imposing some discipline on discussing the problem of individual variation, an excursion into the mix of strategies we use to determine what motion pictures our children can and cannot see. The current industry system for rating motion pictures is one of the most familiar and fully articulated approaches to the problem of individual difference, family choice, and age-grading for youth. "G" pictures are made for kids, and on occasion, their parents might enjoy a "G" picture as well. But "G" ratings are the stuff of Walt Disney and Saturday matinees. A "PG" rating is the essence of family liberty theory: my child can see the film if I don't mind, whether he is 4 or 14. But if I am a conscientious parent, the Parental Guidance rating advises me to do some research. There is something about the film that may be inappropriate for my child. The people at the movie theatre won't stop my child from seeing it, but perhaps I should.

In contrast, the "R" rating is the motion-picture equivalent of nocturnal juvenile curfew. My kids can see an "R"-rated film only if I'm there, too. Unlike the "PG" rating, where parental guidance is requested, the Motion Picture Association demands an adult's personal participation in any decision to allow my child to see the film.

The final stage in this fine-tuned regulation is the "NC" rating. And here, Father does not know best. If you're under 18, no movie, even if Dad says yes. Of course, particular films may be misclassified, and parents may make mistakes. Movie censorship may not be appropriate for 16-year-olds. But the design of the system is an eclectic wonder.

Choosing Strategies

Are there general principles to guide us on the matter of when different strategies for coping with the problem of individual variation are appropriately used? There are, in my view, a few such principles. Competence testing makes sense in public law when one of two conditions is met: (1) extending a privilege creates a danger to the user and to others, or (2) A special privilege is requested—for example, entering practice as a doctor, lawyer, or accountant. Even in these circumstances, because our capacities to test competence are limited, testing alone should rarely be a sufficient condition for allowing a dangerous privilege.

Discretion, particularly parental discretion, is an important part of a well-conceived regulatory scheme, unless there is a good reason to exclude it. This is why we live in a world where 15-year-olds need parental consent for plastic surgery but not for treatment of venereal disease. But parental consent is in many cases not a sufficient condition for granting liberty. The law must allow for stupid parents as well as wise ones, weak as well as strong.

Age-grading within adolescence is particularly appropriate when the capacity to test competence is weak and the consequences of mistakes threaten the individual or others in the community with substantial harm. In such cases, minimum ages may also be necessary to ensure that kids grow up a bit before they risk making the *wrong* kind of mistakes. Age-grading isn't so bad after all, if we don't misuse it!

CONCLUSION TO PART I

The three chapters in this brief introduction have discussed three related aspects of modern adolescence as a concern of public law. Chapter 1 showed how changing conditions in American life—urbanization, expanding the reach of public education and the increasing availability of the machinery of physical mobility—created the social changes that produced adolescence before the law changed to accommodate this new reality. Chapter 2 outlined a central conception of adolescence in a free society, as a learner's permit period when semi-autonomous young people push toward maturity by making decisions on an increasing range of subjects. This trial and error system is a necessary part of the preparation to an adulthood of mature free choice. Chapter 3 concerned legal tactics for how young persons can be evaluated during adolescence, a period when kids vary enormously in their skills and maturity. Age grading is one of several methods of allocating privileges but it is probably a necessary element in any rational governance of adolescent development.

What does all this mean for juvenile courts and juvenile justice? Plenty. It turns out that the juvenile court itself is an "age-graded" institution, restricted to adolescents and mixing the same elements of age grading, individual discretion and competency testing in treating the youth who appear before it. And the theory of adolescence is at the core of why a separate institution is required when criminal offenders are adolescent.

Those wishing a more extensive exposure to the jurisprudence of adolescence are invited to consult Zimring, *The Changing Legal World of Adolescence,* from which the material in Part I was excerpted.

Part II

A RATIONALE FOR AMERICAN
JUVENILE JUSTICE

The two essays in this part deal with the central mission of the juvenile court in delinquency cases and with those aspects of youthfulness that require separate policy from any legal institutions that deal responsibly with youth crime. Chapter 4 is a revisionist history of the juvenile court. I argue that the juvenile court was founded not mainly as a means of facilitating intervention in the lives of young offenders but rather as a means of diverting juveniles under arrest from the harms inflicted by jails and criminal courts. From Day One, those who created the court thought that the best cure for youth crime was the normal process of growing up in the community. What kids who offended needed most was not massive intervention but patient supervision and normal education. Keeping young offenders in community settings was the original aim of the court and has been a consistent goal for over a century. The last years of the twentieth century may have been the juvenile court's most effective era as a diversion from the harms of the criminal system. Chapter 5 explores two strands of legal theory that complement the diversionary institutional strategy that chapter 4 has outlined. The first rationale for smaller punishments for youth is the criminal law notion of diminished responsibility because of immaturity. Young law violators are less culpable, and thus deserve less punishment—no matter what kind of court might try and sentence them. For this reason, immaturity should produce reduction in punishment in either juvenile or criminal courts. Youth and immaturity make young offenders deserve less punishment even though they must be punished. A second legal policy—what chapter 5 calls "room to reform"—is a special opportunity to straighten out that the law extends to the young because of the high value it places on kids receiving every chance to grow up into productive adults. Second and third chances are not merely the result of lesser culpability for youth but also a reflection of the tremendous social benefits that result when offending careers can naturally abate into positive adult behavior. The chances that the legal system takes with young drivers, young drinkers, and young offenders are a long-term investment not merely in the welfare of youth but also in the health of the social system that will depend on the good citizens we hope they will become. The two chapters in this part combine to explain both the institutional strategy of juvenile courts and the jurisprudential principles that justify the strategy of diversion from greater harm. Chapter 4 shows the consistency of the court's strategy of diversion from 1899 to current times. Chapter 5 provides the theoretical justification for diversion—equal parts of reducing punishment because of immaturity and keeping kids away from destructive punishments so that normal development might continue. Both of these chapters depend on the theory of adolescence explored in Part I. Giving young persons "room to reform" into normal adulthood by diverting them from punishments that threaten to interrupt development is using the tools of a special court for the young to facilitate a learner's permit theory of adolescence.

The Common Thread
Diversion in Juvenile Justice

The first idea that should be grasped concerning
the juvenile court is that it came into the world to
prevent children from being treated as criminals.

Miriam Van Waters, 1925

The reputation of the American juvenile court at the beginning of its second century in America reflects a mix of
practical success and theoretical incoherence. On the one hand, the
institution has been a spectacular success in the United States and
throughout much of the world. A juvenile court exists to deal with
youthful law violators in all 50 states. No developed nation tries its
youngest offenders in its regular criminal courts, and almost all the
institutions that have been created in Europe, Japan, and the Com-
monwealth nations have been explicitly modeled in their language,
procedures and objectives on the American juvenile court. No legal
institution in Anglo-American legal history has achieved such universal acceptance among the diverse legal systems of the industrial
democracies.

On the other hand, the philosophy of state intervention that has
been most prominently associated with the creation of the juvenile
court had been effectively discredited for at least a generation before
the centenary. Variously called "child saving," "the omnibus theory
of delinquency," and, most memorably, "the rehabilitative ideal," the
original justification we remember for the juvenile court was as an
institution that would intervene forcefully in the lives of all children
at risk to effect a rescue.[1] Informal proceedings were preferred to formal ones so that the delinquent's needs could be determined. Broad
and vague definitions of delinquency were favored, so that all children who needed help would fall within the new court's jurisdiction.
Large powers could be exercised in all cases, so that help could be
delivered to the deserving.

By the mid-1960s, the naive arrogance of the rehabilitative ideal had been exposed, never again to rule unchallenged in the juvenile courts.[2] Yet the court has thrived since the 1960s, just as it did before. Was this post–child-saving juvenile court just an empty shell, an institution that had outlived its mission but continued to function on sheer momentum? Or is the juvenile court a chameleon, taking on new justifications and theories of function as old theories die? If so, why is this particular judicial weathervane so universally popular?

In my view, a substantial step toward understanding both the institutional status and justifying rationale of the modern juvenile court is to revise our view of the original justifications of the new court for delinquent children. I think that two justifications existed from the start for creating a juvenile court, and I shall call these two different policies the *interventionist* and *diversionary* justifications for a separate children's court. The diversionary justification for juvenile court was always the most important of the two rationales, and it remains so today.

In the foundational period of the juvenile court, when different groups formed coalitions for different reasons, and when many reformers had multiple reasons to support a new court, the diversionary critique of criminal court processing of minors was always stronger and more widely accepted than the interventionist vision of the court. When it much later became apparent that the interventionist justification was in conflict with both the realities of court function and with the principles of legality and proportionality, the diversionary rationale for the court emerged as the central explanation for the court's separate operation. Diversionary principles of juvenile justice are well suited both to a modern theory of adolescent development and to concern about procedural fairness and proportionality in legal response to youth crime. My intention here is to show both continuity and coherence to the diversionary rationale for juvenile courts through the first hundred years of their history.

The first section of this essay sets out the two discrete justifications for creation of a juvenile court and documents the diversionary agenda of turn-of-the-century reformers. The second section shows the extent to which the major programmatic elements of early juvenile justice were consistent with diversionary justifications and methods. Much of the work of the juvenile court, in its early as well as later years, was aimed at allowing kids to grow up in community settings. The third section addresses the modern concept of juvenile justice as reflected in two leading Supreme Court cases.[3] It was a diversionary theory of juvenile court that could accommodate due process rules without sacrifices of youth welfare. The fourth section concerns the contemporary understanding of juvenile justice as a passive virtue. I show that the effectiveness of juvenile courts in protecting youth from full criminal punishment is the heart of the reason the court has so many contemporary enemies.

Two Theories of Change

Those who put their hopes in a new juvenile court that would assume responsibility over young offenders had two reasons to assume the new court would be an improvement on the criminal processing of children. The first belief was that a child-centered juvenile court could avoid the many harms that criminal punishment visited on the young. The reformers believed that penalties were unnecessarily harsh and places of confinement were schools for crime where the innocent were corrupted and the redeemable were instead confirmed in the path of chronic criminality. From this perspective, the first great virtue of the juvenile court was that it would not continue the destructive impact of the criminal justice system on children. I call this theory of justification for juvenile court a *diversionary* rationale, an argument that the new court could do good by doing less harm than criminal processes. And those who believed the criminal courts to be destructive instruments that were best avoided included every one of the new court's prominent supporters.

The signal characteristic of a diversionary argument for juvenile justice is its attention to the harmful nature of criminal punishment for the young. A classic and nearly complete litany of the harms of the criminal law comes on the first page of juvenile court judge Richard S. Tuthill's 1904 account of the treatment of delinquents prior to reform:

> Prior to 1899 little was done in Illinois, and, so far as I know, in any other State in the Union, that was not wrongly done by the State toward caring for the delinquent children of the State. No matter how young, these children were indicted, prosecuted, and confined as criminals, in prisons, just the same as were adults pending and after a hearing, and thus were branded as criminals before they knew what crime was. The State kept these little ones in police cells and jails among the worst men and women to be found in the vilest parts of the city and town. *Under such treatment they developed rapidly, and the natural*

result was that they were thus educated in crime and when dis-
charged were well fitted to become the expert criminals and
outlaws who have crowded our penitentiaries and jails. The
State had educated innocent children in crime, and the harvest
was great. The condition in Chicago became so bad that all who
were cognizant of this condition and were interested in correct-
ing it sought a remedy. A bill was prepared and presented
to the legislature of the State, which, in due time, and after
overcoming much opposition, was enacted into a law known
throughout the world as the "juvenile-court law of Illinois."[4]

A similar rhetoric is reflected in accounts of the criminal justice
system issued before and after the founding of the court by every one
of the major public figures in the movement. Among the more colorful examples was Judge Ben Lindsey's characterization of the criminal court as an "outrage against childhood."[5] William Stead speaks
of a police station where "urchins of ten and twelve who have been
run in for juvenile delinquency have found the police cell the nurs-
ery cradle of the jail."[6] The criminal court was the common enemy
that launched juvenile courts in America.

The diversionary justification for juvenile court can easily be contrasted with what I wish to call the *interventionist* justification for
the new court. While the diversionary approach promised the avoidance of the criminal court's harms, the interventionist argument emphasized the positive good that new programs administered by child
welfare experts could achieve. A child-centered court was an opportunity to design positive programs that would simultaneously protect the community and cure the child. This was the notion of child
saving that made the court's early justifications seem so extreme.
While the diversionary and interventionist justifications are conceptually quite distinct, there seems to have been little awareness at
the juvenile court's founding that these two approaches to justifying
the new court might be in any conflict. The same people who believed in the diversionary virtues of a new court affirmed its interventionist potential as well.[7] Because there was no contemporary
awareness of potential conflict, the court's supporters did not have to
choose between these separate but attractive rationales for the new
institution.

But the diversionary rationale had several obvious advantages
over an interventionist theory as a justification for an untested reform. In the first place, the new court could be counted on to achieve
social good whether or not its treatment interventions worked.

Avoiding the harms of the criminalization of children was a near-term benefit, whatever the programmatic potential of the new court's interventions might prove to be. A second advantage of a diversionary perspective was the way that doing less harm fit the shape and orientation of the new court's major tool, community-based probationary supervision. Community supervision is rarely a heroic intervention; it does not take extensive power over the lives of young offenders when compared to jails, prisons, and work camps. It is also, in addition to its high moral principle, a method of responding to official delinquency that is relatively cheap.

At every level of discourse, then, from prochild rhetoric to economic self-interest, the diversionary perspective was monumentally attractive to those who were organizing a new court. It was an argument for juvenile courts without any known opponents or identified disadvantages, a foundation for the new court that was too obvious to be remembered clearly as a distinctive justification for change.

If the diversion of youth from the rigors of criminal punishment was a dominant motive for the new court, why does this justification not play a larger role in the historical accounts of the creation of the court? While diversionary motives dominate the contemporary accounts of the court's early years, these efforts to reduce the gratuitous harms of the criminal court do not receive much notice in the historical critiques of the court that appeared in the 1960s and 1970s.[8]

Part of the reason later scholars give more attention to the interventionist theory of juvenile justice is that such a claim was both novel and controversial, while child-protective sentiments are so widely shared as to be without any singular importance at any particular historical moment. The diversionary sentiments of 1899 do not set that era far off from 1940 or 1980. The claims of interventionist prowess are considered by contrast a striking historical artifact by the 1960s and 1970s, if not before.

One other historical element that produced more emphasis on interventionist dogma than was otherwise justified was the fact that many accounts of the court's justifications were written by judges with a vested interest in expanding the powers and prestige of this new office. Avoiding harm for children is a modest objective, indeed, when compared to the therapeutic rescue of those about to fall to the lower depths. The rhetoric of Judge Julian Mack, for instance, seems prone to such claims; even the writing of Judge Lindsey, a noninterventionist for his time, was full of accounts of judicial rescue.[9]

However understandable the failure of those who study court

history to give sufficient attention to diversionary motives, this gap has led to a variety of unfortunate consequences. First, much late twentieth-century work underestimates the capacities and misrepresents the motives of founding figures like Jane Addams and Julia Lathrop.[10] These were not naive maiden ladies who lacked respect for the cultural roots of immigrant communities, as I shall show. Second, the failure to give prominent attention to avoiding criminal stigma for children leaves these later histories with no explanation for the worldwide popularity of the juvenile court for delinquents. It was beyond doubt the avoidance of criminal justice damage that spread the juvenile court gospel across the world in the early years of the century, not an interventionist claim to judicial power. The third problem with ignoring the diversionary rationale for juvenile court is that it makes it impossible to understand much of the developing nature of juvenile justice in the first half of the twentieth century by referring to the court's justification.

The Aims and Means of the Early Juvenile Courts

The early years of the twentieth century were not a period when new forms of intensive behavioral therapies were applied to either adults or juveniles brought before the Bar of Justice. The most serious of the commitment options open to the juvenile court was the state reformatory or training school, an institution with a nineteenth-century program and a zero reputation for innovation or behavioral impact.[11] One searches the record in vain for major figures in creating the court who put their hopes in state schools of the industrial variety as an arena for child saving.[12] The sole virtue of the reform school was the fact that it was not a prison.

Where did the reformers rest their programmatic hopes in the first quarter of the twentieth century? On social and educational change generally and on community-based probationary supervision for the delinquent in his or her family setting. Compulsory education and child labor laws were the major objectives of progressive youth policy, not the operations of juvenile court. Within the juvenile court, the major programmatic advantage was probation.[13] The goal of the reformers, in the words of Jane Addams, was "a determination to understand the growing child and a sincere effort to find ways for securing his orderly development in normal society."[14] The dominant outcome of juvenile court process was probation as early as

1908, when probation was twice as likely in Milwaukee as all other court outcomes combined.[15]

The emphasis on probation and community-based supervision fits nicely with a diversionary justification for juvenile courts. The job of the court is first not to harm the youth and then to attempt help in community settings. The same programmatic emphasis does not mesh well with the romantic rhetoric of child saving. Probation is at its essence an incremental social control strategy, one that relies on the basic health and functionality of the subjects' community life.

Even the more ambitious plans of probation advocates to get involved with families and schools amounted to low-intensity social control, particularly given the tiny budgets and volunteer staffs characteristic of the early years of the juvenile court. The only new programs that fit the profile of child saving were the secure Chicago "parental schools" for truants, which hoped to marry coercive means to educational objectives and juvenile detention.[16] But this clearly interventionist institution was not emulated in the proliferation of juvenile courts. In this sense, the parental school may be the exception that proves the rule.

The other major increase in social control was the explicit extension of all juvenile court sanctions to noncriminal behavior, such as disobedience of adults, truancy, and violation of curfew. Clearly, the court was not extending jurisdiction in this direction in the name of diversion. But it was the same jurisprudence of childhood dependency that supported these powers for status offenders that also was a foundation for keeping young offenders out of criminal courts.[17]

There is one final respect in which the role of the juvenile court was more modest in the reform imagination than in some of the court's interventionist rhetoric. If child labor regulation and public education are the important public law enterprises of the new order for the young, both of these are centered in governmental operations that stand apart from juvenile court, as does the settlement house created by Jane Addams. To do less harm than criminal courts, the new legal setting for delinquency did not need to be a superpower, and it was not.

The Juvenile Court and the Rule of Law

It took two-thirds of the twentieth century before the United States Supreme Court considered the procedural protections that due process required when accused delinquents were in jeopardy of secure confinement in state institutions. One important issue in *In re Gault,* decided in 1967, was the need for informality if the court was to achieve its child-saving mission.[18] Justice John Harlan thought that rigid due process could disserve traditional juvenile justice. Dissenting from the *Gault* majority, which held that due process requires recognition of a privilege against self-incrimination, the right to confront witnesses and the right to cross-examination, Harlan argued:

> First, quite unlike notice, counsel, and a record, these requirements might radically alter the character of juvenile court proceedings. The evidence from which the Court reasons that they would not is inconclusive, and other available evidence suggests that they very likely would. At the least, it is plain that these additional requirements would contribute materially to the creation in these proceedings of the atmosphere of an ordinary criminal trial, and would, even if they do no more, thereby largely frustrate a central purpose of these specialized courts [references deleted].[19]

His suggestion was that such procedures such as confronting witnesses and cross-examination could jeopardize the substantive mission of the juvenile court. Yet, Justice Abe Fortas, writing the majority opinion, argued that there was no serious tension between the therapeutic intentions of the juvenile court and procedural protections for the accused who come before it. He argued:

> While due process requirements will, in some instances, introduce a degree of order and regularity to Juvenile Court proceedings to determine delinquency, and in contested cases will introduce some elements of the adversary system, nothing will require that the conception of the kindly juvenile judge be replaced by its opposite.[20]

Procedural protections, in other words, would not, in his view, transform juvenile court into a miniversion of adult criminal court with all the tough sentencing that would apply.

Rather than take one side in this debate, I wish to argue that the contrast between interventionist and diversionary theories of the court will decide whether there is tension between the court's objective and due process standards. For an informal and interventionist juvenile court, standards of proof and defense lawyers are a major drawback to identifying children in need and providing them with help. If that is the mission of the juvenile court, then due process will be a major handicap to its achievement. But if saving kids from the gratuitous harms inflicted by the criminal process is the aim, there is no inherent conflict between due process and the court's main beneficial functions.

The best illustration of the tension between due process and an interventionist court is the issue raised by the case of *In re Winship* in 1970. The state of New York allowed a petition alleging delinquency to be sustained in juvenile court if the state proved such facts by a preponderance of the evidence, the usual standard of proof in civil trials.[21] The appellants, using *Gault* as authority, argued that delinquency could only be established by proof of its constituent facts beyond a reasonable doubt. The Supreme Court agreed with this conclusion.[22]

But what is the justification for requiring proof beyond a reasonable doubt in criminal cases? The usual law-day speech tells us that erroneous acquittals are less socially harmful than erroneous convictions: "It is better that 10 guilty men go free than that one innocent man gets convicted!" But if the juvenile court is there to help delinquents, what is the sense in saying "It is better that ten kids who need help do not get help than that one kid who does not need help is erroneously assisted!" If the dominant purpose of juvenile justice was forceful intervention for the child's own good, the rules in *Gault* and *Winship* were a decisive rejection of the juvenile court's jurisprudence.

But every aspect of due process protection can be consistent with a diversionary theory of juvenile justice. If the main benefit of juvenile court is that it keeps children from the destructive impact of the criminal courts, this benefit may be provided whether or not the new court makes a formal sanctioning decision in a particular case. A high burden of proof and a lawyer to represent the youth will not cost the court its diversionary function. There is also no threat to the diversionary rationale of juvenile court from recognition that terms like *delinquent* carry stigma and that juvenile court sanctions may function as punishments. As long as the juvenile court can be seen as the lesser of evils, a diversionary view of the court can be quite worldly and need not deny that punitive motives might color sanctioning decisions in the children's court.

The interventionist view of court processes was always more fragile. A positive characterization of juvenile court interventions is necessary to justifying the venture. To call what the juvenile court does to delinquents a punishment is to deny the truth of a central premise of the interventionist theory. Viewed in this light, the majority opinion in *Gault* rejected one enduring rationale for a separate juvenile court and elevated a second theory to supremacy. The juvenile court that the United States Supreme Court approved protected children chiefly by keeping them out of prisons and jails.[23] Such an institution could be parsimonious with its own punishments—restricting them to cases with strong evidence and fair procedures—without threatening its own substantive mission. The arrogance of unqualified judicial power was not necessary to this version of the court's purposes. After *In re Gault* in 1967, diversion was the approved version of juvenile justice in the United States and probably in the rest of the developed world. Some juvenile court judges might have shed a tear at the way Abe Fortas deconstructed the interventionist facade of juvenile courts, but the *Gault* majority did not undo or completely reorient the court that Grace Abbott, Julia Lathrop, and Jane Addams supported. The diversionary institution they wished for had passed the tests of *In re Gault* and *In re Winship* with flying colors.

Diversion in the Modern Court

The twentieth century has seen many changes in the culture and institutions of the United States. The juvenile court, itself just an experiment at the beginning of the century, has witnessed changes to its clientele, to its political and legal constituencies, and in its operations.

Nevertheless, the core concern of the court "to prevent children from being treated as criminals" was just as clear in 1999 as in 1899. As the usual period of schooling and economic dependency in adolescence lengthened over the twentieth century, the maximum age for juvenile court delinquency first drifted upward to the eighteenth birthday in most states and then stayed at 18 in most states, reflecting an age boundary close to the mode for high school graduation. The period of semiautonomy that now spans most of the teen years is spent for the most part in the delinquency jurisdiction of juvenile courts.[24] This section will show that a consistent diversion orientation of juvenile justice can be observed in recent policy developments.

Modern Reform: The Juvenile Justice and
Delinquency Prevention Act of 1974

The due process requirements discussed in the previous section were closely followed by the first major federal legislation designed to influence the substantive content of state juvenile justice policy by providing financial rewards to state systems that met the federal standards.[25] The two major targets of the 1974 juvenile justice legislation fit quite comfortably under a traditional diversionary view of the court's objectives. The first push of the federal law was to remove minors from American jails and prisons.[26] The protective segregation of children had been at the heart of the diversion agenda in 1899. While the original reformers would have been disturbed to find that 75 years of American history had not yet achieved this primitive reform, the continuing struggle to attain separate housing for children in confinement was an essentialist diversionary reform in obvious accord with the original vision of the court.

So, too, was the second major objective of the 1974 legislation, the deinstitutionalization of status offenders.[27] The saga of the status offender was one of the great failings of the interventionist theory of juvenile courts. In the original legislation, the noncriminal behaviors later to be called status offenses were simply another behavior that could justify a finding of delinquency, as well as any placement that the juvenile court was justified in ordering for a delinquent.[28] Kids who ran away from home or were disobedient or truant could be committed to the same institutions that were dispositional options for the juvenile burglar and auto thief. Two problems were associated with secure institutional confinement for noncriminal misbehavior: it was grossly unfair, and it was manifestly ineffectual. By 1974, the need to scale back on this branch of the rehabilitative ideal was a near consensus among youth welfare professionals.[29] The direct conflict between not allowing the juvenile courts to order secure institutions for truants and an interventionist theory of the court is obvious.

But there is no necessary conflict between limits on the coercive interventions allowed for noncriminal behaviors and a diversionary theory of juvenile justice. Simply that reformers wish to keep adolescent law violators out of prisons and jails does not mean that the same observers support serious punishment for noncriminal kids. Quite the opposite. While juvenile court treatments for young offenders are found in most developed nations, the strong interventionist claim that produced training schools for truants was nowhere near as widespread in popularity as the juvenile court itself. Foreign courts did not adopt such policies, because diversionary theories did not require them. The federal legislation, like the constitutional cases that preceded it, can be seen as endorsing diversion as the theory of the modern court to the exclusion of interventionism.

Diversion and the Punitive Assault on Juvenile Justice

Perhaps the most dramatic evidence of the efficacy and importance of diversionary policies in modern juvenile justice is the sustained attack on the modern juvenile court by the political forces of law and order. At the federal level, Republican legislative majorities have been attempting to use federal financial incentives pioneered in the juvenile justice and Delinquency Prevention Act of 1974 to push a series of standards designed to create more punitive sanctions within the delinquency jurisdiction of the juvenile court and easier transfers of serious juvenile offenders to criminal courts.[30]

The rhetoric in support of this legislation uses new phrases to describe the juvenile court outcomes that are desired—terms like *accountability* and *graduated sanctions*.[31] But the common enemy of the transfer policies and the harsher juvenile court punishments proposed in the legislation is a juvenile court tradition that seeks to avoid permanent stigma and disfiguring punishments of delinquents. The terms of reprobation aimed at the court by its critics on the right are a tribute to the court's diversionary intent—"revolving door justice," "slap on the wrist," "Kiddie Court." To the extent that the attacks by its critics are based on empirical truth, those assaults pay tribute to the efficacy of a court that has been seeking to avoid the harshest outcomes for its caseload for the entire twentieth century.

Truth to the Rumor?

But is there any truth to the rumor that juvenile courts protect delinquents from destructive punishments? Looking behind the rhetoric of current debates about responses to youth crime, we find very little analysis that compares sanctions for similar offenses across the boundaries of juvenile and criminal courts, and ignorance of the impact of juvenile court processing on punishment outcomes for different types of crime is not a recent problem.[32] My own belief is that juvenile courts have always generated some diversionary benefits to many classes of young offenders, but that the size and distribution of diversionary benefits varies by period, by type of youth, and by type of offense. There is no excuse for the near-zero research base on this important issue, a situation that makes determining the aggregate impact of juvenile court case processing on punishments into a guessing game.

My best guess is that the protective impact of a diversionary juvenile court on sanctions for youth crime is largest when punitive policies are at their most dominant in criminal courts—that is, in eras like the American present. The larger the punitive bite of the criminal court system, the more likely it is that a separate court for the youngest offenders takes some of that bite out of the state sanctions that the youngest offenders receive.

Figure 4.1 provides fairly careful estimates of public facility confinement for youth age 14–17 and young adults age 18–24 for 1971, 1991, and 1995. For the 14–17 group, I combine juvenile detention facilities, training schools, camps, and so on with the number of those age 14–17 in prisons and jails. Only the juvenile facilities are under the control of the juvenile court, but total secure incarceration is the best measure of total governmental control. The figure is formatted with each age group's rate in 1971 expressed as 100, so that the changes over time are emphasized.

As figure 4.1 shows, the incarceration rates for the two groups were not greatly different in 1971: the 18- to 24-year-olds have a jail and prison rate that is 28 percent higher than the total public incarceration rate of 14- to 17-year-olds. Trends after 1971 for the two groups diverge. The period 1971–1991 was not a typical interlude in the history of American crime policy. It was, instead, the period of the most substantial growth in the scale of imprisonment in the history of the republic.[33] Never was the pressure for confinement as consistent and substantial. Total confinement for the younger group increased by 21 percent, while the incarceration rate of young adults more than doubled. By 1991, the difference in incarceration rates for the two groups was more than two to one, and this very substantial gap is one reason why those who had succeeded in radically altering punishments in criminal courts might have resented the stability in policy and outcome that occurred for younger offenders.

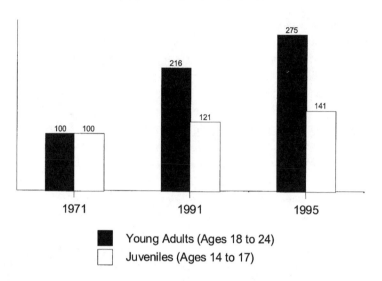

Figure 4.1. Trends in incarceration for juveniles (ages 14–17) and young adults (ages 18–24). Young adult, 1971: 393 per 100,000; juvenile, 1971: 508 per 100,000. *Sources: Children in Custody,* Law Enforcement Assistance Administration (Washington, DC: U.S. Government Printing Office, 1974); U.S. Department of Justice, Bureau of Justice Statistics, *Sourcebook of Criminal Justice Statistics* (Washington, DC: Government Printing Office, 1971, 1991, 1996).

The pattern during the early 1990s is more complicated. The rate at which 14- to 17-year-olds were incarcerated rose almost as much in the four years after 1991 as in the two decades prior to 1991. For that reason, it may look like a significant shift toward toughness had finally taken hold. But the growth in young adult incarceration was much greater than in the younger age group, so that the gap between older juveniles and young adults actually widened in the early 1990s. The incarceration rate per 100,000 grew by about 80 for the 14–17 group, and more than three times that much for those 18–24.

Their consistent incarceration-limiting policy generated substantial political pressure on juvenile courts in the United States, while the criminal justice system experienced two decades of uninterrupted penal expansion. Indeed, the data in figure 4.1 suggest a new explanation for the flurry of legislative activity to create larger punishments for juvenile offenders. The usual account of juvenile crime legislation is based on the concern of politicians and citizens with juvenile crime and violence.[34] But what figure 4.1 shows is that the political forces that had produced extraordinary expansion through the rest of the penal system had been stymied in juvenile courts. In that sense, the under-18 population became the last significant battleground for a get-tough orientation that had permeated the rest of the peno-correctional system. The performance of American juvenile courts over the 1970s and 1980s had been exceptional, and this rendered the system vulnerable to the same attacks that had succeeded decades before in criminal justice.

From this perspective, the angry assaults on juvenile courts throughout the 1990s are a tribute to the efficacy of juvenile justice in protecting delinquents from the incarcerative explosion that had happened everywhere else. The largest irony of the 1990s, from a diversionary standpoint, is that the juvenile courts were under constant assault not because they had failed in their youth-serving mission, but because they had succeeded in protecting their clientele from the new orthodoxy in crime control.

There is a less comforting aspect to the statistics in figure 4.1 as a measure of juvenile court diversion. While the incarceration rate for 18- to 24-year-olds in 1995 was 2.5 times that of 14- to 17-year-olds, the juvenile rate had been only 28 percent below that of the older group in 1971. The optimistic spin on such data is that both the criminal and juvenile courts had been emphasizing diversion in 1971, resulting in the small difference in lockup rates. The pessimistic interpretation is that an earlier and more confident era of juvenile justice was associated with levels of secure confinement that were uncomfortably close to those of criminal courts. In either case, the data from the last third of the twentieth century clearly show that the special policies of juvenile courts were much more significant in their impact on incarceration risks after the War on Drugs and the sharp shift toward general incapacitation in the criminal courts.

Conclusion

For those who see adolescence as a stressful and experiment-laden transition to adulthood, growing up is the one sure cure for most juvenile crime. The policy objective that drew many adherents to the notion of a juvenile court was that it was to be a place where it would be possible "to understand the growing child—and to find ways for securing his orderly development in normal society."[35] A criminal law that removed youth from community settings and thrust them into lockups and jails was seen as a principal threat to adolescent development in normal society. For this reason, the juvenile court "came into the world to prevent children from being treated as criminals." This was and is "the first idea that should be grasped concerning the juvenile court."[36] It is a rationale of tremendous durability, more humble in its ambitions and closer to institutional reality than the rehabilitative ideal ever was. The diversionary theory of juvenile court jurisdiction was not an alternative to helping juvenile offenders, but it was a more particular and more limited kind of help than plenary child saving. It was a modest, focused way of helping young offenders survive both adolescent crime and the experience of social control with their life chances still intact.

The historical record suggests that the diversionary juvenile court was a reform more worldly and sophisticated than historic scholarship has yet acknowledged. There is in the early history of juvenile court the basis for a jurisprudence of patience and restraint, an institutional commitment to do less harm than the criminal courts did to young offenders. This was a very good idea in 1899. It still is.

FIVE

Penal Proportionality for the Young Offender

Notes on Immaturity, Capacity, and Diminished Responsibility

At its core, the Anglo-American criminal law is about punishment, about the intentional infliction of harm on persons who have committed blameworthy acts. We punish because we believe such harm is morally deserved by a particular individual for a particular act. To do this, the criminal law needs to make sense as a language of moral desert, punishing only those who deserve condemnation, punishing the guilty only to the extent of their individual moral desert, and punishing the range of variously guilty offenders it apprehends in an order that reflects their relative blameworthiness. Of course, the perfect satisfaction of these standards is always beyond human capacity, but the legitimacy of a system of criminal punishment depends on recognizing the moral obligations of penal proportionality and attempting to meet them. To the extent that institutions of criminal and juvenile justice make punishment decisions about young law violators, they must be servants of the moral obligations of penal proportionality.

The harm caused by a particular criminal act is one important measure of the seriousness of an offence and thus of the amount of punishment it deserves, but the role of harm done in determining deserved criminal punishment is much less dominant than the influence of harm done in the measure of compensation due or owing in civil law. The level of harm suffered determines compensation in the civil system once a liability threshold has been satisfied. But desert is a measure of fault that will attach very different punishment to criminal acts that cause similar amounts of harm.

The Anglo-American law of homicide is a spectacular demonstration of the wide range of punishments that await persons culpable in causing a death, even though the harm caused is a near constant. The punishments for criminal homicide in most states typically range from probation to capital punishment with a number of intermediate

stops (Zimring, Eigen, and O'Malley 1976). An intentional and culpable killing may be first-degree murder, second-degree murder or
voluntary manslaughter (LeFave and Scott 1986, 605–683). Reckless-
ness and negligence lead to multiple categories of criminal liability.
Blameworthy intended killings under circumstances of provocation
or unreasonable mistake may generate less punishment than some
categories of reckless conduct that cause death. A host of subjective
elements affect judgments of deserved punishment, even though the
victim is just as dead in each different case.

This chapter considers one set of subjective personal factors that
influence the extent to which adolescent defendants deserve punishment for particular blameworthy acts. I will argue that even when a
particular young person possesses the cognitive capacities and social
controls necessary to be eligible for punishment, immaturity should
continue to be a mitigating circumstance for some time.

This chapter is organized into four sections. The first section attempts to create mutually exclusive definitions of capacity and diminished responsibility to avoid a persistent confusion between
threshold issues of capacity and questions of the proper level of punishment for an immature offender. The second section argues that juvenile courts in the United States have been a recognized part of a
punishment system for at least a generation. The third section first
distinguishes between two separate reasons for lower levels of punishment of the immature: penal proportionality and theories of youth
as a protected and privileged status. The diminished responsibility
doctrine in penal theory is then developed at some length and contrasted to changes in adolescent punishment based on youth policy.
The fourth section addresses the relationship between assumptions
about immaturity that animate various conceptions of diminished responsibility and other legal doctrines that govern adolescence in
modern industrial states.

Immaturity and Desert

One fundamental distinction in the criminal law is between conditions that negate criminal liability and those that might mitigate the
punishment deserved under particular circumstances. Very young
children and the profoundly mentally ill lack the minimum capacity
necessary to justify punishment under a system where blameworthiness is punishment's sine qua non. Those exhibiting less profound

handicaps of the same kind that serve as excuses will often qualify for a lesser level of deserved punishment, even though they meet the minimum conditions for some punishment.

Those who were searching for illustrations of the difference between excuse and mitigation in the early months of 1998 need look no further than the sad but well-publicized plea bargain of Theodore Kaczynski, the infamous Unabomber, sentenced to life in prison after a negotiated plea of guilty on the eve of his death penalty trial. A psychiatric diagnosis of this defendant clearly established the existence of serious psychosis. Just as clearly, the defendant was not sufficiently removed by illness from the capacity for moral judgment to excuse his conduct from criminal liability under current law. Under the circumstances of this case, the trial judge would not even have allowed the defense team to raise the defendant's profound mental illness as an absolute defense to the criminal charges.

The general principle that mental illness should not excuse but can mitigate is well established (see American Law Institute 1980 Model Penal Code 210.3[1][b]). Thus, the same disease conditions that could not excuse Kaczynski's conduct might well mitigate his deserved punishment, and this was the prospect that could justify the government in agreeing to a less-than-death sentence. This is most clear in cases involving capital punishment because with respect to the death penalty, there are common law, constitutional, and statutory discussions of mitigation not found in current law on imprisonment or other punishments.

Immaturity, like mental disease or defect, might serve both as an excuse and as a mitigation in the determination of just punishment. But this double duty has frequently led to confusion between the criteria and proper ages for immaturity to function as an excuse, and the criteria and proper age boundaries for mitigation. Part of this confusion is solely linguistic. Terms like "capacity," "culpability," and "responsibility" are quite slippery. For the purposes of this chapter, I wish to use the term "capacity" rather restrictively, to refer to the cognitive and experientially based abilities that are necessary at a minimum before punitive sanctions may properly be imposed in either a juvenile or a criminal court.

In a simple world, the matter of capacity could be a totally binary concept, something a particular youth either has for all purposes or lacks. In the real world, different thresholds of competence may apply, depending, first, on the kind of court and kind of punishment involved, and, second, on the type of task that a finding of competence applies to. But my use of the term "competence" restricts it to binary determinations of minimum conditions of punishment eligibility. Seven-year-olds are too young for only punishment—they lack *penal capacity.*

I want to restrict the term "diminished responsibility" to circumstances where the minimum abilities for blameworthiness and thus for punishment exist but the immaturity of the offender still suggests that less punishment is justified by reason of the offender's immaturity. While the elements of capacity were limited in the previous discussion to moral reasoning and minimal social information and experience, the personal deficits that could count toward immaturity as a mitigation of punishment might be more numerous. A 14-year-old deserves some punishment—he or she has penal capacity—but he or she is not as blameworthy as a 20-year-old who commits the same offense.

The use of restrictive and mutually exclusive definitions makes it possible to make two points that are no less important to legal policy because of their simplicity. In the first place, a finding of minimal capacity is in no way logically inconsistent with concluding that an offender's immaturity is a reason for mitigating the punishment imposed on him or her. The definitions I've imposed would make any argument of this kind a confusion between capacity concerns (excuse in relation to liability) and diminished responsibility concerns (mitigation of punishment).

The second preliminary point is not quite so simple, but involves the systematic relationship between standards for competence and the theoretical and practical importance of diminished responsibility in criminal sentencing. Once personal capacity is relevant to the moral measure of punishment, we should expect to observe an inverse relationship between whether a minimum capacity test screens out troublesome cases and the importance of assessing diminished responsibility for punishment purposes. The more significant the capacity stage, the less significant will be the role of diminished responsibility concerns in keeping the punishment system morally coherent.

The criminal law of mental illness provides an illustration of this theory of inverse importance. Assume two competing standards for when mental illness excuses persons who commit forbidden behaviors from criminal liability. Under a very restrictive McNaughton standard, relatively few mentally ill persons will be excused from criminal liability, since the standard requires that a defendant not appreciate the wrongfulness of his or her conduct before the excuse will hold. Under the much more liberal Durham rule, a larger propor-

tion of mentally ill defendants will be excused from any criminal liability because the excuse will apply whenever it is found that the
otherwise criminal act was the product of a mental disease. If serious
mental illness is a moral concern relevant to punishment, where will
the law and procedure relating to mitigating punishment by reason
of mental illness be more important, in a liberal Durham jurisdiction
or in a restrictive McNaughton jurisdiction?

The relative importance of diminished responsibility should be
greater in the McNaughton jurisdiction, because the more liberal
rules of excuse in a Durham jurisdiction will divert many more defendants away from being eligible for a criminal sentence, including
a large number of those defendants with the most profound mental
illnesses. By contrast, the more restrictive McNaughton rule will
push a much larger proportion of its mentally ill defendants through
to criminal sentencing, including many of the sickest. There will be a
larger number of cases to consider for mitigation of punishment, and
a larger range of types and severity of mental illness to be measured
against the moral compass of the criminal law of sentencing. The
stricter the standard of excluding the mentally ill, the more important the doctrines and procedures that calibrate mitigations of punishment. On this reasoning, the maximum importance for a diminished responsibility system would come in a system that rejects a
defense of insanity but admits the relevance of mental illness (Morris
1982).

With regard to the punishment of the immature, the same inverse
importance principle applies. If no offender under 18 were eligible
for punishment because the system diverted all below that age out at
the capacity stage, the role of diminished responsibility would be
much less important than if a system found minimum capacity at age
12 or 13. The younger the age at which kids were deemed eligible for
some punishment, the more important would be the role of principles of mitigation of punishment based on immaturity.

The implications of any such inverse relationship between excuse
and mitigation for immaturity are substantial in the United States at
this moment in our history. Every trend in recent legislation in this
country seems calculated to increase the importance of doctrines of
mitigation on account of immaturity as an influence on sentencing.
Mandatory and discretionary waiver of adolescent offenders to
criminal courts, lowering of the minimum ages for eligibility for
transfer from juvenile to criminal court, and increasing the severity
and penal context of sanctions administered within juvenile courts

all have the tendency to put additional pressure on doctrines of mitigation to avoid injustice in the punishment of young offenders. The
collective impact of all three trends is to place unprecedented importance on the ability of American criminal and juvenile courts to generate coherent doctrines of diminished responsibility on account of
immaturity for the huge and diverse assortment of young offenders
who are now regarded as eligible for some punishment. Every new
reduction in the threshold of penal capacity makes the role of diminished capacity doctrine more important in maintaining a system of
penal proportionality.

But what should be the content and boundaries of such doctrines?
What aspects of American adolescence are relevant to the proper
punishment for crimes committed by the young? This is a question
not only of analytic matters, but rather of an issue that requires
hands-on knowledge of youth and youth policy to answer. After a
short discussion of further conceptual distinctions in the next section, in the third section I will discuss such an empirically informed
assessment.

Delinquency and the Aims of the Juvenile Court

Is there an age or level of capacity below which no child should be
subjected to the delinquency jurisdiction of the juvenile court? The
answer to this question depends on whether the delinquency docket
of the juvenile court should be regarded as punitive in nature. If not,
there is no need to find any minimum standard of accountability or
ability to assist a defense counsel. No minimum age or level of capacity is necessary for a juvenile court to take dependency jurisdiction or to investigate neglect. If the sole aim of delinquency jurisdiction were the assistance and the best interests of the minor, then
kids of any age and capacity would be eligible for such help, no matter the level of their comprehension.

For this reason, the original theory of juvenile justice probably
would not have required any minimum level of comprehension or
desert prior to a delinquency finding (Zimring 1982, 31–40). Just as
clearly, the U.S. Constitution now requires some minimum level of
penal responsibility and comprehension prior to affixing the delinquency label. The constitutional precedent for this requirement is *In
re Gault* (1967), a case more often noted for its procedural rulings—the
right to a lawyer, to notice of charges, and to confront witnesses—than

for the substantive assumption at the heart of the ruling. What juvenile courts do to young persons classified as delinquent was enough like punishment in the view of the *Gault* Court that a large number of criminal-style procedural regularities were necessary to satisfy the due process guarantee of the Fifth Amendment.

As a matter of constitutional law, then, we have known for a generation that those who administer juvenile court delinquency dockets are in the business of punishing adolescent law violators. Once this is conceded, it is also apparent that juvenile and criminal courts in the United States have been operating a large system with relatively low standards of penal capacity but with reduced sanctions that fit closely a model of diminished responsibility in juvenile courts and probably in criminal courts as well. Compared to systems in western Europe and Scandinavia, we punish youth who offend at younger ages—11, 12, and 13—but one consequence of punishing the very young is that justice requires calculations of diminished responsibility. If this reading of the juvenile court is correct, the dominant impact of immaturity on punishment of offenders in the United States is that punishment is reduced because of diminished responsibility. What is extraordinary about this huge diminished responsibility system operating across two large and independent judicial branches is the absence of either explicit recognition of this fact or any legal standards for describing this diminished responsibility system.

Indeed, many observers deny the character of the system. Transfer to criminal courts is often debated as if it were a precondition for punishing young persons arrested for crime. What the juvenile court does in this view is not "real" punishment, however that term might be defined. The confusion here may be between the character of a sanction and its quantity. Delinquents in juvenile courts may be receiving punishment, but not as much punishment as is administered to older offenders in other courts. But the lower dose does not change the fundamental character of the medicine.

In the United States, there is a massive establishment administering punitive sanctions short of full adult penalties for proportionality reasons that never get mentioned or analyzed. In terms of the inverse significance of capacity and diminished responsibly discussed in the previous section, the major operating principle at work in this country, at least since the 1960s, is diminished capacity—all the more reason to wonder about the substantive standards being used in this unarticulated and un-self-conscious punishment enterprise.

What should be the articulated standards for such a system? That is the topic of the next section.

Foundations of Special Punishments for Adolescents

For a variety of reasons, little has been written about the substantive arguments that support a separate policy toward crimes committed by young offenders. Part of the problem is that debate about procedures and jurisdiction crowds out any issues of the substantive content of a youth-crime policy (Zimring 1998), and another part of the problem is that juvenile court and criminal court issues are usually considered separately, so that little pressure is exerted to examine the same questions across different procedural settings. A further deterrent to substantive analysis is that separate treatment of children seems intuitively right in a way that does not invite further scrutiny from its advocates. Of course kids who violate laws should be treated differently; should we imprison 6-year-olds? Legal nuance and complexity might seem beside the point in this context. For all these reasons, no sustained analysis of the factors that justify separate treatment of adolescent offenders is in the literature to measure against the known facts on serious youth violence.

Some years ago, I suggested that two general policy clusters were at work in youth-crime policy: diminished responsibility due to immaturity and special efforts designed to give young offenders room to reform in the course of adolescent years. The issues grouped under the "diminished capacity" heading relate to the traditional concerns of the criminal law; these matters tell us why a criminal lawyer might regard a younger offender as less culpable than an older offender. The cluster of policies under the heading of "room-to-reform" are derived from legal policies toward young persons in the process of growing up. They do not concern penal desert.

Dimensions of Diminished Responsibility

The consideration of immaturity as a species of diminished responsibility has some historic precedent but little analytic history. Children below age seven were at common law not responsible for criminal acts by reason of incapacity, while those between seven and fourteen were the subject of special inquiries with respect to capacity. Capacity in this sense was not a question of degree, but an "all or nothing" matter similar to legal insanity, as discussed in the first section. Yet diminished culpability logic argues that even after a youth passes the minimum threshold of competence that leads to a finding of capacity to commit crime, the barely competent youth is not as culpable and therefore not as deserving of a full measure of punishment as a fully qualified adult offender. Just as psychiatric disorder or cognitive impairment that does not render a subject exempt from the criminal law might still mitigate the punishment to be imposed, so a minimally competent adolescent should not be responsible for the whole of an adult's desert for the same act.

In the first section, I argued that this notion of diminished culpability as a limiting influence on criminal punishment is not an isolated element of juvenile jurisprudence but rather one expression of a core value in Anglo-American criminal law: the notion of penal proportionality, which requires that less blameworthy offenders—the young, the emotionally disturbed—be punished less harshly.

Yet the absence of analysis about penal proportionality for early and middle adolescents is a particular puzzle. Despite the universal acceptance of immaturity in doctrines of infancy and the widespread acceptance of reduced levels of responsibility in early teen years, there has been little analysis of the aspects of immaturity that are relevant to mitigation of punishment. Again, the intuitive appeal of the result and the separate categories of juvenile and criminal jurisprudence may have deferred the analysis of its rationale. Yet the specific attributes of legal immaturity must be discovered before judgments can be made about what ages and conditions are relevant to reducing punishment on this ground.

In the second section, I argued that the entirety of the delinquency jurisdiction of the juvenile court can be seen as an institutional expression of the diminished culpability of youthful offenders. The lesser maximum punishments of serious crime in juvenile court can be seen as testimony to the belief in youthful diminished culpability, but this set of practices is at best mute testimony, lacking any statement of principles that can be analyzed and criticized. Further, when this concept of proportionality is expressed only in the institutional output of one court system, the transfer of offenders from the juvenile to criminal court would risk changing the applicable penal principles without justification.

What characteristics of children and adolescents might lead us to lessen punishment in the name of penal proportionality? An initial distinction needs to be drawn between diminished responsibilities and the poor decisions such impairments encourage. Most teenaged law violators make bad decisions, but so do most adults who commit major infractions of the criminal law. Anglo-American criminal law is designed to punish bad decisions in full measure. But persons who, through no fault of their own, lack the abilities observed in the common citizen either to appreciate the difference between wrong and allowable conduct or to conform their conduct to the law's requirements may be blameless because of their incapacity. Even when sufficient cognitive skill and emotional control is present to pass the threshold of criminal capacity, a significant deficit in the ability to appreciate or control behavior would mean the forbidden conduct is not *as much* the offender's fault as it would otherwise be, and the quantum of appropriate punishment is less.

How might 14-, 15-, and 17-year-olds who commit crimes be said to exhibit diminished responsibility in moral and legal terms? There are three different types of personal attributes that influence adolescents' decisions to commit crimes. In each case, the adolescent may lack full adult skills and therefore also full adult moral responsibilities when the law is violated.

First, older children and younger adolescents may lack sufficiently fully developed cognitive abilities to comprehend the moral content of commands and to apply legal and moral rules to social situations. The lack of this kind of capacity is at the heart of infancy as an absolute defense to criminal liability. This ability to comprehend and apply rules in the abstract requires a mix of cognitive ability and information. A young person who lacks these skills will not do well on a paper-and-pencil test to assess knowledge about what is lawful and unlawful behavior and why. Very young children have obvious gaps in both information and the cognitive skills to use it. Older children have more subtle but nonetheless significant deficits in moral-reasoning abilities. For most normal adolescents, the ability to reason in an adult style is present by age 16 or, at the latest, 17 (Steinberg and Cauffman 1996, 268).

The ability to pass paper-and-pencil tests in moral reasoning may be one necessary condition for adult capacity of self-control, but it is by no means a sufficient condition. A second skill that is required to transform cognitive understanding into the fully developed capacity to obey the law is the ability to control impulses. This is not the type of skill that can be tested well on abstract written or oral surveys. Long after a child knows that taking property is wrong, the capacity to resist temptation may not be fully operational.

To an important extent, self-control is a habit of behavior developed over a period of time—a habit that is dependant on the experience of successfully exercising self-control. This particular type of maturity, like so many others, takes practice. While children must start learning to control impulses at a very early age, the question of how long the process continues until adult levels of behavioral control are achieved is an open one. Impulse control is a social skill not easily measured in a laboratory. We also do not know the extent to which lessons to control impulses are generalized, nor do we know how context-specific habits of self-control are. Kids must learn not to dash in front of cars at an early age. How much of that capacity for self-control carries over when other impulses—say the temptation to cheat on a test—occur in new situations? The assessment of self-control in field settings is not a thick chapter in current psychological knowledge. The developmental psychology of self-control has been studied by question-and-answer hypotheticals and not by the observation of behavior in natural settings.

There may also be an important distinction between impulse control in the context of frustration and impulse control in temptation settings. If so, the frustration context may be the more important one for study of the determinants of youth violence. When should we expect adult levels of control of violent impulses while angry? Almost certainly the developing adolescent can only learn his or her way to fully developed control by experience. This process will probably not be completed until very late in the maturation process.

To the extent that new situations and opportunities require new habits of self-control, the teen years are periods when self-control issues are confronted on a series of distinctive new battlefields. The physical controls of earlier years are supplanted by physical freedoms. New domains—including secondary education, sex, and driving—require not only the cognitive appreciation of the need for self-control in a new situation but also its practice. If this normally takes a while to develop, the bad decisions made along the way should not be punished as severely as they are for adults, who have already had the full opportunity to develop habits of self-control in a variety of domains relevant to the criminal law. To the extent that inexperience is associated with being error prone, this inexperience is partially excusable in the teen years, whereas it is not in later life. That is the basis for a mitigation for adolescents that is not available for most adults.

The ability to resist peer pressure is yet a third social skill that is a necessary part of legal obedience and is not fully developed in many adolescents. A teen may know right from wrong and may even have developed the capacity to control his or her impulses while alone, but resisting temptation while alone is a different task from resisting the pressure to commit an offense when adolescent peers are pushing for misbehavior and waiting to see whether or not the outcome they desire will occur. Most adolescent decisions to break the law take place on a social stage where the immediate pressure of peers is the real motive for most teenage crime. A necessary condition for an adolescent to stay law-abiding is the ability to deflect or resist peer pressure. Many kids lack this crucial social skill for a long time.

Figure 5.1 shows the percentage of juvenile defendants who were accused of committing a crime with at least one confederate in the New York City juvenile courts of the 1970s. These offenders were all under 16 at the time the act was committed. The percentage of total defendants who acted with a confederate ranged from 60 percent for assault to 90 percent for robbery. (For further examples and analysis, see chapter 6.)

The cold criminological facts are these: the teen years are characterized by what has long been called "group offending." No matter the crime, if a teenager is the offender, he or she is usually not committing the offense alone. When adults commit theft, they usually are acting alone. When kids commit theft, it's usually in groups. When adults commit rape, robbery, homicide, burglary, or assault, they

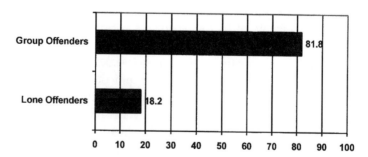

Figure 5.1. Multiple offender cases as a percentage of total juveniles charged, by crime, New York City. *Source:* Zimring 1981.

usually are acting alone. When adolescents commit the same offenses, they usually do so accompanied by other kids (see chapter 6). The setting for the offenses of adolescents is the presence of delinquent peers as witnesses and collaborators.

No fact of adolescent criminality is more important than what sociologists call its "group context," and this fact is important to a reality-based theory of adolescent moral and legal responsibility for criminal acts.

When an adult offender commits rape, his incitement to action may be rage or lust or any number of other things. When a teen offender in a group setting commits rape, an important part of the motive is social—usually "I dare you" or "Don't be a chicken." Fear of being called a "chicken" is almost certainly the major cause of death and injury from youth violence in the United States—the explicit or implicit "I dare you" leads kids to show off and deters them from publicly backing out of committing crimes, even if they would prefer to. "I dare you" is the reason that "having delinquent friends" both precedes an adolescent's involvement in violence and is a discriminant predictor of future violence (Elliott and Menard 1996; Howell and Hawkins 1998).

How does this propensity for group crime amount to diminished responsibility? That social settings account for the majority of all youth crime suggests that the capacity to deflect or resist peer pressure is a crucially necessary dimension of being law-abiding in adolescence. Dealing with peer pressure is another dimension of capacity that requires social experience. Kids who do not know how to deal with such pressure lack effective control of the situations that place them most at risk of crime in their teens. This surely does not excuse criminal conduct. But any moral scheme that gives mitigational recognition to other forms of inexperience must also do so for a lack of peer-management skills that an accused has not had a fair opportunity to develop. This is a matter of great importance, given the reality of contemporary youth crime as group behavior.

I do not want to suggest that current knowledge is sufficient for us to measure the extent of diminished capacity in young offenders, nor do I want to express in detail the types of understanding and control that are important parts of a normative developmental psychology. We have a great deal of social psychology homework ahead of us before achieving understanding of the key terms in adolescent behavioral controls that are relevant to criminal offending in field settings.

There are, however, two important points to be made about age and diminished responsibility, even in the current state of partial knowledge. The first principle about adolescent development and age boundaries for diminished responsibilities is that the age where the legal system can expect adult-level abilities depends on the range of experience that is regarded as important. If only the cognitive capacity to make judgments in paper-and-pencil exercises is important, then adolescents are usually well equipped by their sixteenth birthdays. But if social experience in matters such as anger and impulse management also counts, and a fair opportunity to learn to deal with peer pressures is regarded as important, expecting the experienced-based ability to resist impulses and peers to be fully formed prior to age 18 or 19 would seem on present evidence to be wishful thinking. Becoming an adult is a gradual process in modern industrial societies. Ironically, the process may start earlier but still take longer to complete than in earlier eras (Zimring 1982, 17–22). Partial responsibility for law violation may come at a young age, but full responsibility should take longer. This is the learner's permit perspective discussed in chapter 2.

The second thing to remember about diminished responsibility is that it is not merely a doctrine of juvenile justice but a principle of penal proportionality, wherever in the legal system that calculations of culpability must be made. The nature of adolescent immaturity would raise the same issues we now confront in juvenile justice even if all young offenders were tried in criminal courts. In other words, even if there were no separate youth policy to consult in making decisions about younger offenders, even if there were no juvenile court, the just punishment of young offenders would be a distinctive moral and legal problem. So changes in the jurisdictional boundaries of juvenile and criminal courts do not remove the necessity of determining variations in moral desert.

Room to Reform in Youth Development Policy

The notion that children and adolescents should be the subject of special legal rules pervades the civil as well as criminal laws of most developed societies. A multiplicity of different policies are reflected in different legal areas, as well as important differences throughout law in the treatment of younger and older children. Under these circumstances, to refer to a single "youth policy" generally risks misunderstandings about both the subjects of the policies and the age groups covered.

The policies I refer to in this section concern adolescence, a period that spans roughly from ages 11 or 12 to about age 21. This is also the only segment of childhood that is associated with high rates of serious crime. This span has been described as a period of increasing semi-autonomy, in which kids acquire adult liberties in stages and learn their way toward adult freedoms along the way (see chapter 2).

At the heart of this process is a notion of adolescence as a period of "learning by doing," in which the only way competence in decision-making can be achieved is by making decisions and making mistakes. For this reason, adolescence is mistake-prone by design. The special challenge here is to create safeguards in the environments of adolescents that reduce the permanent costs of adolescent mistakes. Two goals of legal policy are to facilitate "learning by doing" and to reduce the hazards associated with expectable errors. One important hallmark of a successful adolescence is survival to adulthood, preferably with the individual's life chances intact.

There is a popular theory about the etiology of youth crime that provides a rationale for room-to-reform policy. The theory is that the high prevalence of offense behavior in the teen years and the rather high rates of incidence for those who offend are transitory phenomena associated with a transitional status and life period (Elliott 1994). Even absent heroic interventions, the conduct that occurs at peak rates in adolescence will level off substantially if and when adolescents achieve adult roles and status.

That assumption carries three implications. First, it regards criminal offenses as a more or less normal adolescent phenomenon, a by-product of the same transitional status that increases the risks of traffic accidents, accidental pregnancies, and suicidal gestures. This view of youth crime tells us, therefore, that policy toward those offenses that are a by-product of adolescence should be a part of larger policies toward youth.

A second implication of the notion that high rates of adolescent crime can be outgrown is that major interventions may not be necessary to reorient offenders. The central notion of what has been called "adolescence-limited" offending is that the cure for youth crime is growing up.

Related to the hope for natural processes of remission over time is the tendency for persons who view youth-crime policy as a branch of youth-development policy to worry that drastic countermeasures that inhibit the natural transition to adulthood may cause more harm than they are worth. If a particular treatment carries risks of severe side effects, it usually should only be elected if failure to use it would risk even more cost. Those who regard youth crime as a transitional phenomenon see problems of deviance resolving themselves without drastic interventions and are prone to doubt the efficacy of high-risk interventions on utilitarian grounds. So juvenile justice theories with labels like "radical nonintervention" and "diversion" are a natural outgrowth of belief that long-term prospects for most young offenders are favorable.

But what about the short term? The current costs of youth crime to the community at large, to other adolescents, and to the offending kids are quite large. How would enthusiasts for juvenile court nonintervention seek to protect the community? Is a "room-to-reform" policy inconsistent with *any* punitive responses to adolescent law violation?

The emphasis in youth-development policy is on risk management over a period of transitional high danger. As I have shown, the legal theory that adolescents are not fully mature allows a larger variety of risk management tactics than are available for dealing with adults. Minors cannot purchase liquor, acquire handguns, buy cigarettes, or pilot planes. Younger adolescents are constrained by curfews and compulsory education laws. There are special age-graded rules for driving motor vehicles and entering contracts and employment relationships. Many of these rules are to protect the young person from the predation of others. Many are to protect the young person from himself or herself. Many are to protect the community from harmful acts by the young. So there is a rich mixture of risk-management strategies available to reduce the level of harmful consequences from youth crime.

Does this mix of strategies include the punishment of intentional harms? The answer to this question is yes from all but the most extreme radical noninterventionists, but attaching negative consequences to youthful offenders is regarded as good policy only up to a point. Youth-development proponents are suspicious of sacrificing the interests of a young person in order to serve as a deterrent example to other youth if the punished offender's interests are substantially prejudiced. Punishing a young offender in ways that significantly diminish later life changes compromises the essential core of a youth-protection policy. There may be circumstances in which drastic punishment is required, but such punishments always violate important elements of youth-development policy, and can be tolerated only rarely, in cases of proven need. In this view, punishment begins to be suspicious when it compromises the long-term interests of the targeted young offender.

Punishment and the Legal Construction
of Adolescence

The account of diminished responsibility and immaturity presented here is only one of a number of competing proposals for measuring the liability of adolescent offenders. It is a characteristic of the current era that there are sharply different proposals for punishment policies toward young offenders that explicitly or implicitly make quite different assumptions about the moral responsibilities of adolescents.

One of the most discouraging features of this continuing debate about punishing youth crime in the United States is the extent to which it is isolated from consideration of other law-related policies toward growing up. When the issue is transfer from juvenile to adult court or the maximum punishment that juvenile courts with blended jurisdiction should have the power to impose, there is rarely much reference to the age boundaries used in other areas of law, or whether the assumptions about adolescent development that particular crime policies advance are consistent with the assumptions about ages of maturity that are made in other regulatory domains. There is, instead, an ad hoc quality to youth-crime policy discussions, as if the way the juvenile and criminal courts treat young offenders is not related in important ways to other areas of law or to the legal conceptions of adolescent nonoffenders.

I wish to defend a contrary proposition, that one measure of the merit of a punishment policy toward young offenders is the degree to which the legal policy on this topic is consistent with the assumptions about adolescent competencies that can be found in other areas of the law. Even if the crime policy preferences we express are in fact made on an ad hoc basis, one important test of the quality of any punishment policy is whether it says the same things about the nature of growing up in the United States as the legal rules that govern the advancement to adult status in other legal categories.

If consistency with other legal doctrines on age is the criterion, the trend toward early and total penal responsibility is problematic. Failing to regard persons under the age of 18 as anything other than significantly less mature than adults who meet the full adult standard for punishment contradicts the laws regarding the age of majority in every state in every area of nonpenal law. Yet, despite the fact that every state in the United States has legislated some circumstances where persons under 18 face the criminal courts without any explicit recognition that their young age merits a reduction of the punishment, there is no mention in legislative debate of the fact that persons treated as nonadult for all other purposes are presumably held to adult standards upon criminal conviction. Why is this?

There are two circumstances in which the gap between criminal liability standards and other legal standards might be other than problematic, but neither saving circumstance is plausible in the United States of the twenty-first century. In the first place, it could be argued that serious criminal offenders are much more mature that their noncriminal age peers. Of course, to take this seriously would be to suggest that kids who commit serious crimes should also be able to drink alcohol and purchase firearms at an earlier age than ordinary teens. The closest I have seen to this sort of tribute to the maturity of the targets of social control was in an article entitled "In Venezuela 'Year of Rights,' the Police Kill More Youths" (*New York Times*, December 6, 1997), in which a Venezuelan official justified his country's jailing policy by alleging that "Latin American minors are not like European minors. Mentally they are adults." Are juvenile armed robbers in the United States also to be considered a discrete category of precocious mental adults?

The second proposition that could harmonize full punishment at young ages with higher ages of privilege and majority is concluding that immaturity on account of youth should not influence the level of punishment deserved by any persons capable of committing crimes. To the extent that immaturity deprives a person of penal capacity, this theory of the irrelevancy of youth would give way to common law requirements of minimal responsibility, as discussed in the first section of this chapter. But once capacity is established, why not just treat all other levels of immaturity the way the penal law treats bad judgments by adults?

But why would any legal system wish to treat offenses that were partly the result of immaturity as if the immaturity that cooccurs with childhood and adolescence were wholly the young person's fault? One searches in vain for a principled argument to make immaturity a step function of tremendous importance in determining a capacity threshold for punishment but irrelevant thereafter. It may be said that terrible crimes are committed by youths and there is a social necessity for punishment. Whether there is a social necessity for the same level of punishment as for adults is usually not discussed in this context. The implicit assumption is that only two polar alternatives, full penal responsibility or no responsibility, are the field of choice. Certainly the political slogan associated with unmitigated penalties is something of a non sequitur: *If you are old enough to do the crime, you are old enough to do the time.* (Read literally, this refrain would also remove any requirement of any capacity prior to punishment.)

The lack of principle on this question is not limited to the realm of politics. The United State Supreme Court has made important constitutional law on the matter of diminished responsibility by reason of youth in connection with capital punishment with a distressing lack of substantive analysis. *Thompson v. Oklahoma,* and *Stanford v. Kentucky* and now *Roper v. Simmons* are the leading cases on youths and capital punishment, and the results in these cases are much easier to state than the principles on which they rest. No state may execute a person for an offense committed under the age of 18, even though the defendant might properly be found guilty of the highest grade of murder at a younger age than 16. The states may, if they choose, subject persons otherwise guilty of a capital crime to the death penalty if the defendant was over 18 at the time of the offense (*Roper v. Simmons*).

With respect to the death penalty, then, the prohibition against cruel and unusual punishment in the Eight Amendment mandates lesser maximum punishment for 17-year-old murderers than for adults. But not for 18-year-old murderers. The age boundaries imposed in these two cases were, to some extent, attributed to public attitudes as expressed through state legislative standards of minimum age (at the time of the crime) for execution. But there was no attempt to relate the age boundary selected for the death penalty to the views of maturity reflected in other legal rules. As a matter of minimum constitutional standards, a youth can become eligible for what has properly been called the "ultimate penalty in criminal law" three years before he or she is old enough to purchase alcohol or handguns. Some theory of penal proportionality must be at work here, for why else would the Court prohibit imposition of a punishment on a 17-year-old defendant who is properly liable for first-degree murder? But how this implicit theory of penal proportionality can be rationalized with the other age boundaries of growing up in American law is a continuing mystery.

If immaturity on account of youth is relevant to penal desert, then proposing a particular age or set of conditions as appropriate for full punishment should be accompanied by the consideration of other legal boundaries of maturity—a set of assumptions that should be tested against other legal principles that implicitly or explicitly make assumptions about how and when adolescents reach adulthood.

The conception of adolescent punishment discussed in the second section of this chapter is consistent by design with a theory first advanced some years ago (see chapter 2) that sees adolescence as a long period of semiautonomy in which adolescents learn their way toward adult levels of responsibility gradually. This notion is also consistent with relatively early ages of partial accountability—an early age of capacity to be punished—but long periods of diminished responsibility that incrementally approach adult standards in the late teens. The major emphasis of this approach is not the capacity threshold but the less-than-adult punishments that gradually approach adult levels during the late teen years. This system is consistent with the extension of some privileges, such as driving and voting, prior to full adulthood, because these privileges are extended to allow young persons to exercise their responsibility, a "learning by doing" theory (Zimring 1982, 89–96). It is also consistent with staggering ages of majority throughout adolescence rather than making all transitions on a single magic birthday. This is not a view of growing up in American law that would make 16-year-olds eligible for lethal injection as punishment for crime.

Conclusion

Once immaturity is relevant to the punishment that young offenders deserve, there is an inverse relationship between the importance of threshold determinations of capacity and the importance of diminished responsibility in keeping punishments proportional to the blameworthiness of offenders. The younger the age at which a system imposes some penal capacity on its children, the more sensitive the system must be to reducing punishment because of diminished responsibility. If the juvenile court is best viewed as an agency that assigns punishment to delinquents, then the major emphasis in the American system is on diminished responsibility. But no explicit doctrine of diminished responsibility can be found in the statute books and case reports of modern American law.

This analysis has argued for two doctrinal developments in the penal law of youth crime. The first is a sliding scale of responsibility based on both judgment and the practical experience of impulse management and peer control. The second is for establishing as a requirement—for any theory governing punishment for young offenders—an attempt to harmonize assumptions about the nature of adolescent development and responsibility with other legal regulations of the transition to adulthood. The rules of penal responsibility for the young should not be permitted to remain an isolated anomaly in the legal landscape.

Part III

THE ADOLESCENT OFFENDER

This part addresses one further set of facts that should influence policy toward young offenders: the realities of adolescent crime. Chapter 6 shows how peers have a pervasive influence on youth crime much greater than on adult offenders, no matter what crime is analyzed. This dominance of group crime demonstrates the necessity of studying group influence when examining the factors that influence rates of youth offending.

Chapter 7 shows how crime rates rise sharply and then fall back during adolescence, but distinguishes two contrasting patterns of juvenile crime. For offenses such as arson and most property crimes, the peak rates that occur during the teen years are much higher than the rates for young adults. The chapter calls this "phase-specific" criminality and suggests that its attractions seem specially concentrated in the adolescent experience. But offenses of violence have peak rates during late adolescence that are not much higher than the rates found during young adulthood. For such crimes, the increased rates during the teen years seem more likely to be a predictable part of learning adult roles and behavior.

Chapter 8 illustrates how ideological assumptions about disadvantaged children and their risks for later crime produced catastrophic miscalculations about future trends in youth crime over the period after 1994. Just when rates of juvenile homicide were supposed to double during the late 1990s, they instead fell by two-thirds. This cautionary tale should be remembered for decades as an antidote to the assured pronouncements of talking heads about "juvenile superpredators" and "the coming storm of juvenile violence."

All three of the studies reported in this part illustrate the close connection between the factual circumstances of youth crime and public policy debates.

Kids, Groups, and Crime
Some Implications of a Well-Known Secret

Social and policy sciences, reflecting human nature, are rich in contradiction and are occasionally perverse. It is sometimes possible both to know something important and to ignore that knowledge. To do this is to generate the phenomenon of the well-known secret, an obvious fact we ignore. When Edgar Allen Poe suggested that the best location to hide something is the most obvious place, he was teaching applied law and social science.

This chapter is about youth crime and sentencing policy. The "well-known secret" is this: adolescents commit crimes, as they live their lives, in groups. While the empirical evidence for this hypothesis is at least 70 years old, the consequences of this simple and important finding are frequently ignored when we measure crime, pass laws, and postulate theories of criminal activity. The problems associated with ignoring the obvious have grown more serious in recent years, as the study of criminal behavior has shifted from its sociological origins into a wide spectrum of social, behavioral, economic, and policy science disciplinary subspecialties. We have failed to ask the right questions and have risked answering the questions we ask in the wrong way because we have not appreciated what we already know.

The sentiments expressed in this chapter are strong: the burden of proof is mine. I shall attempt to meet that burden in two stages. In the first section, I discuss some evidence on adolescent crime as group behavior that emerged from the pioneering studies of the Chicago School in the 1920s, and I supplement this rich information with more recent crime-specific estimates of group criminality. In the second section, I catalogue some of the things we do not know as a consequence of ignoring the obvious.

Ignoring the well-known fact of group involvement causes us to overestimate the amount of crime kids commit, to generate inaccurate models of deterrence and incapacitation, and to overlook the special character of adolescent motives and vulnerabilities in group settings.

Kids, Groups, and Crime: Then and Now

Clifford Shaw and Henry McKay wrote a major study for the first National Commission on Crime. The year was 1931. The title was *Male Juvenile Delinquency as Group Behavior*.[1] The essay was based on an analysis of all boys who appeared in the Cook County, Illinois, juvenile court charged with delinquency during 1928. The analysis justified the title of their essay, as shown in figure 6.1 (their original fig. 9). Eight out of ten boys accused of delinquency were alleged to have committed their offenses in the company of one or more companions. Shaw and McKay extended this analysis by specifying the number of participants alleged, in the 1928 petition sample shown in figure 6.2 (their original fig. 10).

While these findings were dramatic, they were not surprising. A 1923 study of theft offenders in the same court had found that nine out of ten males charged with theft were believed to have committed their offenses in groups.[2]

More recent data on the relationship between groups and adolescent criminality are needed for two reasons. First, 1928 was quite a while ago. Second, the petty thieves depicted by Shaw and McKay

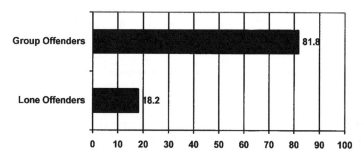

Figure 6.1. Percentage of lone and group offenders among offenders brought to the juvenile court. *Source:* C. Shaw and H. McKay, "Male Juvenile Delinquency as Group Behavior," in *Report on the Causes of Crime,* [II Wickersham Comm'n Rep., no. 13 (1931)], 191–199, reprinted as chapter 17 in *The Social Fabric of the Metropolis,* edited by J. Short (Chicago: University of Chicago Press, 1971).

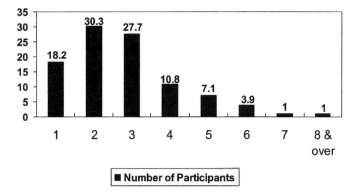

Figure 6.2. Percentage distribution of offenders brought to the court by number of participants. *Source:* C. Shaw and H. McKay, "Male Juvenile Delinquency as Group Behavior," in *Report on the Causes of Crime* [II Wickersham Comm'n Rep., no. 13 (1931)], 191–199, reprinted as chapter 17 in *The Social Fabric of the Metropolis,* edited by J. Short (Chicago: University of Chicago Press, 1971).

hardly fit the contemporary image of serious delinquency in the American city. The authors of one textbook on criminology observe how "quaint" the Shaw and McKay "delinquents seem to us today, in their knickerbockers and cloth caps and pre-Atomic innocence."[3] Furthermore, while group activity is associated with most juvenile delinquency, there is a tendency to revert to individualistic models when discussing serious crime.

Modern evidence is available on the predominance of groups as a distinctive aspect of adolescent criminality, including the serious offenses that are the focus of recent concern about youth crime policy. Table 6.1 shows data collected from a sample of robbery victims in the National Crime Panel in 1973.

For present purposes, the National Crime Panel data are deficient in two aspects. Since the method of the survey was to ask victims to guess the ages of offenders, it was necessary to use crude age categories. Robberies committed by offenders "under 21" are hardly homogeneous events. The second shortcoming of the National Crime Panel data is that when victims are asked to guess ages, a substantial number of incorrect guesses may produce a random error factor that would mute any difference in pattern between younger and older offenders because of improper classification.

Table 6.1. Robbery Incidents by Number of Offenders and Age Groups.

Number of offenders	Under 21 (percent)	21 and over (percent)
1	36%	61%
2	29	25
3	16	10
4 or more	19	4
Total	100%	100%

Note: Cases in which offenders were identified as mixed age groups have been deleted.

Source: National Crime Panel Data, provided by Wesley Skogan, Department of Political Science, Northwestern University.

Despite its drawbacks, the National Crime Panel data show that the relationship between the offender's age and group robbery is striking. Slightly more than a third of the robberies committed by offenders under 21 are committed by a single assailant, compared with 61 percent of those robberies where the victim believes the offender was over 21. At the other end of the distribution, younger offenders commit five times as many victimizations in groups of four or more than do older offenders.

More precise data on youth criminality are available from the recent Vera Institute of Justice analysis of the delinquency jurisdiction of New York's family court. Figure 6.3 is an analysis of a sample of cases leading to court referral of offenders under age 16 and thus eligible for family court processing in New York City. This figure is comparable to the information presented in the first Shaw and McKay analysis. The Vera sample counts each alleged delinquent as a separate case. Thus, if two juveniles are referred for one robbery, this will result in two cases of group robbery, while a single 15-year-old arrested for robbery counts as only one case. For this reason, the New York data overstate the number of offenses that are the product of group participation, but the method allows direct comparison with the Shaw and McKay figures, which were compiled using the same approach.[4] With the exception of assault and rape (n = 8), the bar charts bear what can only be called a striking resemblance to each other and to the theft estimates that emerged from the Chicago area studies half a century earlier.

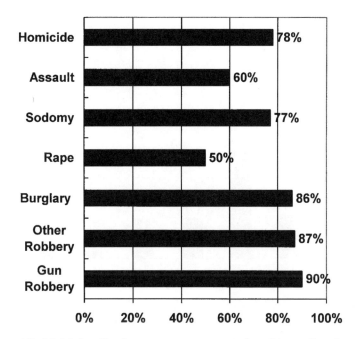

Figure 6.3. Multiple offender cases as a percent of total juveniles charged, by crime, New York City. *Source:* Vera Institute of Justice, Family Court Disposition Study (1981) (unpublished draft).

The predominance of group crime in this sample of young adolescent offenders (under 16) is similar to the earlier studies of juvenile theft, but occurs across a wide variety of offenses. For these age groups, the youthfulness of the offender appears to predict group participation more effectively than the nature of the offense.

The New York data were not coded in a way that could replicate the precomputer precision of Shaw and McKay's distribution of theft offenses by number of offenders.[5] However, a sample of armed robbery arrests referred to juvenile court in Los Angeles collected by the Rand Corporation does permit this further detail, as shown in figure 6.4.

In the Rand study, only 18 of 103 robberies involved lone offenders, yet over half the juvenile robbers were 16 or 17 years old. So the Los Angeles findings show that the impact of multiple offender adolescent crime and multiple arrests on aggregate statistics will be

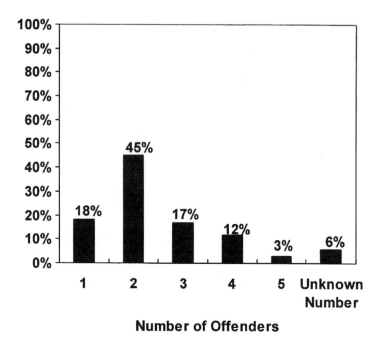

Figure 6.4. Percent distribution of armed robbery offenses involving juvenile suspects by number of offenders, Los Angeles. *Source:* Peter W. Greenwood, Juvenile Records Study (Santa Monica, CA: Rand Corporation, 1979).

very large in serious offenses, and even when juvenile populations include older offenders. To quote Shaw and McKay, male delinquency is still predominantly "group behavior."

So What?

This essay is intended neither as a comprehensive survey of the evidence on group criminality during adolescence nor as an assessment of the importance of this data to criminological theories about delinquent behavior. Empirical studies documenting adolescent crime abound.[6] The criminological literature discussing the implications of "dyadic," "triadic," and "other group" conformations is extensive. Whatever else may be said of modern criminology, the role of "male juvenile delinquency as group behavior" is acknowledged as fundamental, and the extent to which different types of criminality exhibit similar characteristics is well known, although the New York and Los Angeles data presented earlier provide us with larger numbers of serious offenses than many modern delinquency studies.[7]

This well-known pattern has important implications for contemporary research dealing with crime statistics, general deterrence, incapacitation, the construction of models of criminal behavior, the study of criminal careers, and efforts to reform sentencing practices in juvenile and criminal courts. These relatively recent research subspecialties are the intellectual next-door neighbors to traditional studies of crime and delinquency. Lately, however, the neighbors have not been speaking to each other, and the impact of group predominance is not taken into account.

Estimating the Proportion and Volume of Serious Youth Crime

No one doubts that young offenders account for a disproportionate share of most serious crimes. But the question is, how large a share? This cannot be answered with current data. The evidence for this assertion goes beyond fashionable doubts about a "dark figure" of crime or of offenders. The current state of the art for estimating the youth share of serious crime is: (1) to establish the percentage of persons under 18 or 21 arrested for a particular offense, and (2) to assume, explicitly or implicitly, that the percentage distribution of arrests accurately reflects the percentage distribution of crimes.

In the process of passing the Juvenile Justice and Delinquency Prevention Act of 1974,[8] the very first thing that the United States Congress found was that juveniles account for almost half the arrests for serious crimes in the United States today.[9] Does that mean they commit half the crimes? One problem with inferring that juveniles account for half of all serious crime from these statistics is that the crude heterogeneous categories used in crime and arrest reporting lump serious and relatively minor offenses under single rubrics, such as robbery or assault.[10] A second problem is that younger offenders who are arrested in groups for a single crime are counted two, three, or even four times far more commonly than are older offenders. The compound effect of treating minor and major offenses with equal statistical dignity in multiple offender counts is illustrated by figure 6.5, adapted from the previously discussed National Crime Panel data based on robbery victim reports.

Offenders under 21 comprise slightly over 60 percent of all the

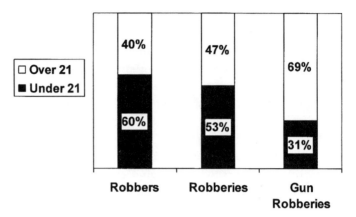

Figure 6.5. Percentage of robbers, robberies, and gun robberies by age (mixed group cases [n = 106] deleted). *Source: National Crime Panel. Survey Report.* U.S. Department of Justice; Bureau of Justice Statistics. (Washington, D.C.: Government Printing Office, 1974.

sample's "robbers," and just over half of all "robberies," but less than a third of robberies committed with firearms. Figure 6.5 is only the beginning. The estimates contained there use the twenty-first birthday as a cut-line, while juvenile court jurisdiction typically ends on or before the offender's eighteenth birthday. The statistics used to compile the congressional findings of fact are FBI estimates of arrests for under age 18.[11] Since the rate of robbery events per arrest increases with age and the proportion of robberies committed with firearms also increases as a function of age, the proportion of firearm robbery events attributable to "juveniles" could plausibly range as low as 10 percent.

In dealing with currently available statistics, using hedge phrases like "could plausibly range" is well advised. We simply do not know the youth share of particular forms of criminal activity, and we *cannot* use arrest statistics to derive estimates with acceptable margins of error.

Measuring Arrest and Punishment Risks in the Study of General Deterrence

The past 30 years witnessed a resurgence of interest in the general deterrent effect of the threat of criminal sanctions, and a variety of efforts to study deterrence by comparing crime rates and punishment levels over time or between jurisdictions.[12] Attempts to use existing aggregate data on offenses, arrests, and punishments are confounded by the overlapping jurisdictions of juvenile and criminal courts, and it is unlikely that researchers can use arrest statistics to "unconfound" matters.

The problem can be illustrated by examining common methods of estimating the risks of punishment and apprehension that are used to measure the credibility of threats in deterrence studies. The "risk of punishment" reported in figure 6.6 is often used and is fundamentally flawed.[13] By expressing adult prison admissions as a proportion of total reported offenses, "risk of punishment" measures no one's actual risk of punishment and will systematically be reduced as the proportion of juvenile offenses to total offenses increases. If juveniles are responsible for a large number of marginally serious offenses that either may or may not end up classified as a particular index offense, variations in police reporting and classification practices, as well as variations in the ratio of juvenile to adult offenses, will produce negative correlations between crime rates and the risk of punishment that have nothing to do with general deterrence.[14] Measuring the risk of apprehension by comparing total gross arrests to total gross offenses in any particular crime category generates similar problems. The measure is of two separate risks of arrest that cannot be segre-

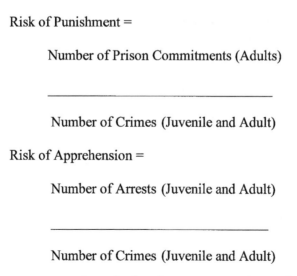

Risk of Punishment =

Number of Prison Commitments (Adults)

———————————————————

Number of Crimes (Juvenile and Adult)

Risk of Apprehension =

Number of Arrests (Juvenile and Adult)

———————————————————

Number of Crimes (Juvenile and Adult)

Figure 6.6. Conventional methods of estimating risk in deterrence research.

gated and a pool of offenses that represents an unknown admixture of juvenile and adult offenses with varying degrees of severity. Unless the mixture of adult and juvenile crimes and risks does not vary over time or from city to city, the result of this mixing will confound attempts to measure deterrent effects.

Under such circumstances, variations in the age distribution of crime or in police policy can successfully masquerade as variations in sentencing policy until we can separately estimate juvenile and adult offense rates. But the lesson of figure 6.5 is that using the age distribution of arrests to attempt this segregation will not succeed. For this reason, it seems unlikely that comparative studies using aggregate data can measure true risks.[15]

Measuring the Incapacitation Impact of Incarceration

The logic of incapacitation is straightforward: lock up people who would otherwise commit crimes, and the general community will experience a lower crime rate.[16] But selecting the appropriate candidates for incapacitation and estimating the number of crimes saved proves to be a tricky business. Efforts to estimate "crimes saved" have proceeded from individualistic models of criminal behavior to what may be inaccurate conclusions. Those studies that found high offense rates in early adolescent target populations have failed to account for the problem of group involvement.[17] Simply put, if one of three offenders is taken out of circulation for one year, we have no current basis for estimating whether, or to what extent, the crime rate is affected. If all three offenders are incapacitated, it is possible to estimate "crime saved" as a joint function of the crimes these offenders would have committed alone and with each other, but not in other groups. Using current methods of incapacitative accounting, however, assigning *each* member of *each* group *every* crime he or she would have committed together or in other groups creates a form of double and triple counting that overestimates "crime saved" in the group-prone adolescent years. The published studies that purport to measure incapacitation effects have not made serious efforts to correct for this bias. They are not merely wrong for this reason; they are very much wrong.

Modeling Patterns of Criminal Behavior

Frequently, attempts to impose simplifying models to explain variations in particular offenses cannot succeed because of the diversity of behaviors subsumed in a single crime category. Robbery is a case in point, and an illustrative example concerns the determinants of whether firearms are used in robbery events. Working from a sample of robberies in Boston, John Conklin concluded that "robbing with accomplices reduces the need to carry a weapon for self-protection, since the group itself acts as a functional equivalent of a weapon."[18] His data evidently did not control for age when relating weapon use to the number of offenders involved. Analyzing National Crime Panel data, Philip J. Cook found the opposite to be true:

> Guns are *less* likely to be used by single offenders than by multiple offenders and . . . this pattern holds for subgroups of offenders . . . as well as for the entire sample . . . ! While it is plausible that a team of offenders has less "need of a gun" than a single offender for a certain type of victim, the data suggest that teams of offenders tend to choose stronger victims.[19]

It may not be necessary to referee this particular dispute, because *both* Conklin and Cook are correctly describing the behavior of different subsets of robbery offenders—Conklin's analysis applies with force to unpremeditated robberies by young offenders. These patterns cannot be detected, however, by cross-tabulating weapon use and number of offenders for the total sample of robberies, as shown in figure 6.7.

It turns out, however, that this flat pattern is misleading. Looking at these data without controlling for age is precisely the wrong way to examine the National Crime Panel data, because of the greater

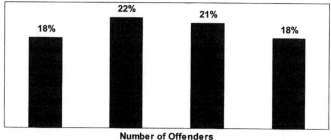

Number of Offenders

Figure 6.7. Percentage gun use in robberies by number of offenders. *Source: National Crime Panel. Survey Report*, U.S. Department of Justice, Bureau of Justice Statistics (Washington, D.C.: Government Printing Office, 1974); see also Cook, note 19 in this chapter.

likelihood that younger offenders (1) will rob in groups and (2) will use guns less often *whether or not* they rob in groups.[20] Table 6.2 displays the results of separate analysis patterns of guns use and number of offenders by age. For reported victimizations where all of the offenders were thought to be over 21, there is a modest increase in gun use as the size of the group increases. For offenders under 21, their youth is a much more powerful predictor of gun use than the number of robberies. Consistently, gun use is about a third of adult levels across all categories of offender group size. Thus, it may be true that young offenders find "courage in numbers" when a preexisting group spontaneously decides to commit a robbery. This is consistent with the low rate of gun use and the low rate of single-offender robberies among younger offenders. Older offenders engage in more planning and exhibit different target selection and accomplice selection patterns. For planned offenses, the target of the robbery has a substantial impact on the size of the group and the weapon used. In spontaneous robberies, the group and armaments have been determined before the target is selected, but failure to control for age of offender completely obscures these patterns.

Comprehending Criminal "Careers"

Almost all American adolescent males commit crimes at some point in the transition to adulthood. Many of these offenses are trivial; most of the time, adolescent criminality does not represent the beginning of a pattern of habitual criminality that will extend through

Table 6.2. Percentage Gun Use in Robbery by Age of Offender and Number of Offenders.

Number of offenders	Under 21	Over 21
1	8	24
2	13	33
3	13	36
4 of or more	12	40

Note: For total robbery event numbers, see table 6.1.

Source: National Crime Panel Data for 26 cities, analyzed by Philip J. Cook; see Cook, op. cit. note 19.

adulthood. It is, however, also true that the majority of those who persist in patterns of predatory crime through early adulthood have started young.[21]

In recent years, the study of criminal careers has been the subject of renewed interest and changing focus. For decades, criminologists have been interested in factors associated with desisting from or continuing to commit criminal offenses.[22] Recently, such studies have been undertaken with ambitions to contribute to policy: finding characteristics that predict continued criminality is now seen as a path to sentencing policy, particularly sentencing policies that emphasize the incapacitative effects of incarcerative sanctions.[23] Similarly, if social scientists can find characteristics of adolescent offending that are associated with a lack of recidivism, this information can be used to allocate scarce penal resources more efficiently and avoid unnecessary social control.

All of this, of course, depends upon the development of accurate discriminant indicators of future behavior. The Wolfgang, Figlio, and Sellin (1972) cohort study of Philadelphia boys who turned 18 during 1963 has provided some promising preliminary cues but stopped far short of predicting adult criminal careers.[24] The follow-up study of that Philadelphia sample provides some further information.[25] More recent retrospective study of individuals imprisoned as adults provides a list of characteristics associated with persisting criminality in the adult years but cannot, by the nature of the sample, provide data on what factors are associated with nonpersistence of criminal activity.[26]

The distinctive group character of adolescent criminality may provide a perspective that can increase the capacity of research to empirically test the degree to which prior behavior predicts future offenses. At some point in adolescence or early adult development, most of those who have committed offenses in groups either cease to be offenders or continue to violate the law, but for different reasons and in different configurations. Either of these paths is a significant change from prior behavior. The transition from group criminality to noncriminal individual behavior is obviously worthy of sustained study. The equally important transition from adolescent to adult patterns of criminal behavior should also be a particularly important period in the analysis of criminal careers.

At the outset, it is important to identify *when* transitions from juvenile to adult criminality and from adolescent criminality to desistance occur. This is not to suggest that the search is for a particular day when crime is abandoned or when patterns of criminality change; rather, both transitions should be expected to be processes that occur over substantial periods of time, and occur at different stages in the life history of different individuals. But identification and study of these transitional periods, in individual cases and cohorts, could enhance our understanding of criminality as a developmental event and sharpen the empirical focus of the questions to be asked in predicting future criminality.

One critical contribution of this focus would be to discriminate between predictive attributes or events that occur early in an adolescent career and those predictive events that occur more proximately to the transition out of crime or into different patterns of crime. A complete accounting scheme should separately consider the following.

1. Characteristics of the individual, such as age, location, and family structure, that antedate or accompany the early adolescent years
2. Aspects of the individual's involvement in early adolescent crime, including the kind of crime, age at first arrest, the type of group participating in crime, and the nature of the individual's role—dominant or passive—in adolescent group activities
3. Events or influences that occur later in adolescence that predict the nature of the change in the individual behavior

Aggregate statistics on the distribution of arrests suggest that the transition out of criminality is not a random event spread over the late teens and through the midtwenties, but rather clusters in late adolescence. However, my previous remarks suggest that aggregate arrest statistics are an insufficient foundation for studying this phenomenon. Those years in which gross arrest rates decline are also periods when arrest statistics underestimate the extent of criminal participation when arrest rates of older age groups are compared to those of younger groups.[27]

When looking for the transition to "adult-style" individual or planned group crime, there is no reason to select a priori any single 1- or 2-year period when we expect such a transition to occur. Case history studies and cohort samples can collect data on the nature of each individual offense coming to the attention of the police, and other supplemental methods, such as self-report studies, can be used to determine the period of transition, its duration, and its significant concomitants.[28]

Determining Appropriate Sanctions for Youth Crime

Statistics on the sanctions administered to young offenders in juvenile or family courts strike many observers as a classic instance of social noncontrol. The most impressive numbers come from New York City, a criminogenically congested urban area where only offenders under 16 are referred to the family court. One study of nearly 4,000 juvenile robbery arrests found that more than half of these charges were dismissed without formal referral to the family court, and over three-quarters of all charges are eventually dismissed.[29] Barbara Boland and James Q. Wilson cite the end result of this study with evident disapproval: "In short, only 3 percent of the juveniles arrested for robbery and only 7 percent of the juveniles actually tried in Family Court received any form of custodial care, whether with a relative, in a Juvenile Home or training school, or in an adult prison."[30] In Los Angeles, another study estimated the chances of a formal determination of delinquency at 17 for every 100 arrests.[31] This kind of statistical portrait lends itself nicely to fears of an army of young, violent offenders roaming the streets unchecked. The observer may also be tempted to conclude that the philosophy and youth welfare policies of the juvenile court are the explanation for such epidemic leniency.

Serious study of the relationship between age, crime, and punishment has only recently been undertaken. But the early returns suggest that the forces that produce such apparently alarming examples of "case mortality" are at once more complicated and less dependent on juvenile court philosophy than many had supposed.[32]

The animating philosophy of child protection in the juvenile court undoubtedly reduces the number of arrests that result in formal adjudications of delinquency and postadjudication commitment in secure facilities. However, a number of juvenile court policies *not* clearly related to leniency toward the young also contribute to high rates of informal disposition. In marginal cases, police might arrest juvenile offenders expecting the case to be "adjusted" at intake but relying on the arrest as a sanction and an opportunity for compiling a dossier.[33] The juvenile court's well-documented use of detention after arrest as a substitute for formal adjudication represents a troublesome social control device that is not visible when only the posttrial sanctions are examined. This is important because nationwide detention is about seven times as frequent as postadjudication commitment to secure facilities.[34] It is difficult to view detention practices as part of a sentimental general theory of youth protection.

Aggregate statistics on juvenile arrests reflect more than the distinctive policies and style of the contemporary juvenile court. The offenders processed in juvenile justice systems are different from other criminal defendants—they are younger, and their youth is an important influence on sentencing policy in criminal as well as juvenile courts.[35] Furthermore, and of central importance for this discussion, the offenses committed in early and middle adolescence also differ qualitatively from the criminal activity that is characteristic of older offender populations. The propensity of adolescent robbers to commit less serious forms of the offense than their elders must be taken into account in providing an explanation for the New York and Los Angeles statistics discussed earlier.[36] It is far from clear what the most just or efficient social response should be to adolescent garage burglaries, fistfights, and schoolyard extortions.

The pervasive problem of the adolescent accessory aggravates the difficulty of determining appropriate sanctions for youth crime. One useful example occurs early in the cohort study volume, when its authors are discussing the proper assessment of "seriousness scores":

> Let us suppose that three boys have committed a burglary. They range in age from 12 to 16 years. The oldest is the instigator and leader who actively committed the offense with one of the others: the youngest is an unwilling partner who was ignorant of the plan but was present because he happened to be with the others at the start of what began as an idle saunter through the streets of the neighborhood. Suppose the event is given a score of 4. Does this score, when applied to each participant, accurately measure the involvement of each? Should the oldest boy and his active partner be assessed this score, but the youngest given a lower one?[37]

In any system of justice that considers the magnitude of the harm done and the degree of the individual offender's involvement, the attempt to determine an appropriate sanction will confront the same difficulties as the researcher attempting to determine an appropriate score. In discussing this case, Wolfgang and his colleagues say that all three offenders are equally guilty "from a legal point of view."[38] This statement is correct but potentially misleading. Assuming that a trier of fact determines that the youngest was a reluctant but voluntary partner who aided and abetted the offense, all three adolescents can be found delinquent in a juvenile court.[39] This kind of group crime would also generate criminal liability for the appropriate degree of burglary in a criminal court through the magic of the doctrine of accessorial liability.[40] But prosecutorial discretion in selecting cases for prosecution, determining charges, and pressing for punishment, combined with judicial discretion in determining sentences in both juvenile and criminal court, creates ample opportunity for differences in punishment policy that are not reflected in the formal substantive law of either crime or delinquency.

When sentencing policy is dispensed by a series of low-visibility discretions, a system can have a policy toward accomplice problems in adolescence without announcing it and, not infrequently, without knowing it. In the Rand study of the Los Angeles juvenile court, lone offenders arrested for armed robbery experienced a 3-in-10 chance of commitment to the state's youth authority, while only 13 percent of those who acted in groups received this most serious disposition available to the court. It seems plausible to suppose that much of this difference can be attributed to prosecutorial and judicial leniency toward individuals at the periphery of spontaneous adolescent crimes. But the discretionary decisions characteristic of juvenile justice hide rather than announce the real reasons they are made.

This chapter's ambitions fall short of resolving the complicated set of problems generated by the juvenile accomplice; instead, it is sufficient for this discussion to note the novelty and importance of these issues in the study of dispositional policy toward youth crime and realistic efforts to reform the law. To study dispositional patterns in juvenile court without paying careful attention to policies toward group offenses seems foolhardy. To assign to each of the three youths arrested in the hypothetical burglary discussed earlier the same seriousness score, and to use that score to predict the level of sanctions, will create the impression that serious crimes go unpunished if any of the group is excused because his participation was relatively minor.[41] This kind of research procedure will also continue our ignorance about how participants in group crime are sanctioned.

Attempts to reform sentencing practices in the juvenile court, especially efforts to lead sanctioning models away from the jurisprudence of treatment and toward concepts of making the punishment fit the crime, will find the myriad problems of sanctioning the adolescent accomplice very close to the top of any sensible priority list for deliberation. These issues are important because they confront whatever set of institutions will process young offenders in a majority of all cases. The issues are novel because the nature of group criminality in adolescence bears scant resemblance to the classic image of the criminal conspiracy or the conceptual foundations of the common law of accessorial liability. The intelligent law reformer thus must take a short course in criminology as a preliminary to setting his or her agenda. My own review of recent literature and debate suggests that this sequence of events is infrequent.[42]

Conclusion

The problems we generate by failing to remember the pervasive importance of group participation in youth crime can be grouped under two headings. There are, first, the technical mistakes we will produce when we use arrest prevalence as an estimate of what share of crime young persons commit, or when we forget about group crime when measuring crime risks or estimating incapacitation effects. These are serious mistakes, of course, but not fundamental mistakes.

The deeper substantive problem with ignoring group involvement and all its implications when discussing either the sociology or the policy analysis of youth crime is that this displays an ignorance of an essential feature of juvenile offenders and offenses. The group context of most juvenile offending is not simply one characteristic of youth crime, it is an essential feature of the juvenile offender, and a major distinction between juvenile and adult offending. To ignore the group context of youth crime is to display ignorance of a central characteristic of the phenomenon under study. No serious student of juvenile behavior can ever afford to forget the well-known secret of group criminality during youth.

SEVEN

Two Patterns of Age Progression in Adolescent Crime

Franklin E. Zimring and Jeffrey Fagan

This chapter shows that the widely acknowledged fact that rates of crime peak in the late teen years should not be regarded as a single pattern of increase in the middle teen years followed by a peak rate and a sharp drop during the early twenties. Instead, we show two patterns. For one set of crimes—including arson and most property crimes—rates of arrest increase sharply to a rate much higher than that observed among adults and drop sharply after age 18 or 19. These crimes with a high peak rate in adolescence we will call "phase-specific criminality"—arrests are concentrated in the teen years, as if committing such crimes were a rite of passage, and rates of "phase-specific" crimes are much lower in young adulthood.

A second group of crimes—including most offenses of violence—have relatively low peak rates in the late teen years. Instead of arrest rates that are two and three times those found in young adults, these "low-peak" patterns show teen rates only 30–50 percent higher than for young adulthood. For these crimes, the increases during early and middle teen years are not a phase that ends when offenders come of age, but rather an increasing rate of crime that seems more closely linked to rates of crime among young adults. We predict that the rates of such crime found among adolescents will be powerfully influenced by rates among adults. If teens grow up in an atmosphere of high adult homicide, then teen homicide rates will be higher. Teens coming of age in lower homicide environments will show lower teen homicide rates. We call this pattern "general rate dependence."

The first section of this analysis shows support for two discrete patterns of age effect using FBI arrest data—an adolescent "high-peak" effect for property crimes, where the behavior of teens is sharply different from that of young adults, and a "low-peak" pattern for crimes of violence, where most of the teen increases in arrest rate are close to arrest levels that also characterize the early and middle twenties. We theorize that the general rate dependence found for homicide should extend to other crimes of violence but not necessarily to offenses with very high concentrations in adolescent age groups. The second section shows the relative distribution of homicide arrests by age in four countries with very different general homicide rates. Some potential differences between high-peak and low-peak patterns are discussed in a concluding section.

Two Ways of Looking at Age Data

Table 7.1 reports arrest rate peaks and their relation to arrest rates for seven index crimes from the Uniform Crime Reports for 1997. The lefthand column reports the age group with the highest arrest rate for each offense. For 2000, the peak age of arrest for violent crime was spread between 18 and 21, while the peak ages for the three nonviolent property crimes were 16, 17, and 18. Arson arrests, in sharp contrast, had a higher arrest rate at ages 13–14 than at any other age. Comparison with earlier years show that peak arrest rates are now experienced at later ages than even in the mid-1990s, but the peak ages of arrest for all the major crimes remain young, leading some observers to hypothesize a unitary "age-crime" relationship (see Hirschi and Gottfredson 1983, 557–559).

The data in the righthand column put the reader on notice, however, that more than two years of peak age separate most violence of-

Table 7.1. Peak Age of Arrest and Ratio of Peak Rate to Rate at Age 20 = 100, United States, 2000.

	Peak age	Ratio to age 20 = 100
Homicide	19	129
Aggravated assault	21	101
Rape	20	100
Robbery	18	137
Burglary	18	153
Motor vehicle theft	16	166
Larceny	17	164
Arson	13–14	286

Source: U.S. Federal Bureau of Investigation, *Uniform Crime Reports* (Washington, D.C.: Government Printing Office, 2000).

fenses from property offense age patterns during the adolescent years. Rates of homicide, rape, and assault arrest at peak age are within 30 percent of the arrest rates found at age 20 in 2000, while arson, car theft, larceny, and burglary arrest rates are sharply higher than the age 20 rate. This bimodal clustering suggests that the skewness of different offenses in the teen years is significantly different from a single "age-crime" relationship.

Figure 7.1 compares the curve for arrest rates for homicide and motor vehicle theft for 1997, as displayed in what we call a relative age distribution curve. For each offense, the arrest rate at each age is expressed as a number based on 100 times the rate divided by the arrest rate at age 20 for the same difference. This strategy permits precise comparisons of age patterns for different offenses with different base rates, as well as comparisons of age patterns in different settings where base rates of a particular crime are quite different. The advantage of the curve is that only variations over the course of age are visible in the slope of the curve.

Figure 7.1 shows that much more than a 2-year gap in peak age of arrest separates the age pattern for homicide and for motor vehicle theft. The rate of arrests for each crime is trivial prior to age 13. Auto theft arrests shoot up in the early teen years, with a very high peak

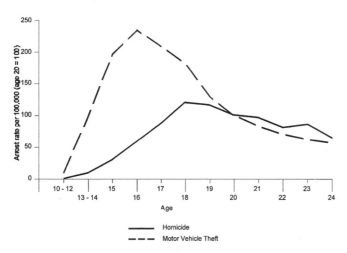

Figure 7.1. Homicide and motor vehicle theft arrests per 100,000, United States, 1997. *Sources:* U.S. Federal Bureau of Investigation, *Uniform Crime Reports*, 1997, table 38; U.S. Bureau of the Census, *Statistical Abstract of the United States,* 1998.

rate at age 16 and a very sharp drop thereafter. By age 23, the volume of arrests for auto theft is less than one-third the rate generated for age 15. This is a typical "high-peak" pattern. Homicide arrests grow more slowly over the years of the midteens, reach their high rate at age 18, and then drop off slowly from that high rate through the early twenties.

The peak rate for homicide is much lower relative to the arrest rates at older ages. Further, rates in the midteens are a smaller proportion of rates in the twenties. While the ratio of homicide arrests at age 15 to those at age 23 is 0.4, the ratio of auto theft arrests at 15 to rates at 23 is 3.67. The relative prevalence of auto theft arrest in the younger age category is *nine times* that of homicide (1/.4 x 3.67 = 9.17).

We think this shows rather clearly that the two offenses have significantly different age patterns. Not only is the peak rate of auto theft well within the adolescent years but also the arrest rates at ages 15 and 16 are much higher than rates noted in early adulthood. This "high-peak" rate relative to early adult pattern is a characteristic of what we will call a *phase-specific* pattern, where the levels of a crime during adolescence are much higher than later in the life cycle. We will argue later that the conditions of adolescence probably have a controlling influence on rates and patterns of offenses, with distinctively high rates during the teen years.

For homicide, by contrast, the peak rate at 19 and 20 is not much higher than rates noted in the early twenties. The elevation in arrest rates during the period from 12 to 18 never climbs much higher than the rates found in the early twenties. The motives and character of adolescent violence may differ from those of adult violence, but the rate of violence in the late teen years is not greatly different. The increase in arrest rates found in the teen years can best be comprehended as *transitional* to adult patterns rather than *phase specific*.

Figure 7.2 uses the ratio of age 15 arrests to age 23 arrests as a shorthand measure of the youth concentration of the eight "index" offenses in 1997. Seven of the eight index offenses are distributed in a clearly bimodal fashion. The three offenses of violence, other than robbery, are distinctly "low-peak" offenses, where the arrest rate at 15 is less than at age 24. These look like textbook cases of a growth in arrest rates during adolescence that peaks in the late teens at rates close to those of young adults. The three "pure" property crimes and arson are all offenses where the age 15 rate of arrest is more than 2.8

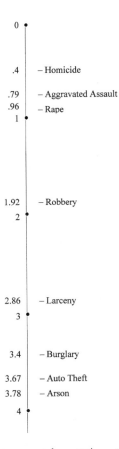

Figure 7.2. Youth propensity to arrest (age 15/age 24) by offense, United States, 1997. *Source:* U.S. Federal Bureau of Investigation, *Uniform Crime Reports* (Washington, DC: Government Printing Office, 1997).

times the arrest level at age 24. These look like phase-specific crimes for most of those who are arrested in 13 years. Only robbery, with a ratio of 1.92, has a ratio value on this measure greater than 1 and less than 2.8. To what extent this singular pattern in the aggregate is a product of different patterns from different subtypes of robbery being lumped together is unknown, and we will not resolve the peculiar status of robbery arrests in this study. Rather, the theoretical implications of the bimodality of the other seven index offenses is the focus of this chapter.

The Youth Share of Index Arrests

Analysis of the relative importance of youth arrests to total crime provides another indication of two distinctively different patterns. Figure 7.3 shows the percentage of total arrests attributable to defendants under 18 for the eight index crimes in 1997.

The relative concentration of arrests in the youngest group show the same bimodal tendency that was observed in figure 7.2. The three offenses of violence, other than robbery, have low concentrations of arrest in the youngest age category, with about one-seventh of all arrests involving suspects under 18. Robbery again occupies a middle position, with a 24 percent concentration in the ages below 18. All three "pure" property crimes average one-third of all arrests involving suspects under 18. For arson, fully half of all total arrests are under 18. The concentration of arrest under 18 thus varies by a factor of five among the eight index offenses.

The differences identified in this aggregate arithmetic are important for theoretical as well as practical reasons. In the aggregate, under-18 behavior is more than twice the proportion of total criminality for arson and nonviolent property offenses as it is for homicide, rape, and assault. Put another way, there is twice as much difference between the share of burglary attributable to juveniles and the share of murder attributable to juveniles (20.8 percent) as between the current share of juveniles arrested for murder and zero

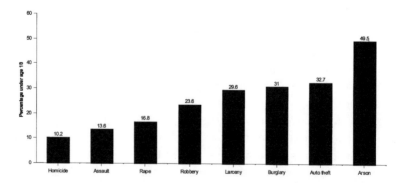

Figure 7.3. Percentage of total arrests under age 18, eight index crimes, 2000. *Source:* U.S. Federal Bureau of Investigation, *Uniform Crime Reports* (Washington, D.C.: Government Printing Office, 2000).

(10.2 percent). Again, the conclusion must be that there are important differences between the typical violence pattern and the typical nonviolent crime pattern in adolescence offenders. Assuming that the three offenses at the left in figure 7.3 document the same trajectory over time as do the four offenses at the right glosses over statistical differences of very high magnitude.

Phase-Specific versus Transitional Patterns

As a first approximation of the developmental significance of high-peak versus low-peak age distributions, we would suggest that intense concentration in the teen years—the high-peak pattern—shows an offense that tends to be *phase-specific* to adolescent offenders. The strongest candidate for a phase-specific crime is arson, where the arrest rate at 15 is 3.8 times the arrest rate at 20. Since most of the offenses involve younger teens, this means that most of the people who commit arson when young do not do so in later life. The pattern for crimes with a high *phase-specific* tendency is that of sharp increase early in adolescence that is accompanied by significant drops in arrest rates in late adolescence. Auto theft is a second offense where both sharp up-slopes and down-slopes occur during adolescence.

A second group of offenses show significant increases in adolescence and then only drop off slowly. These "low-peak" offenses include all the violent crimes except robbery. Homicide, for example, increases significantly in adolescence but stays quite close to its peak arrest rate through the early twenties (see fig. 7.1). We interpret the sharp increase in the early and middle teen years as a transition to rates and risks that are typical of young adulthood rather than a pattern of criminality that is concentrated in teen years. The increases after age 12 are transitional to adult levels rather than phase specific.

Cross-National Homicide as a Case Study
of Age Distribution Analysis

In order to study the age distribution of arrests on a cross-national basis, we obtained complete arrest data by age for homicide by offenders under age 21 in Canada, the United Kingdom, and New South Wales, the most populous state in Australia (no national-level arrest data are available for Australia). Multiple-year samples were compiled for the non–United States data to provide ample numbers in the analysis. Figure 7.4 uses recent data to compare reported homicide rates in the four nations.

The variation in homicide rates among these four English-speaking nations is substantial—an order of magnitude separated the U.K. rates from the U.S. rates in 1990, while the Australian and Canadian homicide levels are more than double the British and about one-fourth of the U.S. rates.

Figure 7.5 shows the pattern of relative age distribution for homicide arrests in the four sets of arrest data we obtained, with each nation's arrest rate at age 20 assigned a value of 100 and the arrest rate of each age group in that national sample as a fraction of that value. If the arrest rate of Canadian 16-year-olds is 70 percent of the rate of Canadian 20-year-olds, the entry for age 16 for Canada will be 70.

The pattern of relative participation of each age under 20 in criminal homicide is strikingly similar from country to country. All the samples show sharp increases in the early and middle teen years, a maximum level of arrest at 18, and levels quite close to that maximum for ages 19 and 20. The largest deviation in pattern is lower

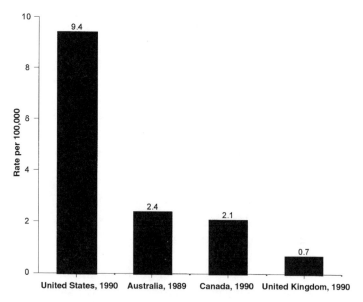

Figure 7.4. Recent homicide rates per 100,000 population. *Source:* Zimring and Hawkins, *Crime Is Not the Problem*, 1997, chapter 3.

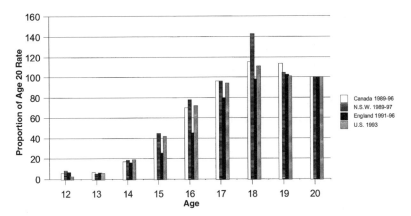

Figure 7.5. Homicide arrest by age, four distributions (age 20 = 100). *Sources:* Canada (Statistics Canada); New South Wales (Bureau of Criminal Statistics, special study); England (Home Office, special study); United States (Federal Bureau of Investigations, Supplemental Homicide Reports).

relative levels of arrest in England at 15, 16, and 17. The only other deviation greater than 10 percent from the general pattern is a high value for age 18 in the smallest sample from New South Wales. The relative age distribution of homicide arrest experience is remarkably similar in the four samples.

What this remarkable similarity does *not* show is that levels of lethal violence are similar among teens in the United States, Canada, the United Kingdom, and Australia. The magnitude of homicide arrests is seven times as high in the United States as in the United Kingdom at age 17, despite the similar relative values in figure 7.5. What the similar relative age distributions throughout the teen years suggest to us is that most of the substantial differences in adolescent homicide that are observed among these four nations are a result of the general level of violence in each nation rather than any distinctive feature of adolescent violence. In each country, there is an almost constant distribution by age in the teen years, and the only major influence in the actual rate of homicide is the general homicide rate in each nation. We call this a *general rate dependence* phenomenon. Variations in arrest prosperity within adolescence seem to account for very little of the cross-national variation in patterns of lethal violence.

The general level of lethal violence is set as a function of adult behaviors and values. Adolescent rates of lethal violence ascend toward that young adult level at a pace that seems nearly constant in the four different national settings where we compared age progression. When so little of the country-to-country differences in rates of lethal violence results from any difference in the proportionate share of total violence that is teen violence in a culture, the view of the rate of adolescent homicide as a function of adult rates and roles seems highly probable.

Applying the Distinction in Prediction and Classification

The distinction between transitional offense distributions that stay close to young adult rates and those where both onset and most desistance occur within and shortly after adolescence may be of value in interpreting and predicting crime trends and in seeking out meaningful classifications of categories of criminal behavior.

Assume that teen arrest rates for a particular offense have been increasing by 80 percent, while adult rates have been stable or declining. If the offense is a "high-peak" behavior such as arson or auto theft, the divergent recent trends may not be of value in guessing what is likely to happen next. When half of all arson arrests are concentrated in the very few teen years, it is a signal that there is substantial difference between teens' and adults' involvements in the offense, and movements in one may not be a good prediction of movements in the other age groups.

But what if the offense is one where the rates during the late teen years are normally close to young adult levels and where cross-national comparisons show that differences in general rates of homicide are the only important factors in predicting cross-national variation in adolescent homicide? In such circumstances, the most likely prediction after an unprecedented increase in only the teen rate is for regression of sorts to a situation where teen rates resume fluctuating in concert with adult rates. If the teen rates have risen much faster, we would expect them to decline more sharply than adult rates in the next time period.

With some variation, this abnormal increase in teen arrest for killings (1985–93) followed by a sharper-than-adult decrease in teen homicide arrests (1994–99) was the pattern in recent American history. The larger than normal drop is a natural prediction if adult levels of arrest are usually good predictors of teen levels but diverge for a time.[1] For what we have called general rate dependent adolescent crimes, long-range divergence in youth and adult trends should not be expected. Indeed, a longstanding divergence would undermine the factual foundation for thinking of an offense pattern as one where the general crime rate predicts the relative level of adolescent offenses.

We don't think that an increase in adolescent auto theft or arson— two "high peak" crimes—could lead us to confidently predict that teen rates will soon fall because adult rates have remained stable. Adult rates of arson have no important link to teen rates of arson. For high-peak phase offenses such as vandalism, arson, and auto theft, the best place to seek behavioral linkages and similarities with teen offenses is with other adolescent behavior systems. But thinking of an adolescent crime pattern as dependent on general rates invites a search for analogies between teen and adult crime patterns. Observers have been searching for the roots of school shootings by focusing on teen motives and adolescent resort to instruments of violence. Since the volume of adolescent homicide as a class seems to depend on the general homicide rate, perhaps more informative comparisons could be made between school shootings and analogous adult behavior such as recent workplace shooting sprees and day-trader shootings in a stock brokerages.

Yet it may be that the volume of homicide in adolescence is a function of general levels of homicide among adults but the types of killing of teens and adults differ. Still, the transitional perspective can be helpful if carefully applied, and the parallels we use as an example here of school and workplace shootings seems to us a good candidate for further analysis. When the level of adolescent offending is closely linked to that of adults, we are on notice that parallels between adolescent and adult offending patterns may be helpful. The utility of specific comparisons will vary substantially.

The Recent Dynamics of Youth Arrests

When homicide arrests of adolescents and young adults increased disproportionately in the 1980s, the statistics received substantial media and public attention (Zimring 1998). What has not yet been noticed is that during the crime declines of the late 1990s, the drop in juvenile arrests was even more substantial than the drop in non-youth arrests. Because the sample of agencies reporting arrests varies from year to year, the best comparisons over time that control for

Table 7.2. Percentage of Arrests under Age 18, by Crime, Eight "Index" Offenses, 1995 and 2001.

	1995	2001	Percentage change
Murder and non-negligent manslaughter	15.3	10.2	-5.1
Rape	15.8	16.8	1.0
Aggravated assault	14.7	13.6	-1.1
Robbery	32.3	23.6	-8.7
Burglary	35.1	31	-4.1
Larceny	33.4	29.6	-3.8
Auto theft	42	32.7	-9.3

Source: U.S. Federal Bureau of Investigation, Uniform Crime Reports (Washington, D.C.: Government Printing Office, 2000).

population coverage will focus on the percentage of all arrests involving offenders under 18. Table 7.2 provides this information for reported arrests in the Uniform Crime Reports for 1995 and 2001. Over the six years, the proportion of the population that was 13- to 17-year-olds expanded from 7.1 to 7.2, so that a modest expansion in the youth arrest total would be expected (Zimring 1998, 52). But that is not what happened.

During a period when the crime drop was significant across the board, the youth share of high-volume offenses like robbery and burglary dropped quite substantially, indicating a decline in youth arrests at least half again as high as the adult arrest trends. For auto theft, the drop in juvenile arrests was over twice that in the over-18 population. With homicide, the disproportionate drop could be a progression toward the long-term mean, since the rate had increased so much after 1986 (Fagan, Zimring, and Kim 1998). But the distinctively more intensive downturn in youth arrests is broader over the period since 1995 than the increase was during the late 1980s and early 1990s. Just about the time when criminologists were predicting a "coming storm of juvenile violence" in 1995, the youth population was entering the longest and most substantial decline in serious youth criminality that has ever been recorded in the United States.

Conclusion

The commission rates of all common crimes increase in the early and middle years of adolescence, but the age distribution observed in adolescence and early adult years fall into two discrete patterns. For one group of property offenses and for arson, the peak rate of arrests occurs early—around age 16. And the drop in arrests by age is swift, so that rates at ages 15 and 16 are between two and four times as high as at age 23. These high-peak offenses are *phase specific,* concentrated in adolescence as in no other period of life.

Another group of crimes, the three violent crimes other than robbery, increase during the teen years but stay quite high through early adulthood. The increase in the teen years appears to progress toward a young adult rate, and the specific level that is maintained at ages 18–20 for homicide and assault is close to the level of young adult offending in the particular population under study. The age distribution of these offenses can be seen as an offshoot of adult levels rather than a peak in adolescence determined mainly by conditions of adolescent life.

So the two superficially similar increases in adolescent offending may be caused by different cultural and social factors. The "high peak" in the teen years is evidence that the specific circumstances of adolescence are driving rates up, but rates will usually go down sharply after age 18. The "low-peak" pattern of most violent crime seems a characteristic not of the particular circumstances of adolescence but rather an increase of rates of violence to whatever the expected level is in early childhood. This is why the major influence in the four-nation homicide sample examined in this chapter is the general rate of homicide in the population—the teen rate is high or low in direct proportion to the all-ages homicide rate. It is not the character of adolescence that causes difference in violence when we compare societies; it is the general rate of violence in the population.

EIGHT

The Case of the Disappearing Superpredator
Some Lessons from the 1990s

A remarkable part of the current dialogue about youth violence in the United States has been its future orientation. In an earlier book, I showed that the concerns and rhetoric about youth crime in the mid-1990s paralleled earlier alarms in the mid-1970s, with one significant exception. Missing from earlier eras was a focus not on current conditions but on future developments (Zimring 1998, ch. 1). In 1995, a large number of analysts began to project increases in the volume and severity of youth violence into the next century. Demographic data about adolescent populations were combined with assumptions about the crime rates of future cohorts of teen offenders. For this reason, projections about the number of teenagers expected in coming years and their social characteristics became important elements in debates about policy.

One of the earlier versions of this type of warning was issued by James Q. Wilson (1995, 507):

> Meanwhile, just beyond the horizon, there lurks a cloud that the winds will soon bring over us. The population will start getting younger again. By the end of this decade there will be a million more people between the ages of fourteen and seventeen than there are now; this increase will follow the decade of the 1980s when people in that age group declined, not only as a proportion of the total but in absolute numbers. This extra million will be half male. Six percent of them will become high rate, repeat offenders—30,000 more young muggers, killers, and thieves than we have now. Get ready.

One year later, John Dilulio (1996, 1) of Princeton pushed the horizon back 10 years and upped the ante: "By the year 2010, there will be approximately 270,000 more juvenile super-predators on the streets than there were in 1990."

James Fox (1996) of Northeastern University described the projected volume of homicide involvements in 2005 as "a blood bath."

The National Center for Juvenile Courts projected a doubling of juvenile arrests by 2010 (Snyder and Sickmund 1995). The Washington-based Council on Crime in America (1996) warned of "a coming storm of juvenile violence." What all of these estimates have in common is that demographic projections play a central role in predictions about the volume of youth crime. Suddenly, population statistics have become an important element in criminal justice policy planning.

Too Many Teenagers?

This chapter considers the two types of demographic measures that have caused concern over trends in youth crime in the next 15 years. This section examines available data on the number of adolescents, focusing on the age group 13 to 17. The next section addresses some concerns about the ethnicity and poverty of children. The last section examines the deterministic logic of these projections.

There are two important methods of measuring the impact of a particular population subgroup on a social environment. One is to count the number of persons in the age group, a natural way of determining its impact. Figure 8.1 provides that information for the actual and projected youth population between the ages of 13 and 17 in the United States from 1960 until 2010. Of course, the last 14 data points are estimated, but because most of the people counted in these estimates already reside in the United States, the margin of error is small. Those aged 13 to 17 are the focus of this time series, because they have the highest juvenile arrest statistics.

This teen population increased rapidly during the 1960s and early 1970s and then peaked in 1975 at 21 million. The 15 years of sharp growth were followed by 15 years of decline, with the midteen population bottoming out in 1990 at 16 million. The reasons for these ups and downs were high birth volume through the late 1950s, followed by declining births in the 1960s and 1970s. Now, the Census Bureau expects the number of teenagers to grow 16 percent over the 15 years ending in 2010, to a total of 21.5 million. The growth rate for this period is projected at about 1 percent per year, slightly more than a third of the growth rate experienced during the 1960s. By 2010, the United States will have just under a half million more teenagers than were in the population in 1975. On the sheer number of teenagers, the United States will have spent 30 years breaking even.

The simple counting of a teenaged population in the style of figure

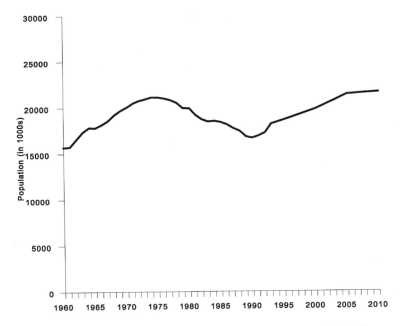

Figure 8.1. Trends in youth population, ages 13–17, 1960–2010. *Source:* U.S. Department of Commerce, Bureau of the Census, 1960–1994, 1995.

8.1 is poor demography in one important respect—it provides no information about the social setting of the United States in the various years for which there are population estimates. Figure 8.2 provides an easy, if partial, cure for this condition by reporting the proportion of the total U.S. population between the ages of 13 and 17 for the half-century beginning in 1960. It provides an important context for the growth of the youth population in the 1960s and early 1970s, a period when the teenage population was expanding far more quickly than the population as a whole. At its 1975 peak, the 13–17 age group was 9.9 percent of the total population, having grown twice as fast as the rest of the population. From 1975 to 1990, the proportionate share of the population in the midteens dropped even faster than it had expanded in the previous 15 years; at 6.7 percent, the older juvenile share of the U.S. population had dropped 3.2 percent. Thus projected increases in the youth population might look large from a 1990 base, because the proportion of youths in the U.S. population was at its low point for a generation.

The most important lesson from figure 8.2 concerns the impact of

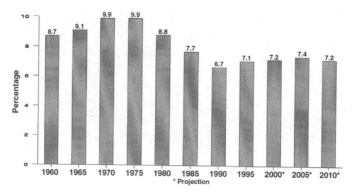

Figure 8.2. Proportion of U.S. population, ages 13–17, 1960–2010. *Source:* U.S. Department of Commerce, Bureau of the Census, 1960–1994, 1995.

expanding numbers of youths on the population as a whole. From 1990 to 2010, the share of the population in the 13–17 age group will expand from 6.7 percent to 7.2 percent. The 7.2 percent share expected for 2010 is significantly less than the 8.7 share noted for 1960, before the huge growth associated with the crime-prone 1960s.

This relatively low concentration of middle teenagers occurs even when the number of youths expands to a record high for a simple reason—the growth of the U.S. population. The 21 million youths in the United States in 1975 lived in a nation of 213 million. The 21 million–plus youths in 2010 will live among a U.S. population of 300 million.

In this context, it does not seem that the age structure of the U.S. population in the coming years should be of particular concern. The modest expansion of the adolescent share of the total population will be neither abrupt nor extreme. There will be no large bulge in the young end of the age scale, challenging with sheer numbers the institutions that socialize youths. The increased burden on schools and youth-serving institutions will be more than offset in due course by a modest expansion in the working-age population needed to support the retirement years of baby boomers. Why all the fuss?

Fighting the Last War?

Once the demographic data on the age structure of the U.S. population are placed in long-range context, it is difficult to comprehend why the expansion of the youth population is perceived as a particular problem. However, even the modest expansions just outlined have produced concern among commentators—for three reasons.

The first concern is the arithmetic of the interaction of the expanding population with high or increasing rates of arrest. If rates of serious violence do go up, a 16 percent expansion in the youth population would make a bad situation somewhat worse (see Fox 1996). There is no flaw in the arithmetic of this type of projection, but putting the emphasis on the small increase in population rather than on the high crime rates that such projections assume is incorrect. If juvenile homicide rates double, the situation would be troublesome even if the volume of teenagers were to decline 5 percent. Population trends are not the real problem.

A second concern comes from memories of the 1960s, when the explosive growth of the youth population was one of many simultaneous criminogenic changes in the American urban landscape. Wilson, who was the first to sound an alarm in the 1990s about a million extra teenagers, had earlier written about the huge impact of demography in the 1960s:

> Well before the war in Vietnam had fully engaged us or the ghetto riots had absorbed us, the social bonds—the ties of family, of neighborhood, of mutual forbearance and civility—seem to have come asunder. Why? That question should be, and no doubt in time will be, seriously debated. No single explanation, perhaps no set of explanations, will ever gain favor. One fact, however, is an obvious beginning to an explanation: by 1962 and 1963 there had come of age the persons born during the baby boom of the immediate postwar period. A child born in 1946 would have been sixteen in 1962, seventeen in 1963.
>
> The numbers involved were very large. In 1950 there were about 24 million persons aged fourteen to twenty-four; by 1960 that had increased only slightly to just under 27 million. But during the next ten years it increased by over 13 million persons. Every year for ten years, the number of young people increased by 1.3 million. That ten-year increase was greater than the growth in the young segment of the population for the rest of the *century* put together. To state it in another way that focuses on the critical years of 1962 and 1963, during the first *two* years of the decade of the 1960s, we added more young persons (about 2.6 million) to our population than we had added in any preceding ten years since 1930.
>
> The result of this has been provocatively stated by Professor

Norman B. Ryder, the Princeton University demographer: "There is a perennial invasion of barbarians who must somehow be civilized and turned into contributors to fulfillment of the various functions requisite to societal survival." That "invasion" is the coming of age of a new generation of young people. Every society copes with this enormous socialization process more or less successfully, but occasionally that process is almost literally swamped by a quantitative discontinuity in the numbers of persons involved: "The increase in the magnitude of the socialization tasks in the United States during the past decade was completely outside the bounds of previous experience."

If we continue Professor Ryder's metaphor, we note that in 1950 and still in 1960 the "invading army" (those aged fourteen to twenty-four) were outnumbered three to one by the size of the "defending army" (those aged twenty-five to sixty-four). By 1970 the ranks of the former had grown so fast that they were only outnumbered two to one by the latter, a state of affairs that had not existed since 1910. (Wilson 1974, 12–13)

The experience in the 1960s may well have alerted observers to the potential role of population changes. But why the alarm over very modest growth in the period 1990–2010? Two clichés compete to provide an explanation. The first is "Once bitten, twice shy," suggesting a reluctance on the part of policy analysts to let another population-led crime wave sneak up on them. But the second cliché, the complaint that too many strategists seem always to be fighting the last war, seems closer to the truth. The coming of age of the baby boomers in the 1960s is in no important sense a precedent for the demographic shifts expected in the next 15 years.

Some Qualitative Concerns

A third reason is offered for worry about the growth in youth populations in current analyses—the theory that a large proportion of current and future teens will be at risk of high rates of crime and social disadvantage. This type of concern is based not just on the number of young persons in the population but also on their social characteristics. Because a large proportion of tomorrow's children and youths may be at special risk, it can be argued that increases in the teen population that might ordinarily not cause trouble should now be regarded with alarm. Whether the focus of concern is poverty, single-parent households, educational gaps, or ethnicity and color, this is a concern about changes in the composition of the nation's population rather than about numbers.

Many important characteristics of the youth population of 2010 cannot be predicted with confidence long in advance. Among these are youth poverty and educational status and attainment. But the racial and ethnic composition of 1997's two-year-olds is a pretty good indication of the racial and ethnic profile of 15-year-olds in 2010, and expected changes in the racial and ethnic mix of the youth population have played an important role in the concerns of many people about "the coming storm" of juvenile crime. The data in figure 8.3 show the changing mix in the proportion of 13- to 1-year-olds classified African American, Hispanic, and all others.

The growth pattern is quite different for the African American and Hispanic segments of the youth population. The former's share of total adolescent population aged 13 to 17 increased 2.3 percent in the

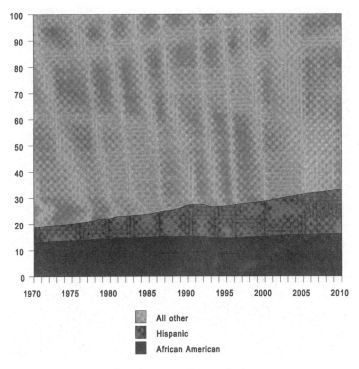

Figure 8.3. Percentage distribution of population, ages 13–17, 1970–2010. *Source:* Projections from U.S. Bureau of the Census, *Current Population Reports: Estimates of the Population of the United States by Age, Sex and Race* (Washington, DC: Government Printing Office, 1995).

17 years from 1970 to 1987. In the 23 years after 1987, it is projected that the African American share of the youth population will grow less than a point, from 15.5 percent to 16.4 percent. The number of African American teens will grow substantially, but three-quarters of the increase will be just keeping pace with the growth of the total youth population.

The Hispanic teen population, in contrast, is in the middle of a growth pattern much larger than that of the rest of the youth population. In 1970, there were 1.14 million Hispanic-surname youths between the ages of 13 and 17 in the United States, according to the Census Bureau's estimate, or 5.7 percent of the population in that age group. By 2010, the number of Hispanic teens is estimated to be 3.63 million, and the Hispanic share of the 13–17 age group is expected to have tripled, to 16.9 percent.

The theory that the racial and ethnic composition of the youth population should influence the rate of youth violence is straightforward but untested. It is thought that since particular segments of the population have higher than average risks at any one time, the larger the share of that high-risk group in a future population, the higher the rate of violence we can expect in the future.

Thus, since African American youths are currently arrested for homicide at a rate much higher than youths from other backgrounds, one of two quite different conclusions might arise, as follows.

1. An increase in the African American percentage of a future youth population can be noted as a feature of the future youth population that might tend to push rates of total youth violence somewhat higher than they might otherwise be.
2. A total youth homicide rate for some future date could be projected by multiplying this year's rate of African American homicide arrests by 2010's expected volume of African American teens, then multiplying this year's rate of white teen homicide arrests by 2010's expected volume of white teens, and adding the totals together to estimate total homicide arrests. (A separate calculation for Hispanics would also be possible in this pattern, except that reliable data are not available.)

The first tactic is, I believe, justified, as long as the considerable limits of using population characteristics to project rates of behavior are acknowledged (Zimring 1975). The second approach is doomed to catastrophic error. It is unjustified precisely because race, ethnicity, gender, and other social factors are not the determining characteristics of the rate of lethal violence in a population over time.

Rates of serious violence are much higher in big cities than in towns and suburbs, among males than among females, and among African Americans than among Caucasians. What this means is that, all other things being equal, a larger concentration of a future population in the higher risk category will be associated with a higher rate of serious violence than will a future population with fewer males, fewer city dwellers, and fewer blacks. The problem with assuming that last year's rate of arrests for African American males will hold steady for the next two decades is that "all other things" are rarely equal for two years, let alone twenty years. Figure 8.4 shows the fluctuations in male arrest rates for homicide over the period 1980–95.

What the gyrations in figure 8.4 show is how many other influences over time have a substantial impact on the particular rates at which risk groups are arrested and presumably also are committing offenses. The early 1980s are a sobering case in point. The African American share of the youth population went up by seven-tenths of a point in four years, and the homicide arrest rate of males in the age

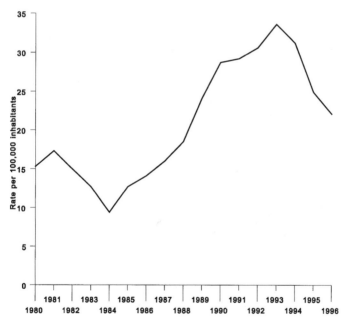

Figure 8.4. Trends in homicide rate for male offenders, ages 13–17, 1980–1996. *Source:* U.S. Department of Justice, Federal Bureau of Investigation, *Uniform Crime Reports*, 1980–1993, 1994a, 1995–1996.

group dropped 38 percent. In contrast, the African American share of the total youth population was stable from 1985 to 1993, whereas the youth homicide rate was climbing by unprecedented lengths. Fluctuations in the percentage of the youth population that is black do not track movements upward or downward in the youth homicide arrest rates over the past 20 years very well, because they play a very minor role in determining arrest rates for serious crimes of violence; in addition, the changing social environment of youths has had a substantial impact on these rates in relatively short periods of time.

To project any single year's aggregate arrest rates forward for 15 years seems unjustified as a projection technique (Zimring 1998, ch. 3). The lowest homicide rate in the last 17 years is less than one-third of the highest (5.3 versus 17.9). The 1996 rate is 11.4, almost at the midpoint between these extremes. Which rate should we use for a projection?

The high margin of error in projections can be illustrated from very recent history. James Fox (1996) of Northeastern University produced a series of projected rates for 1994 through 2010. Two projections were provided: a lower series, which assumed that all future years would experience youth homicide arrests at 1993 rates, and a higher series, which assumed a continual growth in homicide arrest rates. His estimates were obsolete before the ink was dry on the report. The projected lower estimate is 33 percent higher than the actual homicide total for 1996; the higher estimate is more than 40 percent higher. The reason for these gross short-term errors is clear. The variations in the homicide rate in two years—1995 and 1996—were much more important than the growth of the youth population would be for 15 years in determining the volume of homicide arrests. Since the future homicide rate is a guess, so, too, is the projection of future homicide volume.

There are three further points to be made about qualitatively informed projections of future homicides by teens, even though none is as important as the fundamental imponderables that preclude predicting future homicide rates. First, one significant risk characteristic for criminal homicide is diminishing over time in the United States—presence in a large central city. The homicide rate inside the city limits of the 20 largest cities in the United States was four times as high as in the rest of the nation (Zimring and Hawkins 1997, 65), and youth homicides were even more intensely concentrated in major cities in the early 1990s (see Blumstein and Rosenfeld 1998). The long-established trend is toward a smaller proportion of the youth population to be found in major cities. Over the 20 years between 1970 and 1990, the proportion of all U.S. youths aged 10 to 17 who lived inside the 10 largest cities dropped from 9.29 percent to 8.34 percent (U.S. Department of Commerce, Bureau of the Census 1970, 1990). Although this may seem like a small drop, the 10.2 percent reduction in the proportion of all youths in the highest risk environment means that the total youth population could expand by 10 percent without *any* more youths living in the highest risk areas. This dispersion of the population away from large central cities should reduce youth homicide rates, if everything else holds constant.

But this shrinkage in the big-city share of the youth population was overwhelmed after 1985 by the soaring rates among those teens who remained in big cities. So the good news about population dispersion must be tempered by the same inability to predict homicide rates from risk factors that we observe when tracing the impact of changes in race and ethnicity.

Second, the subset of the population with the largest change—Hispanic origin or surname—is not a population group in which homicide offense propensities can be determined reliably from available sources, let alone projected into the future. What makes a 14-year-old a "Hispanic"? His or her last name? The national origin of one of his or her parents? There is no database on homicide from which good estimates of arrest or offense rates can be projected for this group in any single year, let alone over time. There is thus very little improvement in projections that disaggregate minority populations, because the major changes in the population will involve a population group without any reliably documented risk propensities.

Third, none of the factors of concern about family structure—illegitimacy, single-parent status, and so on—can be used to inform homicide projections, because none of these characteristics has any known link to the expected volume of adolescent homicide in the United States or anywhere else. Without any data on social risk factors, the "qualitatively informed" projections of future homicide volume are, in reality, matters of accounting for gender and ethnicity.

Still, is it not better to make these estimates with detailed data about race and ethnicity than without such data? Not necessarily. If the race-specific projections of homicide volume are going to overestimate the actual volume, as every one of them would do for 1995 and 1996, omitting the racial and ethnic details will actually reduce the level of error. More details in projections can just as easily compound a statistical error as reduce it.

I do not mean to suggest that the circumstances of the youth population in the next 10 years are irrelevant to the life opportunities or criminal behavior of the teenagers of 2010. But projecting levels of an infrequent and variable behavior like juvenile homicide from estimates of a youth population in future years is foolhardy. It is not that we do not know enough about the causes of youth homicide to make reliable estimates of future homicides. Quite the opposite. We know too much about the variability of homicide to engage in such numerological guessing games in the name of science.

Determinism without Portfolio

The social scientific evidence for the current argument that a fixed percentage of a population of males will constitute a predatory menace in the year 2010 is a classic case study of compounded distortion. The story begins with a finding by Marvin Wolfgang, Robert Figlio, and Thorsten Sellin (1972) that about 6 percent of Philadelphia boys would accumulate five or more police contacts before their eighteenth birthday. This was first noted with respect to a large group of boys, born in Philadelphia in 1945, who turned 18 in 1963. Rates of violent crime were relatively low in those days, even in Philadelphia, but whatever violent crime was found in the cohort was concentrated among the most arrested 6 percent of the male population. The correct label for this group of juveniles is *chronic delinquents*. Many had some form of violent crime in their police records; many did not.

Many other studies in other settings and in other periods have found that a high proportion of whatever delinquencies are found in a large group of boys will be concentrated in the most active delinquents. In Philadelphia, where there is a good deal of life-threatening violence, the rate of violence in the most active 6 percent of delinquents will be fairly high. In Racine, Wisconsin, the rate of serious violence, even among the most active boys, will be much lower (compare Wolfgang et al. 1972 with Shannon et al. 1991). The fact that offenses tend to concentrate in small subsegments of a juvenile population does not predict what forms of offenses will be found in the subsample or how many acts of life-threatening violence will occur. The finding of concentration thus has no validity in predicting the particular components of juvenile crime.

The concentration of delinquency is the foundation of James Q.

Wilson's (1995, 507) prediction of "30,000 more muggers, killers and thieves than we have now." Wilson gets the 30,000 figure by estimating 6 percent of 500,000 extra adolescent males. This formulation has a substantial capacity to mislead. The three types of criminals are listed in a way that invites the reader to conclude that muggers and killers will be as numerous as thieves. This recalls the classic English recipe for horse and hare stew: "Equal parts horse and hare: one horse, one hare." The reader is further invited to assume that the expansion in the youth population is the dynamic that will generate a larger volume of killing and robbing in the juvenile population: "Get ready!" The next stop toward the prediction of a "coming storm of juvenile violence" is Dilulio's exponential exaggeration of James Q. Wilson's prediction. Whereas Wilson (1995) speaks of 6 percent of juvenile males as "muggers, killers and thieves," Dilulio (1995) coins the phrase "super-predator." Thus we have had a category of young children years away from adolescence transformed from future "chronic delinquents" to prospective "muggers, killers and thieves" to tomorrow's "juvenile super-predators" on sheer rhetorical horsepower. And suddenly, Wilson's 30,000 has become an army of "approximately 270,000 more super-predators." Why does Dilulio estimate an increment eight times as great as Wilson's?

A detailed answer to that question tells us much about the lack of scrutiny of data in the policy debate about juvenile justice in the United States today. Both James Q. Wilson and Dilulio estimate an additional population of hard-core juvenile offenders based on the 6 percent figure from Wolfgang and others (1972). But Wilson (1995) concentrates on the 1990–2000 period, which makes a small difference in his estimate and restricts it to youths who will be old enough to be committing offenses by the year 2000. Dilulio (1995) arrives at the figure of 270,000 extra superpredators by noting that the number of boys under 18 in the United States is expected to grow from 32 million to 36.5 million from 1996 to 2010. By assuming that serious delinquents will be 6 percent of that population, he arrives at the number 270,000 (.06 x 4.5 million = 270,000).

One clue that something is wrong here is that this arithmetic would suggest that there are already 1.9 million juvenile superpredators on U.S. streets (32 million current boys x 0.06 = 1,920,000). That happens to be more young people than were accused of any form of delinquency last year in the United States. The special error here is that Dilulio (1996) assumes that not merely 6 percent of teenagers but also 6 percent of all youths are superpredators. In 2010, fewer than

30 percent of the population under 18 will be 13 years of age and over in the extra cohort and just as many will be 5 years of age and younger. Since 93 percent of all juvenile crime is committed by youths aged 13 and older, fewer than a third of the "extra 270,000" will be active at all in 2010. But the rest, argues Dilulio, will be waiting in the wings, coming at us "in waves." Thus we are to believe that the youths born in 2009 are just as surely superpredators-in-waiting as the 10-year-olds who are behind in reading or the 14-year-olds with a first arrest for petty theft or drug use. We may not know who they are, but we know that they are there, because 6 percent of a male population will meet the criterion.

There are three things to say about this *reductio ad absurdum.* First, even though the numbers involved in this exercise are rather extreme, the predictions and terminology were not seriously challenged for many months after the analysis first appeared in February 1996. That July, the Republican candidate for president made a radio speech on juvenile crime, using the term "superpredator," and informed his listeners that the juvenile arrest rate would double by 2010 (see Zimring 1998, ch. 4). Even extreme claims survive easily in an environment that lacks quality controls for forecasting techniques.

Second, the saga of juvenile superpredators has enormous political benefits. To talk of a "coming storm" creates a riskless environment for getting tough in advance of the future threat. If the crime rate rises, the prediction has been validated. If the crime rate does not rise, the policies that the alarmists put in place can be credited with avoiding the bloodbath. The prediction cannot be falsified, currently or ever.

Third, the wild arithmetic and colorful language of the Dilulio (1996) scenario should not distract observers from the central fallacy of his prediction, a fallacy that animates the James Q. Wilson (1995) work as well. The only proper inference to be drawn from knowing that an extra million teenagers will be present at some future time is that there will be a larger group of teenagers. If delinquency is concentrated in 6 percent of the male population, an increase in the youth population will also increase the number in that 6 percent. How many muggers or killers will be in that population is not known or predicted by the concentration finding.

Thus, even if their adjectives were carefully chosen and their numbers were realistic, the prediction technique used by James Q. Wilson (1995) and John Dilulio (1995) is empty of logical or empirical content. If the argument implied is that the number of homicides or robberies generated by a youth cohort can be easily predicted by its relative size, this is far from obvious in the record of recent American history. The rate of youth violence increased in the late 1980s even as the youth population declined, and the volume of youth violence decreased after 1993 as the youth population grew.

But a deeper point must be made. The reason we cannot currently estimate the volume of juvenile homicide in the United States in 2010 is not merely that we lack an appropriate technology or sufficiently fancy social science. Prediction is beyond our capacity because the conditions that will influence the homicide rates among children now 4 years old when they turn 17 have not yet been determined. The incidence of homicide and other forms of life-threatening violence varies widely over time and is not susceptible to good long-range actuarial estimates even for large groups. It is not possible to know about the homicide rate in 2010, because so many of its key determinants are part of an American history that has yet to happen. Will the schools get better or worse? What patterns of juvenile handgun availability and use will we experience toward the end of the first decade of the twenty-first century? What levels of street drug traffic will urban areas have and with what resultant lethal violence? Most of what will determine the homicide rate among today's 4-year-olds has not yet occurred.

A Manifesto for Disinvestment

To imagine otherwise is to live in a world where a label like "violent delinquent" becomes a hereditary title, an inverse earldom of the urban ghetto. That pattern of thought has two troublesome consequences. To adopt a hard determinist account of lethal violence 15 years down the road makes efforts at improving the environments that influence violence seem far less urgent. If school does not divert youths from hard-core juvenile violence, why care about educational improvements? If future violence is preordained, why waste efforts and resources in trying to stop it? A fatalistic determinism can be an excuse for disinvestment in urban youth development.

Blaming the Toddler

Another latent function of deterministic accounts of criminal violence is rather peculiar. If we really believed that the shape of serious criminal careers were determined early in childhood, future predators would not deserve unqualified blame. After all, the ruthless forces that shaped their careers were much more powerful than their personalities.

But just the opposite view seems to be at work in the rush to identify tomorrow's superpredators before their diapers are dry. In the current juvenile justice debate, it often seems that people use descriptions of future criminality as a device to look past the current dependency and tender years of children, to blame them in advance for the terrible crimes we imagine they will some day commit. This type of projection is certainly not morally coherent, but fear and resentment have never been effective teachers of moral principle.

Conclusion

There will be a middle-sized increase in the youth population over the period 1995–2010, but the percentage of the population in the crime-prone ages of 13 to 17 will be much lower than in the mid-1970s. The percentage of the youth population that is African American will increase by less than 1 percent over the period 1987–2010, whereas the percentage of the youth population that is Hispanic will increase substantially.

The impact of all these changes in the number and composition of the youth population on rates of serious violence is not known. A 19 percent increase in the population will have a modest impact on crime volume. If the rate of serious violence goes down at the rate of the early 1980s or mid-1990s, a 19 percent population increase will not dilute the decline of crime dividend by much. If the rate of serious violence increases substantially, the additional population will make the problem somewhat worse. But population will not be the big story in violent youth crime in the foreseeable American future, and concern about crime should not be a major issue in planning for changes in the youth population.

The Terrifying Toddlers in Retrospect: A 2004 Addendum

The epidemic of alarm about future rates of youth violence was a case study in catastrophic timing. Rates of crime and violence had already declined for three years by 1996 (when the alarms were still being sounded) and continued to decline for the rest of the 1990s. The Great American Juvenile Crime Panic soon became The Great American Crime Decline.

During the crime decline in the United States, rates of youth violence dropped faster than rates of violence by adults. From a high of 26.5 per 100,000 in 1993, the rate of homicide arrests for ages 10–17 dropped by 75 percent to 6.6 in 1999, as shown in figure 8.5.

There are three lessons to be drawn from the data reported in figure 8.5. The first is that rates of arrest are *vastly* more important than the size of the youth population in predicting rates of serious violence. The second is that rates of arrest cannot be projected or predicted successfully from current trends or demographic profiles. The entire period after 1980 provides no time segment that would lead to good middle-range predictions if continued as a straight line projection. There is simply no good "straight line" for projections that will be anything other than ludicrous over time.

The third lesson is not as obvious as the first two, but is of great importance. One reason that homicide rates dropped among teens in the 1990s was that the general rate of homicide declined as well. This is the phenomenon of general rate dependence discussed in chapter 7. But why did youth homicide decline even more than the adult rate? The very divergence in trend between youth and adults

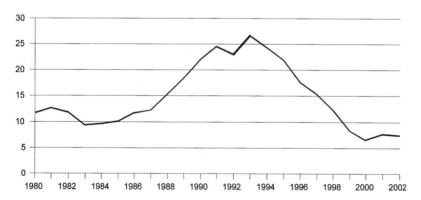

Figure 8.5. Homicide arrest rate for males age 10–17, 1980–2002. *Source:* "Juvenile Arrest Rates by Offense, Sex, and Race (1980–2001)," prepared for the Office of Juvenile Justice and Delinquency Prevention by the National Center for Juvenile Justice; available online at: http://ojjdp. ncjrs.org/ojstatbb/excel/JAR_o53103.xls (May 31, 2003).

that was noted in the late 1980s and early 1990s may have meant that rates among the young would be pushed back toward the long term consistently with adult homicide rates.

If the gods had set out to punish criminologists for their hubris in predicting juvenile "bloodbaths" or epidemics of "juvenile super-predators," they could not improve on the actual data displayed in figure 8.5. The lowest arrest rates in the era after 1980 are in the period after 2000. There is simply no foundation for any prediction of future danger in the first nine years of the period after 1993, the era that was supposed to lead the bad new days of juvenile violence.

Part IV

POLICY PROBLEMS IN MODERN JUVENILE JUSTICE

At any given moment in American history, it is a safe bet that one or more legal issues about policy toward adolescents will be a prominent public worry, but which questions will pop up in tomorrow's headlines is impossible to know. A major national debate about firearms and youth seemed far from the horizon in 1997, but a cluster of school shootings culminating in the Columbine disaster of 1999 pushed that topic to center stage and forcefully reminded us how much of our agenda for legal policy is a hostage to current events. But while the public concerns about the problems addressed in this part may ebb and flow with newspaper headlines, the problems themselves are chronic concerns produced by long-range trends in developed nations.

Teen pregnancy is a wonderful example of a structural problem often mistaken for an issue of sexual morality or health education. Modern history has been conspiring to lengthen the age span of adolescence at both ends. In developed nations, sexual maturity happens at a much earlier age than in previous centuries, but the educational and job training preparation for adult roles lasts at least until the early twenties. So the peak ages of sexual interest begin when it is socially inconvenient to encourage lifetime commitments and the sacrifices of self-development that child rearing requires of the adolescent parent. There is an obvious incentive to discourage teen parenting, but there are also duties to protect the teen parent from governmentally imposed harm.

How best to combat the harms that are produced by minority overrepresentation in juvenile justice is yet another chronic problem that will become a prominent concern from time to time. What steps can we take that are consistent with the priorities of juvenile justice generally that can best reduce the harms so obviously linked to filling our courts and detention centers with youth from disadvantaged minorities?

Each of the five chapters in this part attempts to produce an analysis of policy options that integrates the data available on specific issues with the priorities of youth policy developed in Part II of this book. Even thought each topic occupies its own policy domain, there is the additional need to create consistent theories of adolescent capacities and limits across different policy rubrics. So consistency across the domains of law is a requirement of a coherent set of policies toward youth. The exercises in this part try to push toward that consistency of vision.

There is a very wide range of problems considered in these five chapters, from girls who might get pregnant to the punishment of murderers under 18. But each of the policy analyses in this part reaches back into the earlier parts of this book in an attempt to integrate knowledge and perspectives about adolescent development with the wide variety of specific contexts where government must act. Chapter 9 shows how the concern with premature parenting is centrally linked to the needs for adolescent development to occupy the attention and resources of the teen years. Chapter 10 traces the need for judicial transfer of some serious cases as a necessary "safety valve" to a youth-protective juvenile court but shows that transfer cannot serve justice well unless criminal courts also consider the diminished responsibility of the young.

Chapter 11 argues that many of the general strategies that juvenile courts have for all offenders may be a more effective tool for reducing the harms from minority overrepresentation than rules designed to equalize justice system exposure. Chapter 12 reveals the central inconsistency of using "adult" penalties for juvenile gun possession is that prohibiting gun access to youth is justified because of the same immaturity that requires reduction in deserved punishments. But the wide variety of controls available to keep guns from youth are probably more effective than the exclusive reliance on large penalties.

The final chapter in this collection examines the policy problem where special legal concerns about youth are overwhelmed by other demands: the law's treatment of adolescent homicide offenders. But careful analysis suggests both that diminished responsibility is of great importance to just results when adolescents kill and that the frequently encountered juvenile accomplice discussed in chapter 6 may also require special doctrinal consideration. So the materials assembled in the first three parts of the book are relevant to the full range of legal policies toward youth.

NINE

The Jurisprudence of Teen Pregnancy

This chapter attempts to use some of the same perspectives on adolescence that inform modern theories of juvenile justice to evaluate policies toward teen pregnancy. The concerns that provoke special policy toward teen pregnancy were an important part of the first two-thirds of the twentieth century, when girls at risk were frequently classified as "status offenders." The problems associated with severe punishment for status offenders led to a tactical withdrawal of delinquency classifications and institutional placement for girls at sexual risk (Friedman 2002). But teen pregnancy remains a policy problem of concern. This essay first discusses the reason why teen pregnancy might be regarded as a special problem and then examines a range of potential public policies that have been proposed to prevent or respond to teen child bearing. A final section emphasizes the hazards of punishment as a tool to discourage teen childbearing.

I believe that our recent experience in reforming the ideas and programs of the juvenile justice system can contribute to a prudent and humane policy toward adolescent pregnancy and parenting. Reform efforts in juvenile justice also provide a broader context in which ideas about teenage pregnancy and its outcomes can be examined and evaluated.

Adolescent Childbearing: A Core Concern

A rigorous delineation of what might make teenage parenting a special problem for public law is more than a formal preliminary to the policy analysis of particular kinds of programs. It is important to locate the current concern about teenage childbearing in the modern legal conception of what adolescence is and should mean in the personal development of those who pass through it. We can then use what we regard as the values being protected in worrying about adolescent childbearing as a guide to programs of prevention. Anchoring concerns about teenage childbearing in a specific conception of adolescence helps define the kind of programs that can be justified in the name of this special concern. Moreover, the identification of proper program elements helps us evaluate the consequences of the state's going into the business of discouraging teenage childbearing—consequences, I shall later argue, that do not uniformly operate to the benefit of all young people.

The legal conception of adolescence that I have argued for elsewhere is a period when those not fully adult are engaged in the processes of becoming adult (Zimring 1982). During a period of legal semiautonomy, young persons are progressively given opportunities to make a variety of decisions for themselves, even though it is understood that their relative lack of maturity will lead to a number of errors. This process is justified because trial and error in decision-making constitute one necessary part of learning adult competencies in any society where the freedom of choosing the path of one's own life is the hallmark of legal adulthood. This "learner's permit" perspective is discussed in chapter 2.

The more complex and multifaceted adult roles become, the longer the learning process to full adult competency, and thus the longer the period of adolescence required for transition into adulthood. This linkage explains the irony that modern adolescents are simultaneously precocious and retarded when compared to earlier cohorts of youth. Much of the rhetoric that accompanied the extension of the franchise to 18-year-olds in the early 1970s celebrated the achievement of modern youth, often in contrast with earlier generations. And children today do have more formal education and more exposure to a wider world at earlier ages than the preceding generations.

But there is a contrast between absolute and relative development that characterizes the careers of many modern adolescents: the 18- or 19-year-old of the 1990s typically has achieved more in many spheres of training and development than the 18- and 19-year-old of the 1920s. But the modern adolescent also typically has further to go to complete the process because of the increasing complexity and variousness of the adult choices that must be made in contemporary American life.

The absolute advantage of the modern adolescent over young people in earlier generations is an argument for earlier exercise of some privileges that depend on minimal competence. However, on a relative basis, intellectual and social development among today's 18-year-olds is certainly no closer to the completed process of adult development in 2005 than was the case in the 1920s or earlier. Young people may have come further, but they also have further to go. The gap that still exists between the equipment for choice possessed by a modern adolescent and what we expect for contemporary adulthood is particularly problematic when we consider those decisions made in adolescence that will have substantial and permanent effect on the life opportunity of young people, decisions such as whether to become a parent.

The juxtaposition of relative and absolute accomplishment is, then, central to the concern about teenage parenthood. In the United States in 2005, public concern is expressed not merely about out-of-wedlock pregnancy or pregnancy in the early teens but also about married 18- and 19-year-old women having babies. This concern has increased, even though the incidence of childbearing in the teen years has not increased recently.

The problem with 18-year-old childbearing from this perspective is that early parenthood interrupts the parents' process of development and impinges on the parents' future choices and life chances. This will be true for all mothers maintaining custody and for any father with custodial or financial responsibilities. Having and keeping a child lock an 18-year-old parent into duties and foreclose opportunities. It is this sense of childbearing as arrested development that animates the advertising slogan "Children having children."

Of course, having a child at any time can lock a parent into commitments of care-giving and will foreclose opportunities for other kinds of development. Having a child before finishing the process of growing up means that the choices between commitments to parenting and to other life opportunities will not be made with the degree of social experience that we associate with adult competence. The decision-making that leads to adolescent parenting may be flawed by lack of experience and maturity and is therefore a proper concern of public policy. We want adolescents to accumulate more experience for longer, making decisions with less fateful and permanent consequences in their lives before crossing the threshold of altruistic permanent commitment.

In this account, the central problem of premature commitments to parenting relates to the quality of decision-making. Persons who become parents give up other opportunities as a consequence, at whatever stage in their social development the decision is made. The problem of teenage parenting is that the decision to forgo other opportunities is not made with the same wideness of worldview and the same experience in making decisions that are the hallmark of adulthood in democratic society.

There are, of course, some persons who make decisions in the same way at age 18 that they would at age 25 or 30. This may well be as true of some 16-year-olds. But for most modern adolescents, the world widens dramatically during the years of secondary school and just beyond. In an ideology of adolescence that places great emphasis on mobility and choice, there is great personal cost in making binding choices earlier than when the range of choice available is well known.

This broad objection to adolescent parenting can be contrasted with two narrower sets of concerns that focus on the association between teen parenting and manifest pathology. One concern about "children having children" is that an interruption in the maturing process of the teenage parent will lead to unfortunate near-term consequences. Thus, we hear that those who become parents at young ages will interrupt their educations and forgo economic opportunities as a consequence of childbearing.

Two points can be made about this. First, becoming a parent carries opportunity costs throughout the life cycle. Adult decisions to bear and raise children also frequently lead to sacrifice in educational and economic opportunities for parents. A measure of respect is frequently paid to adult citizens who choose to make the sacrifices associated with becoming parents. Why, then, our paternalistic hostility to the sacrifices of teenage childbearing? The emphasis on the quality of decision-making involved in becoming a parent provides an answer. The social plaint about adolescent decisions to forgo other opportunities in order to become parents is "You don't know what you're missing."

A second point is made that there are some lost opportunities associated with premature childbearing that do not occur in later periods. Even if the young mother manages to finish school and find a desirable job, the process of deciding to become a parent will lack the resonance of maturity. Having come to parenthood too early, she will find that the path to making the decision will not contain the experienced-based reflection that itself then becomes one of the positive aspects of later parenthood. In this view, immaturity can render the decision to bear children as lacking truly informed consent.

An even narrower set of concerns about adolescent childbearing involves a high incidence of particular identified pathologies, such as low birth weight, impaired maternal and child health, welfare dependency, illegitimacy, near-term divorce, and the like. These special problems exacerbate adolescent pregnancy far too often, and additional resources should be invested in programs aimed at postponing parenthood beyond the adolescent years on account of these related pathologies (Hamburg and Dixon 1992).

But if this litany of pathologies is the heart of the matter, then a special concern with adolescent pregnancy is both overinclusive and underinclusive. It is overinclusive because some adolescent childbearing will avoid serious pathology. This is particularly the case when public resources are invested to support childbearing. And a targeted concern on adolescent pregnancy is also underinclusive, in that the majority of children from divorced and welfare-dependent families are not the direct result of teenage childbearing. A focused concern on pathological outcome would seem to be as much directed at support for parenting by young persons as for postponing parenting. It would also miss some aspects of adolescent development that are worthy of notice.

Cause for Concern?

There is ample room on the basis of currently available data to disagree about the importance of early childbearing as an independent problem meriting public intervention. Many of the handicaps associated with early child rearing are not necessarily caused by pregnancy and parenting (Luker 1995). And many of the educational and experiential options we could wish for middle and late adolescents would not be widely available to many young mothers in any event, because of their limited economic means and educational background. In this sense, the theory of adolescence that animates a general objection to early childbearing can be seen as restrictively middle-class.

Yet the aspirations that most urban households of all classes have for their children are also rather middle-class, and there are few enclaves in late twentieth-century America where an 18-year-old's pregnancy is regarded as good news by parents and peers. While becoming a parent in the late teen years can be something less than a disaster (Furstenberg, Brooks-Gunn, and Morgan 1987), a public preference to keep the teen years occupied with the adolescent's personal development can be justified. Nobody yet argues that teenage childbearing facilitates choice and mobility. The fact that

early childbearing is by no means the only restriction on development faced by adolescents at risk requires broader programs than just
pregnancy prevention. But social comfort with other people's children being locked into permanent roles while our own children preserve middle-class options seems a far from benign double standard.

That the costs of teen parenting may have been overestimated becomes an argument against public investment in prevention only if
such prevention programs hurt young people. This highlights the important relationship between the justification for public programs in
this area and the content and effects of the programs. My own conclusion is that as long as a public program pays proper regard to the
interests of the kids it is trying to protect, a policy to encourage postponing childbearing beyond the teen years can be justified.

Implications for Program Strategy

The decision to have children at any age carries significant opportunity costs. In America, the opportunity costs of adolescent childbearing are seen to be higher than for childbearing in later years. But
whether or not the burdens encountered by an adolescent parent are
greater, there is a separate justification for special public concern
about adolescent parenting, because adolescents lack the life experiences that would prepare them for making so fateful a choice in an
authentically adult way. Adolescent parents do not know what they
would be missing.

If this concern functions as the justification for special state programs, I argue that the programs designed to respond to this problem
should be: (1) general in scope rather than simply targeting the
earlier years of adolescence; (2) preventive rather than just ameliora-
tive; (3) paternalistic in preferring postponed parenthood; and (4)
protective of the adolescent at risk rather than punitive or neutral in
approach.

Generality

A concern with the quality of decision-making about childbearing
can support programs that encompass the full range of adolescent development rather than the earlier adolescent years, which are of particularly high biological and economic risk. No matter what one's
special orientation, early adolescence presents particularly high risks

for pregnancy and parenting. The concern for "children having children" is most acute when those children are 13-, 14-, and 15-year-olds, still early in the secondary education process, still not physically mature, and great distances away from the experiential base that should be the background for decisions about marriage and childbearing. Any program especially concerned with adolescent pregnancy should make young adolescents a special priority.

But a concern about the proper experiential background for decisions about having a child need not be restricted to younger adolescents. Publicly supported programs that are based on the concerns outlined earlier can and should target older adolescents, as well as younger ones, and express concern about decisions made by high school graduates as well as younger adolescents. In this sense, adolescents who are not obviously regarded as still "children" should be the object of concern about childbearing decisions, even if they are already acquiring job experience, voting in national elections, and further along the way to authentic adulthood than the younger teens (Zimring 1982).

Prevention

Another feature of the public programs that can be justified on this ground is that they are concerned with prevention as well as the amelioration of the problems associated with adolescent pregnancy and childbearing. If only the lack of prenatal care would justify special concerns for adolescent pregnancy, why not concentrate public funding on providing prenatal care instead of attempting to reduce the incidence of pregnancy? Similarly, if the limited economic opportunity associated with teenage parenting was the major concern, why not just invest public funds to provide counseling and other supportive services?

Concern for premature judgment suggests the investment of resources to prevent pregnancy, not just to support teen pregnancy and parenting. This is especially true for younger adolescents, but is also justified for those of our children who are well launched in college and a variety of experiences in travel, education, and dating.

Paternalism

The special justification for postponing adolescent child rearing permits a degree of paternalism in the administration of prevention programs, although there are important practical and principled limits to the degree of paternalism that should be allowed. The limited paternalism I support is one of a state program that can persist in preferring the postponement of childbearing among adolescents even if the adolescents disagree. If the problematic nature of adolescent judgment about childbearing is the justification for a special program, it would be inconsistent to simultaneously premise a special program on notions of immaturity of judgment and to exempt all adolescents who wish to have children from a public judgment that family responsibility should be deferred.

But it is only in this special case that notions of adolescent immaturity provide an automatic basis for substituting public judgments for personal preferences. Once pregnancy is an accomplished fact, any presumption that the state knows best should probably be inoperative. The limited case paternalism I support is limited to preferring that children do not get pregnant.

Why not let notions of adolescent immaturity license more forceful varieties of state intervention? Let me defer this issue briefly while finishing the list of themes implied by the central concern outlined in the first section.

Protection

My final implied dimension of public programs is the most important. State initiatives in this field should protect the individual adolescent at risk rather than be punitive or neutral with respect to her immediate welfare interests. If the reason we worry about adolescents becoming parents is the risk to their welfare as adults, then the welfare of the individual adolescent should remain central in a special program. Public programs designed merely to reduce welfare rolls or infant mortality or divorce rates should not be targeted especially at adolescents. The special concern of adolescent childbearing is adolescent welfare, and the obligation that the state authority assumes in taking special power over the lives of adolescents on this account is to do so with their welfare as a central policy goal.

With this point about youth welfare in mind, we can return to the real-world context of limited paternalism. What prevents society from implementing paternalistic programs aimed at adolescents at risk for childbearing that are both compulsory and therapeutic? The objection to this combination of coercive state programs as the means and youth welfare as the end is a practical one. Three-quarters of a

century of juvenile court reform efforts have been founded on the fu-
tility of coercing cures among the young. More specifically, the adolescent at risk of pregnancy has long been considered what the law
calls a "status offender" and was made the subject of compulsory
public programs that were celebrated failures in protecting the adolescent and the larger community (Zimring 1982, ch. 5). There is in
this history no evidence available that compulsory programs that
greatly restrict the liberty of adolescents at risk achieve benefits
worth their substantial costs.

The history of efforts to coercively cure status offenders suggests
that the burden of persuasion should be substantial on those who
would return to government efforts in that direction. But history also
suggests that new emphasis on a peril to adolescent development is
frequently accompanied by new bursts of faith in coercive intervention. Changing the problem label seems to reinvigorate enthusiasm
for policies of coercion.

Broad powers were delegated to the juvenile courts to deal with
large categories of adolescents at risk. Institutions were built and
staffed, programs were funded and widely praised on the assumption
that paternalistic and coercive programs could rescue adolescents
from the danger of living criminal, immoral, and dissolute lives.

The best historical evidence demonstrates that coercive intervention programs never worked well (Friedman 2002; Schlossman
1977). The contemporary effort to rethink government's role in dealing with status offenders emphasizes reduction in forced intervention while attempting to minimize the real dangers that status offenders face in unregulated environments with voluntary programs
and limited crisis intervention.

The consensus that supports this direction of reform for status offender programs is all the more remarkable because of society's reluctance to accept the limited capacity of the state to help adolescents at risk. A sense of limit conflicts with the persistent American
optimism that only the right set of programs need be identified for
problems to be solved.

Thus, there is more than a small danger that the relabeling of problems and the programs designed to respond to them can lead to a
repetition of the mistakes that characterized earlier adventures with
status offenders. With each new threat to adolescent well-being—be it
an epidemic of teenage pregnancy, the threat of crack cocaine, or the
specter of AIDS—impulses to intervene run high. Often, the institutional memory of program failures does not carry over to the new in-

stitutions participating in policy discussion and in the arena of legislative change. For this reason, one hazard in public policy toward adolescents in the United States is that it is merely old wine in new bottles.

The Perils of Prevention

Those who design and execute criminal laws have a much easier task than the practitioners of juvenile justice in one important respect. The goal of criminal law is to stigmatize particular forms of proscribed behavior, as well as the persons who engage in that behavior. To cast both the act and the actor in the same negative light is often possible. But the law gives those who practice juvenile justice an unattainable goal, the objective of stigmatizing behaviors without stigmatizing those young persons who engage in them. The goal is unattainable, because negative social judgments about particular' behaviors inevitably spill over to become social evaluations of the persons who engage in those behaviors.

This social fact has placed a contradiction at the heart of the operation of modern juvenile justice: What the formal law demands—stigma-free treatment of the alleged delinquent—cannot be achieved when the system simultaneously wishes to attach stigma to delinquent behavior. Even in an age that has witnessed a so-called Teflon presidency, social judgments about delinquent behavior inevitably rub off on those who engage in the behavior.

The same conflict can be seen at the center of programs that seek to reduce rates of adolescent pregnancy yet ameliorate the difficult life settings of adolescents who are involved in the process. Effective prevention programs will stigmatize teen childbearing. That negative social judgment puts pregnant and childbearing adolescents at greater risk. One consequence of this is that a major secondary goal of preventive programs in this area should be the correction of the negative effects that are by-products of a primary prevention thrust.

Do successful prevention programs really stigmatize adolescent parenting? Of course. Any program that seeks to redirect voluntary adolescent behavior is an exercise in marketing. With respect to adolescent parenting, the marketing task is to focus attention on the negative aspects of pregnancy, childbearing, and child rearing. Some analogues in our recent experience are public and private campaigns to dissuade teenagers from cigarette smoking and, more recently, using drugs. The antismoking campaign research found that the most successful appeals to an adolescent audience involved short-term rather than long-term effects and emphasized the dumbness of smoking. The marketing task is to convince young persons that those of their peers who smoke should not be emulated. The mechanism is stigma.

So one necessary element of discouraging teenage parenting is stigma. But negative messages about adolescent pregnancy and child rearing inevitably spill over into negative judgments about pregnant and parenting teens. Programs that effectively dissuade young persons at risk of becoming parents do so at the price of further lowering the social standing of those who are pregnant and parents.

One case study in the manifest and latent effect of stigma involves teenage marriage. If the decades after 1950 of American demographic experience were to become a Perry Mason adventure, it could be titled "The Case of the Disappearing Bridegroom." As figure 9.1 shows, the proportion of girls, aged 15 to 19, who are currently married has declined in each census year since midcentury and now stands at miniscule levels (Hayes 1987; U.S. Bureau of the Census 1953). Behaviorally, teenage marriage was social deviance in the late 1980s, which seems to have reduced the birthrate somewhat among teenage girls, thus deferring childbearing to later years for many young women (see, e.g., Weeks 1976).

But as marriage rates decline, a larger proportion of those pregnancies that do occur during the teen years will occur outside of marriage. In this sense, an increase in the proportion of all live births among teenage girls that are illegitimate is evidence that policies that stigmatize teenage marriages are working, but working at a substantial cost to a group of young women who are pregnant, unmarried, and the object of social stigma.

Consider, for example, the social environment in which an 18-year-old male high school senior makes a decision in 2005 about how to respond to the fact that his 17-year-old girlfriend is pregnant. Demographic statistics suggest that the young man bent on "doing the right thing" in the 1950s frequently reached different decisions from those he reaches now. And one important reason for this is that the social status of marrying at 18 in order to raise a child has declined precipitously. However difficult in other respects, one of the nice things about "doing the right thing" is the positive judgment one obtains from one's social group after embarking on that course of action. That kind of positive reinforcement for 18-year-old males mar-

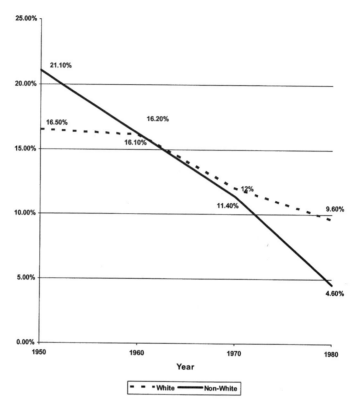

Figure 9.1. Percent of women, 15–19, who have ever been married, by race and census year. *Source:* data for 1950 are from: U.S. Bureau of the Census (1953); data for 1960, 1970, and 1980 are from Hayes (1987).

rying seems to have disappeared from adult society and from most adolescent peer cultures in the United States.

The simple point is this: the war on adolescent pregnancy necessarily inflicts casualties, and today these casualties are often pregnant and childbearing adolescents. These teenage girls were always at the highest risk of suffering the bad outcomes that come with early parenting. One negative consequence of stigma-based programs is increased difficulties suffered by those most at risk of negative social consequences from teenage pregnancy. What to do?

There is a direct contradiction between the negative effects of stigma-based prevention programs and any sentiment that initiatives in this field should be protective of the individual adolescent at risk.

One way to cope with this kind of conflict is to deny the protective obligation of state policy. Thus, in dealing with delinquents, some contemporary observers now use the blameworthiness of individual delinquents to deny any obligation to take their interests into account in the juvenile justice process. Can a parallel argument be constructed for disowning those who are dumb enough to get pregnant or to stay pregnant? I hope not, but blaming the victim is tempting in social policy toward adolescents at risk.

Instead, a balanced social agenda requires programs to ameliorate the risks experienced by girls who experience pregnancy in adolescence. This obligation should be a reason to avoid inflicting gratuitous stigma in programs (i.e., by excluding adolescent mothers from educational programs). The obligation to protect provides another reason to justify programs for those males and females who choose adolescent parenting as the lesser evil.

But is it not inconsistent to support both programs that seek to prevent adolescent parenting and programs that seek to support young persons who have children? The answer is no. As long as youth welfare is the goal of pregnancy prevention programs, the same reasons that underlie committing resources to prevention programs counsel us to help those of our older children who now have children themselves. If we value the developmental options of young people, we should seek public policies that foster the development of pregnant as well as nonpregnant young women.

The true inconsistency is pursuing youth welfare only to the water's edge, by using the needs of young persons as a justification for prevention programs but ignoring those needs when pregnancy and childbirth occur. Both support of adolescent parenting and steps toward prevention are necessary elements of an evenhanded policy that addresses the central social harm of premature parenting.

TEN

Juvenile or Criminal Court?
A Punitive Theory of Waiver

Transferring defendants still young enough for juvenile court into the criminal courts is a compound legal arrangement of a special character; it is a universal exception to a universal rule. The first universal is juvenile justice itself. In every American state, juvenile courts have been created to respond to criminal charges against offenders under a maximum age that varies from 16 to 18.

The use of a juvenile court for youth crime is in fact almost universal throughout the developed nations. No major industrial democracy incorporates the processing of very young offenders into the normal operation of its criminal courts. A century after its creation, the juvenile court is the uniform major premise in policy toward youth crime in every advanced legal system.

While juvenile court is the universal rule, every American jurisdiction has provided for exceptions to it—circumstances and procedures that transfer those within the age boundaries of juvenile court to criminal court instead. The particular procedures used and the circumstances that justify their use vary, but the provision for some transfer of cases is, in the United States, just as universal as the general policy that it modifies.

Both the policy of juvenile court jurisdiction and the exception to it are puzzling American universals. Why the ubiquity of juvenile courts for trying our youngest offenders? What is the special advantage of a court for children in criminal cases? Why does such a court continue everywhere, despite widespread doubts about its capacity to rehabilitate youth on the terms of the court's original philosophy? If juvenile court is a good place to process and sanction most young offenders, why not all young offenders?

My account of the answers to these questions will be delivered in four installments. The first section argues that the necessity of transfers must be understood in the context of the functions and limits of juvenile courts. The modern juvenile court is an institution that holds juveniles accountable for intentional wrongs but is restrained in both the kind and amount of punishment it can administer. The strong pressure to remove cases from juvenile court comes when older adolescents are accused of conduct so serious that the minimum punishment felt necessary exceeds the maximum punishment within the power of the juvenile court. It is the limited capacity of the juvenile court to punish that leads to transfers as a universal exception to juvenile court jurisdiction in the United States.

The second section examines three different structural accommodations to the need for serious punishment for a few youths: wholesale transfer of jurisdiction to criminal courts; the expansion of punishment powers available within the juvenile court so that even the most terrible crimes can meet their just deserts in a juvenile court; and the selective transfer of cases. I regard selective transfer as the obviously superior method to respond to the need for serious punishment in extraordinary cases.

But selective transfer can be achieved in many different ways. The third section contrasts three different mechanisms for transfer: (1) legislative standards that define both the necessary and sufficient causes for transfer; (2) a legal framework that delegates power to judges to decide whether a particular case requires transfer; and (3) a system that delegates total power to prosecutors. In practice, I show the real choice is between judicial and prosecutorial final authority.

The concluding section of this chapter describes a few of the minimum conditions necessary to justice at the interface between juvenile and criminal court. Without appropriate substantive provisions for the treatment of transferred cases, no procedural restrictions on the method of transfer can rescue the system from incoherence.

One further point is necessary as an introduction to this chapter. The question of transfer from juvenile to criminal court is the very opposite of an independent issue. The design of sensible provision for transfer depends on clearly understanding the functions and limits of juvenile and criminal courts, and the differences between these two institutions. Finding the appropriate methods of transfer from juvenile to criminal courts thus demands that we comprehend the entire context in which such decisions must be made.

The Mission and Limits of Juvenile Court

The universal popularity of juvenile court jurisdiction for very young criminals suggests a widely shared perception that the very youngest law violators are different from other criminals, as well as agreement that a special judicial institution is better suited to adjudicating cases involving the young than is a criminal court. In the original theory of the juvenile court, young law violators were considered just one class of child in need of help, and the only official reason for any legal response when children committed crimes was to help the child. On this theory, interventions in the lives of delinquent youth were no different from the responses that the legal system would choose for noncriminal children in need of supervision, and wholly different from those appropriate to adult law violators (Mack 1909). In theory, the special province of the juvenile court flowed automatically from the solely youth-serving purposes for intervention in the juvenile court.

But was there ever really a time when the legal system's response to the youthful burglar and car thief was wholly nonpunitive? Historical accounts from the earliest years suggest that help without blame was never the court's sole basis for intervention (Platt 1969; Schlossman 1977). Punitive motives seem to have been an inevitable part of juvenile court responses from the start, and by the time *In re Gault* was decided in 1967, the punitive content of juvenile court sanctions for delinquency was the central factual premise on which modern procedural protections were based (Zimring 2000, pt. 2).

For at least a generation, then, the official jurisprudence of the juvenile court's delinquency jurisdiction has included the punishment of wrongdoing. Even with the reduction in culpability that the young may deserve because of diminished responsibility, why not administer such punishments in criminal rather than juvenile courts? Why is punishing the young in the juvenile court style so different and so much better than the sanctioning that criminal courts can deliver that every legal system chooses the juvenile court forum?

The advantages of the juvenile court are two. The first distinguishing feature of a juvenile court is expertise on youth and youth development. The court and its affiliated institutions have expertise in the special needs and special responses of young persons. In the modern understanding of juvenile justice, such special information on youth is not only relevant to a narrow band of issues concerning rehabilitation but also informs the character of appropriate supervision, of assessments of dangerousness, and of judgments about culpability (Allen 1964, 52–53).

But more than expertise is involved in the uniform choice of a juvenile court. The second advantage of the juvenile court is restraint from the imposition of destructive punishments. Even in the post-*Gault* era of legal realism about its mission, the American juvenile court has been characterized by a qualified but very significant commitment to the welfare of all minors who come before it. The juvenile court, in setting the terms of punishment, must stop short of destroying the objects of its attention to preserve its legitimacy.

In other writing, I have used the phrase "room to reform" to describe the objective of juvenile courts even when they punish. The policy of the juvenile court is to punish offenders without sacrificing the long-term life chances and developmental opportunities of the targets of punitive sanctions (Zimring 1998, ch. 5). The key distinction here is between punishments that hurt and those that permanently disfigure. Discomfort and restriction are elements of juvenile sanctions, but permanent stigma is to be avoided at great cost, and a juvenile residential facility that did not offer schooling and life preparation to its subjects would be in irredeemable conflict with the purposes of the modern juvenile court.

This search for nondisfiguring punishments is by no means the equivalent of seeking out only the best interests of the convicted juvenile burglar. All of the customary aims of criminal punishment can be served while providing room to reform, including deterrence, short-term incapacitation, and retribution within limits. But the limits of punishment are also very important. The problem with extending secure confinement far into adulthood to punish juvenile crime is the destruction of any chance for a normal young adulthood. The typical maximum sanction in juvenile court will leave time for a young adult to emerge from confinement to enter the world of work, to mate, and to form a family. The high value placed on the future life opportunities of the delinquent is a defining aspect of the juvenile court that sets it apart from the open-ended punishment portfolio of the criminal court. The two courts may serve the same inventory of purposes of punishment, but with very different limits.

The commitment to limit punishments to preserve the juvenile's life chances is at once the singular appeal of the juvenile court and the characteristic feature of juvenile justice that inevitably produces pressure to transfer some serious cases to criminal court. The reason for this dual importance is that the mix of sanctions limited in this way is the best result for the overwhelming majority of all youth law violations, but a serious problem for a very few of the most serious of juvenile crimes. If the unwillingness of a juvenile court to disfigure is a defining characteristic of its orientation to its subjects, the very serious crime committed by a 16- or 17-year-old is exactly the kind of hard case that the juvenile court cannot easily accommodate while preserving its nondestructive mandate.

On this account, the limited range of sanctions is not an oversight or an unimportant detail of the juvenile court's organization but rather a fundamental element of juvenile court philosophy that is the court's great strength in most cases. But there are, it seems, cases where the most severe secure confinement that the normally constituted juvenile court can permit itself falls far short of the minimum punishment that the community will tolerate. The typical worst case in a metropolitan juvenile court with a maximum jurisdiction age of 18 will be intentional homicide (Zimring 1998, table 7.1) committed by a 16- or 17-year-old. These are visible cases where punishment responses that avoid impinging on the offender's life changes may fall short of the community's sense of minimum desert. What to do?

To ignore demands for a special punitive response is an act of will that leaves the juvenile court vulnerable to swift legislative change in a democratic government. While "worst case" events are a small part of the juvenile court's business, they are recurrent phenomena. Some accommodation to the pressure for additional punishment in serious cases has become universal in the United States. But the structural changes that have been made to account for hard cases differ, and these different systems carry very different mixes of cost and benefit, as the next section will demonstrate.

Of course, not all of the cases transferred out of juvenile court are superserious. In this regard, it is necessary to distinguish between the type of case that makes transfer necessary and the much wider variety of cases that get transferred. Once transfer out of juvenile court is institutionalized, the practice is often not restricted to the superserious cases that rendered it necessary. All manner of older, recidivist, and recalcitrant juveniles are pushed into criminal courts once the channel between the two institutions has been opened (Feld 1987; Ferguson and Douglas 1970). But my argument suggests that only one class of cases makes transfer necessary, and substantial effort should be invested in restricting the practice to cases that meet the criterion of core necessity.

If waiver is restricted to cases where the sanctions available in juvenile court are clearly inadequate, the great majority of cases close to the waiver border will be homicide charges, but not all homicide charges will be strong candidates for waiver. In my view, even murder charges are better thought of as a necessary but not a sufficient condition for transfer of juvenile defendants to criminal courts. So the number of cases where waiver might be necessary is small, but the importance of finding a principled basis for waiver is much larger than the number of cases would suggest. How juvenile and criminal courts deal with these most serious cases is one significant element of the legal framework of juvenile and criminal justice.

Structures of Accommodation

A very few young offenders will commit crimes that demand, at minimum, more punishment than a juvenile court that seeks to avoid debilitating injury can administer. There are three basic structural mechanisms that might change the ordinary operation of juvenile justice to meet the need for extra punishment in such extreme cases. The delinquency jurisdiction of the juvenile court could be cut back or abolished to minimize the number of extremely serious cases with only limited punishment power available. Or punishment powers within the juvenile court could be expanded so that even the punishment suited to crimes of extreme seriousness would be available within the court for children. Or a safety valve procedure for transfer of some special cases could be instituted without changing either general jurisdictional boundaries or limited juvenile court punishment powers. Of the three structural accommodations, the safety valve procedure for transfer in special cases is by far the most common and also the least harmful to the appropriate functions of the juvenile court. Only highly selective transfer systems can avoid needless reductions in the jurisdiction of juvenile courts and gratuitous assaults on the legitimacy of the court.

Jurisdictional Cutbacks

If the juvenile court is a barrier to the just punishment of very serious cases, why not just abolish the court? Such a remedy might be regarded as overbroad, since more than 98 percent of the delinquency petitions in the United States are not transformed into adult prosecutions where the practice is discretionary. But what is the harm in dropping juvenile court jurisdiction when minors commit felonies?

The harm of adopting an overbroad reduction in juvenile court jurisdiction is important only if there is special value in treating most juvenile crime in a distinctively juvenile court. For this reason, the willingness to adopt overbroad restrictions on the jurisdiction of the juvenile court is one significant indicator of continuing public commitment to the ideal of a children's court.

The broadest method of cutting back on the limited punishments of juvenile justice is to abolish the court entirely, thus ending any special restrictions on punishment tied to juvenile courts. For all its punitive simplicity, this has been a reform option without any constituency even in an era of great concern about lenient treatment of young criminals. Nothing speaks as powerfully to the continuing legitimacy of some ideal of juvenile justice than the absence of credible campaigns to disestablish the juvenile court.

Short of abolishing the jurisdiction of juvenile courts, the next most effective wholesale reduction in jurisdiction would be to cut back on the court's maximum jurisdictional age. While the usual boundary between juvenile and criminal courts is the eighteenth birthday, there are many states that use the seventeenth birthday as the jurisdictional end of juvenile court and some that cut off delinquency jurisdiction at 16. Cutting off the oldest age groups from delinquency jurisdiction would have substantial impact on serious crimes of violence because such offenses are more common in the late teens than in younger age, groups. More homicide arrests occur between the sixteenth and eighteenth birthday in the United States than in all the younger age groups combined (United States Department of Justice 1998, 232–233).

Reducing the jurisdictional age of the juvenile court is both overly broad and too narrow as a method of removing serious crimes from the protection of juvenile justice, but only its overbreadth is a decisive disadvantage. Cutting the age of juvenile court delinquency jurisdiction from 18 to 16 would reduce the homicide caseload by 60 percent, but that would still leave hundreds of homicides each year within the age boundaries of American juvenile justice. So reduction in age would not be a complete removal of troublesome cases and would have to be supplemented with other case reduction methods. But that is hardly a fatal defect in any legal restructuring that does not carry significant costs.

It is the overbreadth of age reduction reforms that must explain the reluctance of American states to adopt them in large numbers even during the youth crime panic years of 1991–97, when new legislative countermeasures to youth violence were an annual event. The problem with age reductions is that they indiscriminately sweep nonviolent and violent offenders alike into the ranks of criminological adulthood, flooding the criminal courts with nonserious cases. But what is the great harm in tens of thousands of adolescent thefts and house break-ins being processed in criminal courts?

The lack of recurrent efforts to lower age limits is powerful circumstantial evidence that unnecessary expulsion from the jurisdiction of juvenile courts is currently still widely regarded as a significant disadvantage. My argument here is that general cutbacks in jurisdiction would be a natural method of responding to concern over serious cases if there were no strong preference for juvenile court jurisdiction in garden-variety delinquency cases, including many cases of juvenile violence. The prospects of this kind of cutback are worth our attention in analyzing the treatment of serious cases not because they have been a popular method of diverting troublesome cases, but precisely because they have not been embraced in the war against juvenile violence.

The failure to launch radical experiments in the reduction of delinquency jurisdiction tells us that juvenile court processing of youth crime is still a normative system. In this sense, the absence of abolition and age reduction as popular causes is the dog that did not bark in juvenile justice reform. The only explanation for no serious proposals to cut back juvenile courts is the continued legitimacy of the ideal of juvenile courts for young offenders.

There is one further respect in which the absence of any trend to reduce the maximum age of delinquency jurisdiction provides data of value on public opinion about adolescent development. The eighteenth birthday has been a consensus boundary in juvenile justice for some time, but the original subjects of delinquency jurisdiction were much younger than that (Zimring 1982, ch. 3). The age of both modal and maximum delinquency jurisdiction expanded throughout most of the twentieth century. There is no sign that the current conditions of American life carry any strong countervailing tendency. While legal reforms provide that youths accused of particular serious crimes can be transferred at earlier ages to the criminal court, the absence of any broader cutback in maximum age argues against concluding that younger offenders are being transferred because they are regarded as more mature than in previous generations. Earlier maturity would support a general reduction in jurisdictional age. The selection only of serious crimes suggests the need to punish rather than any developmental maturity of the object of punishment is the motivating factor.

So the political slogan "If you are old enough to do the crime, you are old enough to do the time" is not about maturity. It is instead a denial that issues like immaturity should be relevant to the appropriate punishment for criminal offenders. The lack of consistent momentum toward lower jurisdictional age limits in the United States shows us that the shift toward punitive responses to serious youth crime is not grounded in a conception that adult levels of responsibility are acquired either earlier or more easily than in past generations. The political conflict in the United States is not about adolescent maturity but about the relevance of immaturity to the proper punishment of young offenders.

Expanding Punishments in Juvenile Courts

Once the problem presented by serious youth crimes is identified as the limited punishment powers of juvenile court, one natural remedy would be to expand the maximum punishment available in juvenile court until the gap between what the community demands and what the court can provide has been closed. For many years, the notion of expansions of penalties within juvenile courts was a road not taken in juvenile justice reform, and criticism of this strategy was a hypothetical exercise (Zimring 1981, 1991). More recently, several jurisdictions have authorized special trial procedures and expanded punishments in some branches of juvenile court under the rubric that Redding and Howell (2000) call "blended jurisdiction." The details of "blended jurisdiction" schemes vary, but most such systems share three characteristics: (1) cases are assigned to special divisions within juvenile courts where jury trials and other nonstandard procedural protections are provided; (2) very long periods of penal confinement are available after conviction, but usually the confinement extending past majority is assessed conditionally, with further proceedings and findings necessary to confirm long sentences; and (3) these blended alternatives within the juvenile court are not an exclusive mechanism for extending punishment—every jurisdiction with blended jurisdiction provides for transfer to criminal court for homicide prosecutions as well.

The Byzantine complexity of the laws creating blended jurisdiction sentencing demands scrutiny. In an era where truth in sentencing is popular and hostility to indeterminacy is rampant, the Texas provisions create nominal 40-year sentences that can nonetheless result in the release of a juvenile at age 18 unless the longer penal term is extended at a separate hearing when the offender turns 18. The Minnesota blended jurisdiction sentencing provisions are among the most dauntingly complicated in the history of criminal sentencing. Both the complexity and the conditional nature of typical "blended" sentences may be the result of intentional efforts to design systems that sound much tougher just after conviction than they turn out to be in the hard currency of time served in custody. There is a long tradition in the United States of creating sentencing systems that bark much louder than they bite. To some extent, both the contingency and complexity of blended sentencing may just be deliberately false advertising by drafters who want legislation to sound stringent.

But more than that must be at work to create sentencing structures that are distinctively inconsistent with the prevailing style of sentence determination. I would suggest that the contingency in most extended sentencing systems is an attempt to resolve the central dilemma of extended punishment power in juvenile court—any sentence long enough to satisfy the retributive demands of the community in extreme cases is too long to be consistent with the juvenile court's fundamental commitment to the life opportunities of its subjects. The only plausible escape from this dilemma is a form of doublespeak in which long prison sentences can be announced but not enforced.

I do not wish to recite in these pages the considerable litany of disadvantages associated with extended punishments in juvenile court that are mentioned in my earlier analysis (Zimring 1998, ch. 9) and discussed elsewhere in this book. I do want to emphasize that if limiting the destructive impact of punishments on youth is a central tenet of American juvenile justice, then any juvenile court sentence of 20 years' time served turns out to be a contradiction of that central element of the juvenile court's philosophy. Criminal courts can ignore the future life chances of the defendants before them and, in fact, do so quite frequently. There is no violation of the criminal court's mandate in 25-year-to-life sentences as long as such punishments are administered in ways consistent with penal proportionality and the offender's dignity and personhood. But when the juvenile court sacrifices its obligation to limit the destructive impact of its sanctions, it creates a crisis of mission, with implications that spill over from the subunit of the court that assigns the extended punishments to the whole of the juvenile court. Once that institution gets into the business of unlimited destruction of the offender's life chances, the sincerity of its orientation to limits is open to question across the whole spectrum of delinquency jurisdiction. When the juvenile court becomes the instrument of open-ended incapacitation, the damage is to its core commitment: the court has not shot itself in the foot, it has shot itself in the heart.

One reason I believe that the complex and conditional nature of blended sentences is more denial than deception on the part of its drafters is that the false advertising of blended sentences has been totally ineffectual. In no jurisdiction where conditional sentences have been used has the new blended jurisdiction system ended transfer to criminal courts. In this important sense, extended sentences in juvenile court have been a supplement rather than a substitute for transfer. If blended sentences were too transparent to serve as a displacement of transfer to criminal court, it is plausible to search for other constituencies that might see benefit in the complex contingencies of the new provisions. One such benefit would be to reassure those who would be gravely troubled by the long shadow that "real" 40-year sentences would cast on the legitimacy of the juvenile court.

Selective Transfer

The vice of expanding punishment power in juvenile courts is that it undermines the mission of the entire juvenile system. The vice of across-the-board cutbacks in juvenile court jurisdiction is gross overbreadth, because there is still a preference for juvenile court processing of youth crimes, where this does not conflict with the community's sense of minimum commensurate desert. The best outcome is to transfer only those cases where high-magnitude punishments are required over to criminal courts, through a process that minimizes the transfer of juvenile court subjects where a transfer is not necessary. The optimal outcome is a system that produces selective transfer only of cases where there is direct conflict between the upper bounds of juvenile court punishment and the minimum punishment deserved by an offender if guilty of the charged offense. That highly selective transfer is a preferred result follows easily from finding positive value in the juvenile court processing of most young offenders. But who is to select the candidates for transfer and what processes should govern the transfer decision? These are the topics of the following section.

The Right Kind of Safety Valve

The traditional juvenile court structure in the United States developed with a discretionary system of waiver, where the juvenile court judge could elect to waive his court's primary jurisdiction over an accused juvenile, and only such a waiver would allow charges to be adjudicated in the criminal court. In the post-*Gault* era of prosecutors in juvenile courts, the division of authority between prosecutor and judge in juvenile court waiver decision-making is much like the division of labor in sentencing decisions. The prosecutor is the moving party who advocates the superiority of a waiver to criminal court, and the judge is an umpiral authority with wide discretion to decide the matter and very little prospect of reversal by an appellate court. It has traditionally generated a low volume of transfers to criminal court.

An alternative or supplemental approach to discretionary waiver is legislative provision for transfer to criminal court. Two types of legislative standard setting on transfer should initially be distinguished. One type of legislation creates minimum conditions that must be met before waiver is possible. The typical legislative standard of this type will state the minimum age and list the predicate charges that can support a discretionary transfer. This sort of law provides only the necessary conditions for transfer, and usually reserves the decision in particular cases to a juvenile court judge. Such provisions narrow somewhat the discretionary power of judges and prosecutors to select candidates for transfer.

When legislative standards turn prescriptive, they attempt to set both the necessary and sufficient conditions for transfer to criminal courts. The attempt in prescriptive standards is to create binding standards for transfer based on categories of criminal offenses. As Barry Feld points out, legislation providing such prescriptive standards has been a growth industry in the 1980s and 1990s, either supplementing or replacing judicial waiver as a method of channeling juvenile defendants into criminal courts. When legislative standards are the exclusive basis for transfer to criminal court, the list of crimes that generate transfer grows rather long. Because only a minority of even homicide charges end up being waived to criminal court in discretionary systems, the impact of automatic waiver standards is to sharply expand the volume of waived cases, even when the literal terms of the statute are partially nullified by prosecutorial discretions.

There are two contrasting patterns of impact that lists of automatic waiver provisions might produce. If the provisions of prescriptive transfer statutes are substantially enforced, a much larger volume of cases is transferred than under a discretionary system, and the range in severity of cases transferred to criminal court will be substantial. Robbery and assault are very heterogeneous crimes. Automatic waiver of arrests for even aggravated forms of these offenses will transfer many cases into criminal court that will have relatively low prosecution priority. These are cases where the minimum levels of punishment that the community would tolerate are far lower than in the extreme cases that make transfer unavoidable. The vice of this type of wholesale prescriptive transfer is the same type of overbreadth associated with abolition of the court or reduction in jurisdictional age, though perhaps not to the same degree. The transfer of large categories of heterogeneous felony charges to criminal courts might reproduce within the criminal courts institutional arrangements for adjudicating such cases that much resemble juvenile courts. This is one take on the impact of New York's 1978 legislation and the "youth docket" that has evolved in the New York City criminal court (Singer 1996).

If gross overbreadth is one outcome of broad prescriptive transfer standards, subterranean discretion is a second mode of adaptation. When only 1 to 4 percent of nonlethal violent felonies were being transferred prior to prescriptive standards, laws mandating that all serious assaults and armed or injurious robberies should be transferred to criminal court might be substantially nullified by the exercise of prosecutorial discretion (see Zimring 1998, ch. 7). Few practical controls exist on the prosecutor's power to select charges and thus to avoid charging crimes that would generate automatic transfer consequences.

If automatic transfer standards merely shift discretion from juvenile court judges to prosecutors, there is little to recommend these automatic devices as a juvenile justice law reform. Prosecutors may favor such laws, even if they do not intend to enforce them literally, because prescriptive transfer statutes both enhance prosecutorial power and reduce the prosecutorial work effort needed to obtain transfer in judicial waiver regimes. But a juvenile court judge would seem a better umpiral authority than a prosecutor on the minimum level of punishment that would be deserved in a particular case; if waiver seems more like a sentencing than a charging decision, then maintaining judicial authority seems preferable to the concentration of all power in the prosecutor. Further, prosecutorial power is harder to observe; about the only kind of power that is less visible and reviewable than a discretionary judicial decision is an exercise of prosecutorial discretion.

Even with the manifest problems of unchecked prosecutorial discretion, a good argument can be made that aggressive prosecutorial reduction in the scope of prescriptive legislative standards is preferable to the wholesale overcriminalization that comes with the literal enforcement of broad legislative transfer categories.

Can it at least be said that prescriptive transfer statutes compensate for the tendency to be overinclusive by providing some coherent principle on which to base the transfer decision? Probably not. There is a tendency to include crimes in a prescriptive transfer list if any form of the offense appears likely to require high-magnitude sanctions. This worst-case methodology does not represent a judgment that the wide variety of different types of conduct and levels of participation that each statutory definition of a crime encompasses are all or mostly in need of exceptional punishment. The legislators will tend to provide for transfer of aggravated battery cases not if all such cases justify such a result but if any cases in the class are believed to merit transfer. This sort of legislation is often passed as a response to a well-publicized actual case.

A worst-case methodology may be appropriate when deciding on the appropriate minimum ages and crimes necessary for transfer to criminal court; the method misfires when the worst imaginable form of an offense becomes the motivation for deciding that all juveniles accused of any form of such an offense should be transferred to criminal court. The confusion, in this way, of necessary with sufficient causes is grounds for failing a course in elementary logic, but such confusion is also the usual foundation for using public worries about particular frightening youth crimes as the basis for wholesale reassignment of juvenile defendants to criminal courts.

So prescriptive transfer standards that move entire crime categories into criminal court are unprincipled and overbroad; the best that can befall such systems is prosecutorial discretion being exercised to select only the most serious of within-crime charges to process in the criminal courts. But even this best-case adaptation to categorical transfer legislation is inferior to the allocation of power that animates traditional judicial waiver procedures. The best we can hope for from categorical transfer edicts is high levels of prosecutorial discretion and very low-visibility decision-making. In both substance and procedure, this seems clearly inferior to the judicial waiver mechanism as it has evolved over nearly a century in the American juvenile court.

The error of using broad crime categories as a conclusive presumption of particular levels of deserved punishment cannot be cured by more careful statutory drafting. If the central issue in transfer to criminal court is a matter of deserved punishment, the appropriate unit of analysis for making that punishment decision is almost always the individual case. Transferring entire crime categories on the basis of presumed desert is a repetition of the mistakes legislatures make with mandatory minimum penalties and fixed-price sentencing schemes (Tonry 1996). Only gross calculations of deserved punishment can be made without knowledge of the offender's characteristics, his or her particular role in the criminal event, and his or her prior involvement with 'the justice system. There may be instrumental motives for punishment policies that do not vary within crime categories, but calculating deserved punishment at that level of abstraction is obviously arbitrary.

Justice in Criminal Courts

The processes of judicial waiver that prevailed over the first century of the American juvenile court were in many respects a well-functioning way of selecting out small numbers of cases that might otherwise create tension within the juvenile court and leave the court vulnerable to hostile outside forces. But the standard judicial waiver system I endorse as the least bad method of dealing with extremely severe cases has two major failings that should be a focus for reform efforts early in the juvenile court's second century. The first failure has been the absence of legal standards to inform and control decisions made by juvenile court judges. The second failure has been the absence of appropriate recognition of the special treatment the criminal courts owe to their very youngest defendants. The prospects for improvement soon in either of these two problem areas are not good.

The lawless character of judicial waiver decisions is as easy to explain as it is difficult to remedy. Discretionary decisions are by definition not closely connected to principles that can predict outcome, and discretionary decisions about deserved punishment have been notoriously difficult to regularize into a review procedure that assures that like cases are treated alike. Appellate review of criminal sentences is neither politically popular nor conceptually easy—because appellate judges lack clear standards of comparison (Zeisel and Diamond 1977).

These inherent difficulties have been compounded by the number and variety of criteria that judges were authorized to take into account when deciding about waiver, everything from age and offense seriousness to amenability to treatment and "sophistication." With so many different types of potentially decisive criteria available to choose from, any decision on waiver would be easy to support, even if a written opinion were required (Twentieth Century Fund 1978, 55–57). Without such an opinion requirement, a reviewing body will rarely have a basis for overturning a judicial waiver decision. It should come as no surprise then that appellate courts are quite reluctant to reverse lower court decisions on waiver (Clausel and Bonnie 2000).

Two changes in the legal environment of the waiver decision might improve the chance for meaningful appellate review, but still leave enormous discretionary power in the initial waiver decision maker. The first needed reform is a requirement for extensive written justifications of decisions to grant or to reject a waiver motion. This will make the reasons for an initial decision known, and can isolate key factual issues and assumptions for the attention of subsequent reviewers. Further, the discipline of writing such an opinion may also improve the quality of the initial decision-making.

A second improvement on the current environment of waiver decisions would be to place heavy emphasis on a single criterion, the gap between available juvenile sanctions and the minimum deserved punishment if defendant is guilty. A clear focus on desert will reduce the probability that a judge will be distracted by heavy emphasis on other aspects of the case. Of course, many of the same characteristics that judges would consider in decisions about a juvenile's sophistication, attitude, or amenability to treatment will also be relevant to questions of the deserved punishment, but continual emphasis on desert can reduce to some extent the capacity for confusion and self-delusion that accompany traditional juvenile court code words like "amenability" and "sophistication," and long laundry lists of criteria for waiver.

But these interstitial efforts at reform cannot change the essentially discretionary character of judicial waiver decisions and thus will not change the substantial subjective element that will go into each waiver decision. If judges A and B differ in temperament and ideology, the discretionary character of judicial waiver means that which judge hears the waiver petition will have a substantial impact on what decision is made. Inevitably, the great majority of these subjective decisions will be upheld on appeal. If rules of eligibility only identify which cases can be considered for transfer, the actual waiver decision must be a subjective one. Only if rules identify both sufficient and necessary conditions for waiver can the selection of transfer cases be regularized, but the price of regulation by rule is extensive overbreadth. To a distressing degree, the choice in waiver decision-making is between parsimony and principle. Restricting the offenses that create eligibility for waiver is one method of control that can serve both parsimony and principle. Making a criminal homicide charge a necessary condition for waiver would reduce the circumstances that allow judicial temperament to determine waiver outcome. But the general trend is to long lists of eligible charges.

The second major failure of judicial waiver systems lies beyond the boundaries of the juvenile court, but its consequences are a fundamental threat to juvenile justice, as well as to the broader criminal justice system. The problem is the absence of a youth policy for waived juvenile offenders in criminal courts.

There are at least three distinct forms of youth policy in juvenile court, and a consistent legal policy would continue two of these for young offenders waived into criminal courts. First, to the extent that immaturity leads to judgments of diminished responsibility, this should reduce the level of punishment imposed on young offenders in any court (Zimring 2000, pt. 3). A second important aspect of justice policy toward young offenders is to provide age-appropriate institutions, programs, and protections (Zimring 1998, ch. 8). The third strand of policy toward youth is effort to avoid punishments that seriously impinge on the life chances of young offenders. It is this last commitment to avoid permanent harm that may be in conflict with the community's minimum needs for punishment in waiver cases, not the policies of diminished responsibility or age-appropriate institutions and programs.

In principle, a punitive theory of waiver clearly distinguishes be-

tween restraining immature offenders because of the need for punishment in a particular case and treating young offenders as if they
were not young. In practice, there is a tendency to ignore the youth of
offenders once they have been transferred to criminal court, as if the
mandate of a waiver was to regard the offender as an adult.

Yet there are two ways in which a principled and effective juvenile justice system is a hostage to youth-oriented policies in criminal
court. Arbitrary treatment of waived juveniles in the criminal courts
renders the entire justice system for responding to youth crime unprincipled. Waiver in itself is not an arbitrary treatment of young offenders if it conforms to the standards of strict necessity previously
discussed. But the gratuitous removal of youth-oriented protections
in the criminal justice system does generate a pattern of injustice in
which the juvenile justice system had a causal role.

There is a second way in which arbitrary treatment of young
offenders in criminal courts threatens the quality of juvenile justice
in the United States, and this is a lesson of' our recent history. The
experiments with "blended jurisdiction" schemes discussed in Redding and Howell's essay expand the punishment powers of juvenile
courts, risking both a crisis of mission within the court and the rejection of damage limitation as a fundamental principle of juvenile
courts. Why should some of the friends of the juvenile justice system
welcome this punitive Trojan horse into the court for children? To
protect young offenders otherwise at risk of disappearing into the
black hole of the criminal justice system. The failure of the criminal
courts to offer proportional punishment and age segregation leads to
unprincipled efforts to retain jurisdiction over serious young offenders at almost any risk.

While the lawless character of discretionary waiver hearings is an
inherent drawback, there is no inevitable barrier to coherent policies
toward waived defendants in criminal courts. The major obstacles to
principled reform here are political problems, but political problems
of immense proportions.

The best hope for coherent youth policy in criminal courts is elite
and professional leadership in the creation of policy. But professional elite influence is out of fashion in the politics of criminal justice just now, and the network of child welfare and youth interest
groups that has traditionally played a major role in juvenile justice
policy has not involved itself in criminal justice policy other than
age segregation in penal facilities. The coalitions that lobby for juvenile justice have often stopped at water's edge rather than follow

waived offenders into criminal courts. Recent adventures with blended jurisdiction show that the flaws of a criminal justice system in the treatment of young offenders can cast long shadows on the prospects for effective juvenile justice. But creating a youth policy in the criminal court will be no less difficult in the foreseeable future because such a policy will be necessary to the continued coherence of juvenile justice.

There is a special irony in depending on developmental sensitivities in the criminal courts to protect juvenile courts from political risk in cases of great seriousness. While the juvenile court is the legal institution with principal responsibility for respecting adolescence in formulating legal policy, it cannot be the only court to do so, or serious inconsistencies and injustices will result.

ELEVEN

Reducing the Harms of Minority Overrepresentation in American Juvenile Justice

On one critical topic, the materials in the previous 10 chapters of this book appear both innocent and abstract. The overrepresentation of disadvantaged racial and ethnic minorities in the courtrooms and detention cells of American juvenile justice is both an undeniable fact and a serious problem. Throughout the world, the poor and disadvantaged get caught up in the machinery of social control in numbers far greater than their share of the population. In the United States, the long shadow of racism adds another important dimension to concern about young persons already at serious disadvantage. Punishment and stigma make a bad situation worse. What to do?

The issues we confront in trying to fix the damages of disproportion in juvenile justice are a mix of the obvious and the obscure. There can be no doubt that the handicaps imposed on youth by arrest, detention, adjudication, and incarceration fall disproportionately on males from disadvantaged minority groups in the United States. It is equally obvious that the hardships imposed on formally sanctioned youth are substantial by themselves and even worse when they aggravate the other by-products of social disadvantage. But this chapter is about the not-so-obvious choices that we confront when attempting to reduce the harms that disproportionate minority concentration produces. There are a variety of different approaches that can be taken to reforming juvenile justice to protect minority youth, and not all of them are of equal effectiveness.

My ambition in these pages is to identify some of the key policy choices that must be made in reducing injustices found in American juvenile courts. A clear definition of goals and priorities is absolutely essential to intelligent policy planning. My argument is that reducing the hazards of juvenile court processing may be a better approach to protecting minority youth than just trying to reduce the proportion of juvenile court cases with minority defendants.

The chapter is divided into two large segments and then subdivided into smaller units. The first section concerns the conceptual equipment necessary to assess the impact of legal policies on minority populations. A first subsection of this section discusses whether it is best to consider the minority concentrations in juvenile justice as a special problem in the juvenile justice system or as part of the generally higher risk exposures found in criminal justice and other state control systems. A second subsection proposes harm reduction as the principal criterion by which policies designed to respond to minority disproportion should be judged. A third subsection contrasts two competing measures of disadvantage on minorities, relative and aggregate disadvantage, as the appropriate goal of reforms. A fourth subsection compares two overall approaches to minimize harm: cutting back on the harms that juvenile justice processing produces versus cutting back on the number and proportion of minority youth who are pushed through the system.

The second section attempts to apply the apparatus developed in the first section to discuss recent chapters in juvenile justice law reform: changes in transfer policy, the deinstitutionalization of status offenders, and the embrace of diversion programs. A final subsection of this section contrasts the harm to minority youth from exposure to juvenile courts with the harm from criminal courts. If the proper standard for judging the impact of institutions on minority kids is reducing the harms these kids suffer, the current juvenile justice system—warts and all—is vastly less dangerous to minorities than the machinery of criminal justice.

Assessing the Impact of Legal Policies on Minority Populations

Juvenile Justice in Context: A Special or General Case?

The first issue on my agenda is whether the kind and amount of minority overrepresentation is importantly different in the juvenile justice system. How does the African American and Hispanic overrepresentation we observe for delinquency cases in the juvenile system compare to the pattern of concentration of disadvantaged minorities found in the criminal justice system in the United States?

But why should a question about the generality of the pattern that produces minority disadvantage be a starting point for seeking remedial measures? The reason is that the data reveal whether the special organizational and substantive provisions of juvenile justice should be suspected as the proximate causes of the problem, so that shifting the special provisions or procedures of juvenile courts could be expected to provide a remedy. If so, the specific approaches of the juvenile court should be a high priority for reform. If, however, the extent of minority overrepresentation in juvenile justice is about the same as that found in criminal justice, it is less plausible that this pattern is the product of any special characteristics of the juvenile system.

One example of the usefulness of this type of analysis concerns the relative concentration of young girls in incarcerated populations in juvenile justice. Figure 11.1 turns back the clock to compare juvenile and adult incarcerations by gender for 1974, as a familiar example of looking for special patterns in juvenile justice. The 1974 vintage for this data is to summarize patterns at the time when federal legislation first mandated deinstitutionalizing status offenders.

The 23 percent of incarcerated juveniles who were female in 1974 was over seven times the proportion of females then found in prisons. The larger concentration of females in the juvenile distribution is an indication that different motives (including paternalism) and different substantive legal provisions (so-called status offenses) were producing different outcomes in juvenile justice. In such circumstances, reforming these special provisions should be an early priority of those concerned with the high traditional exposure of girls

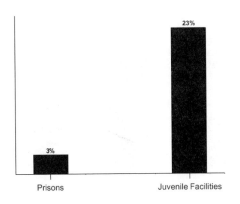

Figure 11.1. Percentage of incarcerated persons who were female in prisons and juvenile facilities, 1974. *Source:* prisoners: U.S. Department of Justice, Bureau of Justice Statistics 1974, 1997; juveniles: U.S. Department of Justice, Bureau of Justice Statistics 1997. Children in Custody.

to juvenile incarceration. The juvenile system's rules and procedures have been clearly implicated in female incarceration by figure 11.1.

Figure 11.2 contrasts the percentage of African American males in
juvenile and adult incarceration facilities in 1997. I dichotomize populations in prisons, jails, and juvenile facilities into African American
and other groups to simplify the analysis. The other major minority
group in criminal justice institutions—Hispanic populations—are
more difficult to define and more uncertain in current measurements.
The 40 percent of incarcerated juveniles who are African American are
grossly out of proportion to the African American percentage of the
youth population (about 15 percent). Thus, overrepresentation is both
obvious and substantial. But the concentration of African Americans
incarcerated in adult criminal justice populations is even greater, with
close to half of jail and prison populations so classified. If we could add
in other minority populations, the size of the total minority shares
would increase, but the contrast between systems would remain close
to that portrayed in figure 11.2.

The importance of finding this general pattern is not to minimize
the problem of juvenile minority overrepresentation but to alert
policy analysts that the pattern extends beyond juvenile justice and
is therefore less likely to have been generated by the peculiar rules
and procedures that the juvenile system uses. The lower concentration in the juvenile system might actually suggest that shifting juve-

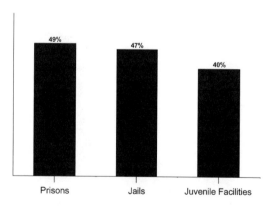

Figure 11.2. Percentage of incarcerated persons that who are are African
American in, 1997. *Source:* U.S. Department of Justice, Bureau of Justice
Statistics 1974, 1997.

nile system priorities and procedures to what the criminal justice system does to older offenders might make things worse for minorities. This is the opposite of the likely impact of using adult rules and procedures for young girls that can be inferred from figure 11.1. So it appears that minority boys are at a disadvantage in the juvenile system, but no more so than minority persons are in the rest of the criminal process. What disadvantages minority kids in delinquency cases is part of a broader pattern that probably should be addressed by multiple system approaches.

Equalize Disadvantage or Minimize Harm?

My friend and teacher Hans Zeisel once published a note showing that a peculiar kind of disproportion was evident in the death sentences accumulating in the state of Florida. Zeisel found that 95 percent of the death sentences in that state were imposed on defendants who were charged with killing white victims (Zeisel 1981). Zeisel showed that some Florida prosecutors believed that the solution to this problem was to add more murder cases with black victims to Florida's burgeoning death row populations (Zeisel 1981, 464–466). The reason for Zeisel's anger at this tactic was that expanding a cruel and inhuman punishment was the last thing he wished to do, and moving closer to proportional representation by adding black-victim cases to death row was a cynical manipulation of the system that again established its arbitrary cruelty. For Hans Zeisel, much more than proportional overrepresentation was wrong with the death penalty system in Florida.

I wonder whether this story has exemplary value for many of us who worry about the overrepresentation of minorities in dead-end detention centers and training schools in 2005. The test question is this: imagine a prosecutor who responds to a finding of imbalance not by releasing minority youth but by trying to lock up many more Anglo-Saxon whites. Would this brand of affirmative action please or trouble the social critic? Why?

Many persons who justly worry about the burden of disproportionate impact on minority youth believe that the deep end of the juvenile justice system harms kids, and they wish to minimize that harm. Expanding the number of kids harmed through an "affirmative action" plan that only adds nonminority targets is perverse from this perspective, for two reasons. First, such an expansion of negative controls does not improve the life chances of any of the minority kids. They continue to suffer the same harms at the same rate. Second, the expansion of harms over a wider population hurts many new kids, placing them in positions of disadvantage close to those that troubled the critics about minority kids. Most of those active in addressing issues of minority overrepresentation care deeply about youth of all colors and backgrounds. This grisly form of affirmative action would be, in their view, a step backward.

My point here is that there are two problems that are rather different when addressing the impact of the system on minority kids: the disproportionate impact of sanctions on minorities and the negative effects that these sanctions have on the largely minority kids who are captured by the system. A critic of the system will have two goals: reducing the harm to kids and reducing the proportion of minority kids in the system. But which goal should have the larger priority?

In my view, the more pragmatic a system reformer becomes, the more he or she will choose measures that reduce the harms that minority kids suffer over programs of better proportional representation. If this is true, then harm reduction creates the opportunity to use concerns about the impact of the system on minority kids as a wedge to reduce the harmful impact of the system on all processed through it. The shift in emphasis from proportional concerns to harm reduction also means that there is no competition between minority and nonminority delinquents, but rather a natural community of interest across group boundaries to make the deep end of the juvenile system less hazardous.

There is also a dark side to the case for emphasizing harm reduction. The sharp edge of the blade in criminal justice almost always falls on disadvantaged minorities, and it is not clear that procedural reform can undo the damage. Some areas of criminal law (traffic and drugs) may respond to administrative controls that reduce the impact on minorities. Spreading traffic stops into nonminority areas can reduce the proportion of traffic arrests and fines that involve minorities. But other arenas, including violence, will remain problematic. Street crimes involve minority suspects more often than white kids for different reasons, and changes in law enforcement procedures will not end the overrepresentation of minority youth arrested for robbery and burglary. As long as minority crime victims are well served by city police, minority suspects will be a disproportionate segment of violence arrests in the United States.

Absolute versus Proportionate Standards of Harm in Choosing Reforms

The choice between harm reduction and proportional approaches to overrepresentation will lead to different judgments about which reforms work best. Assume that one reform will leave the proportion of incarcerated delinquents who are minorities the same but reduce the number of kids locked up by 10 percent. Another approach will lower the proportion of incarcerated minority kids by 10 percent but leave the number of minorities locked up the same. Which is better? The "least worst" outcome for minority kids in some settings will depend on what standard is selected as the most important measure of the problem. If a proportionate approach is most important, an observer will pick the outcome that results in the smallest percentage of total harm falling on the minority youth population. If a harm-reduction standard is used, the observer will try to minimize the amount of harm the minority population suffers, regardless of what share of total bad outcomes are absorbed by minority youth.

If highly selective styles of law enforcement concentrate bad outcomes on minorities, then the law enforcement approach that punishes minority kids in the highest percentage might still punish fewer minority kids than a system that spreads a much larger number of harmful outcomes somewhat more evenly across the youth population. The highly discretionary system may be more proportionally unjust than the system that spreads a larger level of punishment more evenly over the youth population, but the amount of harm the broader system does to vulnerable minorities is greater. A principled argument for preferring either outcome can be made. But more important than pointing to a particular preference is recognizing the potential conflict in standards.

My suspicion is that persons with backgrounds in child welfare will be more apt to choose the aggregate harm reduction standard and discount its distributive implications, while persons with strong legal orientations may be more likely to select higher aggregate harm if it is more evenly distributed.

Whatever might separate those who prefer harm reduction to reducing disproportion when hard choices have to be made, I do not think that different choices can be explained as a liberal-versus-conservative distinction. Instead, I think the conflict highlights the difference between two competing strains of opinion on the left side of the political spectrum that point to different priorities in some circumstances. I will briefly revisit this problem when discussing rules versus discretion competitions in reforming the law of transfer of juveniles to criminal court.

Evening Out versus Softening Consequences in Delinquency Cases

If minimizing the harm that falls on minority youth becomes the dominant standard for choosing policy in this area, there are many different policy levers available to seek this end. One contrast is between trying to reduce the number of minority kids subjected to harmful results without attempting to alter the consequences of a delinquency finding, as opposed to trying to lower the amount of aggregate harm suffered by minority kids by reducing the harm produced by juvenile justice sanctions. The first approach tries to alter the distribution of sanctions; the second tries to take some of the sting out of the sanctions themselves.

Ultimately, which approach to take when choosing how to attempt reform is an empirical question that general statements cannot illuminate much. But there are some generalizations about such a choice that teach important lessons. The first point is that softening the bite of sanctions only becomes a path to a priority reform because harm reduction is selected as a priority. It is only when harm reduction is isolated as a goal that shifts in the content of sanctions rather than their distribution can compete with redistribution strategies on an equal footing in protecting minority kids.

A second point about taking some of the harm out of sanctions relates to its distributional advantage over reducing the number of minorities punished. The benefits of sanction reform reach all of those unlucky enough to be punished after the reform. All minorities who are sanctioned benefit, rather than just those who are spared the punishment as the result of a distributional reform. And all delinquents benefit, not merely the minority population. Further, since most youth held for serious acts of delinquency are at social disadvantage, the nonminority beneficiaries of the process are not all that different than the minority kids who are its core concern.

There is one potential problem with sanction-softening approaches that carries no practical weight in current conditions. A strategy that pushes for reducing the harm in sanctions would generate conflict where the youth advocate feels there are strong social and justice benefits in severe sanctions. However, most youth advocates dislike severe juvenile sanctions, so that it seems safe to discount the prospects that youth advocates would be reluctant to reduce the negative impact of recent levels of sanction in American juvenile justice.

A third contrast between proportional reduction strategies and harm-reduction strategies concerns the inferences about overrepresentation that justify the approach. A focus on reducing the share of sanctions absorbed by minorities may not require the assumption that some form of discrimination has produced the overrepresentation, but it is certainly much easier to justify proportional remedies when discrimination is suspected. But what if the large percentage of delinquents incarcerated for robbery and homicide from minority backgrounds is matched by arrest rates of minorities for robbery and homicide? By contrast, the question of proving discrimination is not implicated by attempts to reduce the negative impacts on sanctions for all delinquents.

I will not speculate here on the political circumstances that favor emphasis on reducing the concentration of minorities, as opposed to reducing the harmful content of sanctions. These two strategies can complement each other in a coordinated program to reduce harm. Here, I suspect, is the reason that one rarely encounters hardline policies toward criminal offenders in those interest groups that serve disadvantaged minorities. Minority interest groups become penal reform advocates by structural necessity.

A further implication of the close connection between concern about proportional disadvantage and concern about the harms of juvenile sanctions is that often our worry about disproportion reflects concern about the justice of the harshness of a penal measure. One reason for special concern about the overrepresentation of minorities on American death rows is the feeling that capital punishment is too degrading a sanction for a civilized nation. Our prison populations are just as skewed racially as our death rows, but ambivalence toward the death penalty makes the concentration in death cases a larger concern.

This pattern of larger distrust of more severe sanctions would predict that the expansion of sanctions in blended-jurisdiction juvenile systems, and the legislative trends toward more frequent transfer to criminal court may exacerbate fears about minority overrepresentation in juvenile justice. Just as lowering the punitive stakes may take some of the bite out of disproportionate minority representation, raising the punitive stakes in the juvenile system can be expected to increase concerns about the extent to which this heavier burden falls on members of disadvantaged minorities.

Minority Disproportion and Modern Juvenile Justice Reforms

The first section of this chapter attempted to provide tools for policy analysis. The aim of this section is to apply the perspectives just outlined to consider the impact of three changes in juvenile justice policy over the past generation: (1) the proliferation of legislative transfer standards to supplement discretionary waiver by juvenile court judges; (2) the attempt to protect status offenders from secure confinement by creating separate legal categories with restricted dispositional options for status cases; and (3) diversion programs to resolve minor delinquency charges without formal juvenile court charges or adjudications. None of these three reform programs was centrally concerned with minority overrepresentation in delinquency cases; but each set of changes has an impact on minority presence in juvenile and criminal justice. Further, evaluating the impact of such changes on minority prospects is a critical task in contemporary policy analysis. A final subsection of this section views the substitution of juvenile court for the criminal process as a law reform that has had a positive long-range impact on minority youth in the United States.

Automatic Transfer Rules and Minority Harm

Almost all juvenile justice systems provide a method for transferring some accused delinquents close to aging out of the juvenile system who are charged with serious crimes into criminal court to face much harsher sanctions than are available in the juvenile system (see Fagan and Zimring 2000). The traditional method of determining whether an older juvenile would be transferred was for a hearing to be held in the juvenile court, and for the judge to decide whether he or she should "waive" the juvenile court's jurisdiction and therefore allow criminal prosecution (Dawson 2000). The issue before a juvenile judge in such a hearing is whether the youth is a fit subject for the juvenile court. This was always a discretionary decision, difficult to review and quite rarely reversed on appeal (Clauson and Bonnie 2000).

This type of discretion would seem to be an ideal breeding ground for attitudes that prejudice the prospects of African American and Hispanic juveniles. No precise studies have been done, but the track record of waiver for transferring high proportions of minority youth is not encouraging (Bortner, Zatz, and Hawkins 2000). At the same time, however, the signal virtue of traditional discretionary waiver was the low rate at which juveniles were transferred.

An almost universal addition to discretionary waiver provisions in recent years has been legislation that provides for automatic transfer of juveniles to criminal court if one from among a list of serious charges is brought against the juvenile. The charges frequently listed include murder, armed robbery, rape and many other serious offenses (Feld 2000). The advantage of this legislative system is that it substitutes a clear rule for personal discretion. The disadvantage is that many more kids of all kinds, including many more minority kids, will be shipped to criminal court under mandatory transfer rules than under systems that only transfer juveniles after juvenile court waiver hearings. Even if the *proportion* of all kids transferred who are African American or Hispanic goes down with automatic transfer rules, the *number* of minority kids disadvantaged will increase. The rule-versus-discretion choice looks, at this first impression, like a competition between proportional representation and harm reduction. When automatic transfer replaces discretionary waiver, the number of minority kids harmed will increase, even if the share of transferred kids from minority backgrounds declines.

A second look, however, suggests that "automatic transfer" standards have nothing to offer minority kids, not even the certainty of the application of a uniform set of rules. The only discretion less reviewable than a juvenile court judge's is that of a prosecutor, and the adoption of automatic transfer standards really substitutes a prosecutor's discretion for that of a judge. A prosecutor can select the charge to bring against a juvenile, and that charging decision will determine whether the case goes to juvenile or criminal court. No review can force a prosecutor to file more serious charges than he or she wants to file, or indeed to file any charges at all.

My guess is that the proportion of minorities transferred might go down somewhat in regimes of prosecutorial rather than judicial discretion, but not because prosecutors are more sensitive to minorities. Instead, as the number of juveniles transferred increases substantially, the population transferred will tend to become somewhat more like the general population of accused delinquents. As a result of disadvantaging a much larger fraction of the youth population, the proportional share of minorities hurt by prosecutorial discretion systems may decline, but this is nobody's definition of youth welfare. The number of minority youth at risk of criminal sanctions will expand, and it is small comfort that they have been joined in this vulnerability by larger numbers of nonminority youth.

Further, there is no enforceable legal principle behind this change, only the substitution of prosecutorial for judicial discretion, a shift that moves the locus of authority from a legal actor with a formal commitment to consider the welfare of the accused to a legal actor under no such obligation.

Deinstitutionalization of Status Offenders

Since the original juvenile court was presumed to be taking power only for the welfare of its youthful clients, that court was given power to order institutional placements, including detention and training schools for young people who were truant or disobedient but had not behaved in ways that harmed others. Since juvenile court sanctions were not regarded as punishment, it was said that there was no need for proportionality limits on power assumed over delinquents, and thus no need to differentiate between burglars and runaways when distributing the juvenile court's helpful interventions.

From the start, this theory suffered from two linked problems. First, the detentions and commitments of juvenile courts were punitive in effect and often in intent, so that imposing them on kids who did not deserve punishment or imposing much more punishment than disobedience would merit was manifestly unjust. Second, there was no evidence that the punitive treatment of delinquents in twentieth-century juvenile justice was effective either as therapy or social control (Titlebaum 2002). The legal realism about juvenile justice that produced decisions like *In re Gault* also demanded that proportional limits be placed on the power exercised by the state over runaways, truants, and adolescents in conflict with parents. The particular target of the Federal Juvenile Justice and Delinquency Prevention Act of 1974 was to discourage the states from the practice of putting status offenders in secure confinement. While the effort to break status offenders out of juvenile jails was neither an instant nor an unqualified success, its core judgment that unlimited detention is unjust and ineffective for noncriminal misbehavior has stood the test of time, even with shifting sentiments about many other aspects of juvenile justice.

The shift in status-offender policy is rarely considered as an important aspect of policies relating to minority group overrepresentation. The paternalistic excesses of juvenile justice were concentrated on girls, but the status offenders pushed into state processes were no more concentrated among minorities than were delinquents.

But did the emphasis on this policy goal help minority kids? Considering this question again raises the contrast between aggregate and proportional measures of minority disadvantage. The number of African American and Hispanic kids locked up in detention centers and training schools decreased as a direct result of successful deinstitutionalization. But the proportion of detained kids who were minorities may have increased as a result of the program. Although fewer African American kids were locked up, a greater proportion of the kids locked up might have been African American. Was this progress? I would suggest the answer to that question is yes.

But didn't the deinstitutionalization of status offenders strip the veneer of child welfare from the court and thus make harsher policy toward other classes of delinquency more acceptable (Empey 1979, 408–409)? After all, the intense pressure to crackdown on "juvenile superpredators" happened after the welfare facade of the court had been removed. So why not conclude that the latent function of status-offender reforms was additional hardship for the largely minority residual of delinquents that stayed in juvenile court systems?

The first problem with such a spin on status-offender reforms is that those who supported such reforms were skeptical about secure confinement for delinquents generally. There was no push to fill empty cells with burglars and joy-riders from the policy analysts who had pushed the 1974 reforms on the public agenda. Nor did a juvenile court crime crackdown stem in any clear way from the status-offender reforms. The get-tough rhetoric and punitive pressure that arrived in juvenile court policy debates in the 1980s was a spillover from crime policy changes in criminal justice that began in the late 1960s (Zimring, Hawkins, and Kamin 2001, ch. 9). The premises and the example of the status-offender reforms probably worked against the push for punitive policy in juvenile justice and thus were consistent with the youth-welfare interests of minority advocates. I will revisit this issue in the last section of this analysis.

Diversion and Minority Justice

What is the impact of reforms aiming to divert first-time and minor offenders from formal processing on minority offenders in juvenile justice? The policy thrust of diversion seems in harmony with lower levels of coercive controls and concern for youth welfare, but what are the results? Here again, the method of score-keeping may determine the result. The aggregate impact of diversion on the number of minority youth in formal processing will be a benefit, unless the diversion program is a complete sham. If substantial numbers of kids escape detention and adjudication, many of them will be African American and Hispanic. But even if the number of minority youth benefited is high, the proportion of those not diverted who are members of disadvantaged minorities will not go down, and it might increase. So a proportionate standard would not produce evidence that diversion had a positive impact on the problem of overrepresentation. Because I believe that harm reduction is the appropriate standard, my conclusion is that diversion programs benefit minority populations.

Juvenile versus Criminal Court

The last comparison that teaches us about harm reduction is between the current rate of minority incarceration from juvenile versus criminal courts. The comparison is instructive for two reasons. First, comparing the exposure to harm associated with these two systems is one way of forming a judgment about the aggregate impact of the juvenile court, itself a special reform in American law, on the welfare of minority populations. The second reason to compare aggregate juvenile versus criminal court outcomes is to provide an indirect test of the effects that reforms like diversion and deinstitutionalization of status offenders have had on the welfare of minority youth. Comparing a system performing with these features against an alternative system for processing accused criminals might help us decide whether these major thrusts in juvenile justice over recent decades have made the system more or less sympathetic to interests of minorities.

Table 11.1 repeats one measure of minority overrepresentation used in figure 11.2, the percentage of incarceration populations who are African American, but adds, for the age groups 13–17 and 18–24, the rate per 100,000 African American males of incarceration in the

Table 11.1. Comparative Indicators of Minority Overrepresentation, Juvenile and Criminal Justice, 1995.

	Juvenile facilities	Jails	Prisons
Percentage African Americans in incarceration facilities	40	47	49

	For ages 13–17	Ages 18–24	Ratio of 18–24 to 13–17
Total incarceration rates			
African American incarceration rates	1,332	4,699	3.5

Sources: U.S. Department of Justice, Bureau of Justice Statistics 1974, 1997 Bureau of Justice Statistics (incarceration population); U.S. Department of Justice, Bureau of the Census, 1997 Bureau of the Census (U.S. populations).

mostly juvenile justice age brackets of 13–17 and the early criminal court age brackets of 18–24.

The juvenile-versus-adult data based on proportionate overrepresentation of African Americans shows that 40 percent of all juvenile incarcerations are African American, a much higher proportion of the total incarcerated population than African American youth are of the total youth population. Still, the proportion of inmates who are African American is 20 percent higher for jails and prisons than for youth institutions.

But the important statistic for my argument is the rate of minority incarceration in juvenile and adult facilities. The incarceration rates for African American kids in the age 13–17 bracket is 1,332 per 100,000. The rate for African American males ages 18–24 is 3.5 times higher than for 13- to 17-year-olds. The adult system is not 20 percent more punitive than the juvenile system for African American youth, it is 250 percent more punitive! I suspect that the same juvenile-versus-criminal court pattern would hold for other discrete and overrepresented minority male populations. The big difference in incarceration rates suggests that the aggregate protective impact of juvenile justice policy on minority youth appears to be substantial when compared with criminal justice impact. To borrow a phrase from legal Latin, *res ipsa loquitur.*

Conclusions

The overrepresentation of disadvantaged minorities in the juvenile justice system is part of a broader pattern observed throughout law enforcement in the United States and in most other places. The particular doctrines and processes of juvenile courts do not appear to exacerbate overrepresentation when compared to criminal courts.

This analysis has contrasted two approaches to the problem of overrepresentation: a legalist view that emphasizes reducing disproportionate impact and a youth-welfare view that attempts to reduce the harms suffered by minority youth.

The major positive reforms in juvenile justice over the past generation—deinstitutionalization of status offenders and diversion—have not had dramatic impact on the disproportionate involvement of minority youth in the deep end of the juvenile system. But the lower levels of incarceration embraced by juvenile courts mean that the harms suffered within juvenile courts by all sorts of youth are much smaller than the harms imposed on young offenders in America's criminal courts. It turns out that the entire apparatus of juvenile justice is functioning as a substantial harm-reduction program for minority delinquents.

What I have called a harm-reduction perspective shows clearly that those concerned about the healthy development of minority youth must also be invested in the continued operation of the juvenile court as by far the lesser evil in modern crime control. That the institutions of juvenile justice need reform should not obscure the fact of their lesser harm or its policy implications.

Choosing a Coherent Policy toward Juveniles and Guns

The most alarming statistics about American youth violence during the youth crime panic of the 1990s concerned the increasing rate of homicide, which was wholly the result of increasing gun use in assaults. During the eight years after 1985, when the homicide rate for persons over the age of 24 did not increase, the total homicide rate attributable to juvenile offenders more than doubled. But this statistic was itself an aggregation of two quite divergent trends. Juvenile homicides committed by all means other than guns were remarkably stable throughout the 1980s and the early 1990s. However, the rate of gun killings resulting in the arrest of an offender under 18 years of age more than tripled over a nine-year period.

The usual pattern in the United States had been that firearms were used in a smaller percentage of homicides by adolescent offenders than in homicides by adults. In less than a decade, this pattern was reversed, with a larger proportion of homicides by offenders 14 to 17 than by adults (Zimring 1996). The increase in adolescent homicides in the United States was all guns, and the public perception about this facet of contemporary youth violence was consistent with the facts.

The public attitude about gun ownership by adolescents is a rare island of consensus in the United States, where any other issue relating to firearms control is not merely controversial but also explosively contentious. The United States is a country where membership in the National Rifle Association has traditionally been regarded as a political asset for a presidential candidate. Unrestricted access to guns and ammunition is a matter of intense ideological importance to many citizens, a sentiment expressed in the phrase "firearms freedom." Academic journals publish statistical arguments that increasing the number of ordinary citizens allowed to carry concealed guns in public will reduce the homicide rate (Lott and Mustard 1997)—a conclusion that organized gun-owning groups regard as obvious and embrace with enthusiasm. Contemporary issues like restrictions on semi-automatic weapons and regulation of gun shows are very controversial in a closely divided Congress.

But there is no support for the "firearms freedom" of 14-year-olds to buy handguns, even among groups otherwise opposed to legal restrictions on gun ownership and use. The first federal law that singled out classes of citizens forbidden to purchase firearms in the United States was passed in 1938, and minors under 18 years of age were among the first groups forbidden to acquire guns. There was no controversy associated with that exclusion at the time, and there has been no sustained effort to remove this prohibition (Zimring 1975). The federal Gun Control Act of 1968 raised the minimum age for handgun acquisition to 21, in one of the least controversial changes wrought by an otherwise contentious legislative restructuring of federal gun control that took place in two installments a generation ago (Zimring 1975). State and local laws frequently parallel the federal standard. By a strict statistical count, persons under the age of 21 are probably 90 percent of all the people prohibited from purchasing handguns in the United States in 2005. On the arithmetic, then, gun control in America is mostly about children and youths.

Although minors are prohibited from acquiring handguns, gun laws have never been an important part of youth policy in America, and policy regarding young persons has never been a significant element of federal gun law enforcement until quite recently. A 346-page summary entitled *Understanding Juvenile Law* was published in 1997 (Gardner 1997). The terms "firearms" and "guns" are not to be found in either the table of contents or the index. My earlier review and analysis in *The Changing Legal World of Adolescence* (Zimring 1982) has no mention of firearms, guns, or gun control. Alcohol and tobacco, in contrast, were each the subject of sustained coverage. Age restrictions on the acquisition of handguns were ignored in the literature because they were regarded as noncontroversial and unimportant until quite recently.

Public policy for armed juveniles is still noncontroversial, but it is far from unimportant. The sharp increase in gun woundings and killings attributed to persons under the age of 18 was the subject of extensive media attention. The armed juvenile offender has become a priority target for state and federal legislatures since the late 1980s, including changes in criminal court transfer (discussed in chapter 10) and special provisions for crimes, gang gun crimes, and drive-by shootings. Then, just as juvenile gun crimes dropped in the mid-1990s, a cluster of school shootings increased public worry.

The range of legislative proposals is extraordinarily broad, and new ones are frequently ingenious and often incoherent. During the past two decades, the U.S. Congress has contributed to constitutional history with two separate versions of what was entitled a Gun-free Schools Act. The first version was passed in 1989. The federal power for this act was explicitly based on congressional power to regulate commerce. The law had been patterned after federal "drug-free schools" legislation that combined the symbolic denunciation of worrisome crime with the hope that the threat of federal prosecution would reduce the presence of guns and narcotics in schools.

The U.S. Supreme Court invalidated a prosecution under the Gun-free Schools Act in *United States v. Lopez* (115 S.Ct. 1624, 1994), ruling that even the federal government's extensive powers under the commerce clause, which had been held to be almost infinitely elastic in more than 50 years of Supreme Court jurisprudence, could not be stretched to justify the extension of federal jurisdiction to the vicinities of local schools under the congressional recitals of the 1989 act. The swift response of Congress was to pass another Gun-free Schools Act in short order, with different factual recitals to justify federal jurisdiction. Whether any of this activity helped to keep America's schools gun-free is not known. But the flurry of extensive legislative activity in the national government was a poignant contrast to the previous century, when the gun-free status of primary and secondary education was not an issue.

Beginnings

One frequently used technique for creating legislation to combat adolescent gun use was to appropriate countermeasures that had been popular in other contexts. Just as Congress dusted off the approach of the Drug-free Schools Act to create gun-free schools, the advocates who had combined long, mandatory prison sentences and baseball terminology to pass a "three strikes" initiative in the state of California started a campaign that would have provided a mandatory 10-year prison term for any person 14 years of age or older convicted of unlawfully carrying firearms (Podger 1995). While the effort to place this proposal on the initiative ballot failed, a cut-back version was passed by the state legislature with the enhanced mandatory penalties for older juveniles intact.

The aim of this chapter is to provide a strategic context for thinking about adolescent gun use as a public policy problem. A first step is to consider the justification of age-specific prohibitions. Why deny handguns to adolescents when we allow them to adults? Do the assumptions we make when we prohibit youths from having guns limit the extent to which we can punish them for violating the prohibition? These are the concerns of the first section.

The second section discusses the potential and limits of partial or age-specific prohibition as a gun control strategy. How much harder is it to keep guns from felons and minors, when most other citizens can have all the guns they want? What types of controls should be imposed on qualified gun owners to deter transfers to the prohibited subjects?

The third section examines the practical problems of prohibiting gun access to the young by examining the record of parallel efforts to restrict access to tobacco, alcohol, and pornography. Is age-specific gun prohibition likely to be easier or more difficult to accomplish? The final section discusses a more particularized topic: whether juvenile courts or criminal courts are better suited to handle adolescents charged with the violation of age-specific gun prohibitions.

Minimum Ages: Justifications and Implications

A disadvantage often associated with widespread social policy consensus is the absence of any searching analysis of its justification. Ninety percent of the people prohibited from acquiring handguns in the United States are currently under the age of 21, yet little of the literature on gun regulation concerns the reason for this ban. However, the reason may be inferred from the terms of the regulations in force, as well as by comparing the restrictions imposed on other disqualified groups, although a fair amount of license needs to be taken in the interpretation of existing statutes.

Restrictions on minors are the joint product of ambivalence about widespread and unrestricted handgun ownership for anybody and a consensus judgment that middle and even late adolescents are not sufficiently mature to be trusted with easily concealed lethal weapons. One common characteristic concerning goods and services that by law cannot be purchased by those below a specific minimum age is anxiety about the easy access of adults to these items. We enforce minimum age restrictions on vices such as gambling, drinking alcohol, and smoking in part because we are uneasy with the notion of free access to these activities for anyone.

A minimum age is an interesting kind of compromise between

prohibition and free access, in which mixed feelings about a behavior produce restrictions designed to protect children and youths. As a historical matter, this can be seen in the strenuous enforcement of minimum ages for alcohol in the decades after Prohibition was repealed. A more recent example of this kind of projection has been the increased focus on keeping cigarettes from children and youths as the social status of smoking has declined in the 1980s and 1990s. Yet another example is the crusade against child pornography that absorbed the energies and passions of groups that were really opposed to hard-core pornography in general (Hawkins and Zimring 1989, 176–179).

A similar type of ambivalence played an important role not in the 1938 minimum age for all firearms but in the 1968 minimum age for handguns. The objective justification for singling out handguns was their higher rate of use in homicides, suicides, and other crimes. But there was a subjective dimension as well. The handgun has a social reputation as a more dangerous weapon than a shotgun or rifle. This problematic social reputation also explains the invention of the term "Saturday night special" to describe cheap handguns and their special regulation (see Zimring 1975).

But why single out persons under the age of 21 for special restrictions? The justification for this is youthful immaturity rather than youthful malevolence. The same federal gun law that prohibits the young from acquiring handguns also bans the acquisition of firearms by convicted felons. The latter ban is permanent in the sense that the disability is never removed. The ban on youth is temporary, suggesting that the reason for the prohibition will be outgrown as the subject grows older. It can therefore be inferred that the disabling characteristic of the young is immaturity, a lack of judgment and experience that presumably would help an adult gun owner to control impulses to use the gun in an unjustified violent act.

An important distinction can be drawn between immaturity of a kind that is used to justify firearm prohibition and one that would denote the lack of moral and cognitive capacity required for minimum levels of criminal responsibility. Irresponsibility is an extreme condition, one that would rarely be found in a normal adolescent aged 14 and above. Various levels of immaturity, while they escalate the risk that members of the group will behave inappropriately, fall far short of the disabilities that would render individuals not accountable to the criminal law. If immaturity is a head cold, irresponsibility is the equivalent of double pneumonia.

There is thus no inconsistency in denying a privilege to a high-risk population and then punishing members of the prohibited class when they violate the terms of the prohibition. Because we believe that 15-year-olds are immature, we can prohibit them from acquiring handguns. If they acquire handguns nonetheless, the immaturity that justified the age-specific prohibition does not forbid their punishment. In this sense, an age-related prohibition may be simultaneously paternalistic and punitive and not be incoherent for that reason.

The legal regulation of youth violence becomes incoherent when the age-specific prohibition on guns is justified because of immaturity but the claim is then made that the 15-year-old who gets hold of a gun and then uses it in a robbery should be punished to the same extent as a fully responsible adult for the same offense (see, e.g., the proposal described in Podger 1995). The inconsistency here is in ignoring the diminished capacity to conform to adult standards of judgment and risk management that is the basis for restrictions on handgun acquisition and ownership. To make the claim for equal culpability is to imagine that an offender is simultaneously (1) disadvantaged by a developmental process not of his or her making, and (2) is in full possession of adult levels of maturity and judgment.

Adolescents are not the only group disqualified from gun ownership on the grounds that unrestricted access to firearms would be dangerous. The other important exclusion in federal law is the convicted felon (Zimring 1975). So the question arises whether convicted felons, excluded from gun ownership because of irresponsibility, should not also benefit from doctrines of diminished responsibility when they obtain guns and misuse them? Any argument that minors and felons should be treated in a similar fashion would be problematic on a number of grounds. The most significant is the failure to comprehend the distinction between minors and adults. Children and adolescents are excluded from gun ownership because they cannot be expected to exercise the judgment and control that make gun ownership a risk worth taking. But the deficiency in judgment is not wholly the adolescent's fault, nor do we expect maturity that early in life.

Criminals are disqualified from eligibility for gun ownership because previous criminal acts suggest an unacceptably high risk that future gun ownership will produce trouble. We impose the same expectation of maturity on adult felons as on other adults. It is therefore appropriate to assess a punishment for conviction of criminal acts without discounts attributable to notions of diminished responsibility. The capacities of the adolescent, in contrast, more resemble those of persons over the age of majority who are prohibited from gun purchase because of a mental disease or defect. In such cases, it is not a prior bad decision but the lack of a fully adult capacity to make decisions that is the basis for the prohibition. In each case, the impairment of capacity argues for a reduction in punishment from the full adult standard.

Wide versus Deep Regulatory Power

The developmental immaturity that justifies much more extensive state regulation of the access of adolescents to guns also limits the extent to which offending adolescents may justly be punished for violating gun laws or for committing other crimes. An inability to impose the most severe punishment on adolescent violators might cause some reduction in the extent to which punishment can control adolescent gun crime. However, the substantial portfolio of additional powers held by the state in regulating adolescent access to guns more than compensates for the need to reduce the punitive bite of the criminal law. In jurisdictions in which adult access to weapons is substantially unregulated, the special powers available to the state to enforce gun restrictions for minors are considerable. The width of regulatory controls over adolescents in current law is really quite substantial. Young persons may be stopped and searched in schools, school lockers may be examined with or without consent, private living space may be searched with parental consent, and access to guns through legal means can be prohibited. Since substantial punishment can also be imposed upon conviction of a crime, including a gun law violation, the loss of penal efficacy is not great. On balance, the tools available to limit gun misuse among the young in the United States are much more substantial than those tools available to regulate the ownership and use of guns by adults.

The Prospects for Partial Prohibition

To say that the prospect for restricting the availability of guns to minors is superior to the prospect for regulating adult use is by no means the equivalent of concluding that age-specific gun controls in the United States work well. Gun control for any target group is difficult to accomplish in an environment where the number of available handguns might exceed 60 million.

There are three different ways in which young persons prohibited by law from obtaining firearms nonetheless may get them, and an effective age-specific prohibition must reduce the availability of weapons in all three sources of supply. The first avenue is the legally regulated retail suppliers, who account for the bulk of the transfers of new weapons in the United States, and many used guns as well. This is the regulated market. Second, there is the unregulated exchange of used guns between individuals in what has been called the hand-to-hand market (Zimring and Hawkins 1987). I include in this category the transfers that occur through theft, as well as sales and gifts between individuals who are not dealers. The persons who originally owned the weapons before transfer were lawfully in possession of their guns, but the transfers were not regulated and did not result in any records that linked the new owners with the guns. This channel of supply can be called the gray market. The third method of supply involves the bulk purchasing of guns followed by their sale to persons who the seller knows are not legally permitted to own them. The people in this business are dealers in an illegal market. I refer to this channel of supply as the black market in guns.

The distinction between the black and gray markets often depends on the sellers' knowledge that a weapon transfer is a crime. In a gray market, gun owners do not specialize in the transfer of weapons to prohibited owners. Instead, there are transfers of privately owned guns to a wide variety of different kinds of users at market rates and without any regulatory formality. In black market transactions, in contrast, sellers supply goods to people they know cannot legally possess them. The price charged for the illegal transfer will be somewhat higher than the market rate that the legally qualified person would be willing to pay because there is a crime tariff, a premium to compensate the seller for the risk that boosts the price on the black market.

Any effective program to keep handguns from minors needs to develop strategies to cut off these rather different kinds of supply mechanisms. This means that any successful program of age-specific prohibition must fight a war simultaneously on three distinct fronts. In addition, different methods of regulation and policing will be needed for these different channels of supply.

The regulated market for the sale of handguns is a very easy place to secure compliance with minimum age regulations. Gun dealers are instructed to require proof of a prospective buyer's age, and photo identification on such documents as drivers' licenses is widely carried and easily consulted. The age on a driver's license can, of course, be forged, but even then prospective buyers might look too young to be thought 21 until shortly before they attain the age of legal possession. If law enforcement puts regulatory pressure on dealers to exercise caution, legitimate retail channels can be effectively closed to underage buyers without great effort.

This case of administration is a happy contrast to the problems in preventing retail sales to convicted felons. Documentary proof of age can be found in the purse or wallet of most adult citizens. Documentary evidence of the absence of a criminal record is not something a citizen carries. For decades, federal law was frustrated by the fact that only a sworn statement by the purchaser about the absence of a disqualifying record was required. The provision in current law for "instant checking" of criminal records was an attempt to close a gap for felons that did not exist for underage buyers. It is a compromise between the waiting period the Brady Bill of 1993 initially provided and the absence of verification procedures under previous law.

Preventing the gray market supply of handguns to minors is more difficult and more costly than securing compliance in the regulated market. More used guns are acquired by transfers from individuals than from dealers (Newton and Zimring 1969). The law could require the same documentation and reporting from private individuals as from dealers. Enforcement of this requirement would be a problem, however, because dealers are repeat players in the gun transfer business who have strong incentives to learn and observe the rules, whereas individuals are not. They are difficult to reach through official communications and hard to motivate except with the threat of draconian penalties. Of course, record checks are not likely in the sale of stolen weapons. As hard as it might be to motivate a casual gun owner to check the credentials of a purchaser, obtaining cooperation from a burglar or fence would be harder still.

Whereas regulatory efforts are the principal resources used to secure compliance from retail dealers, trying to reduce the flow of guns to youths in the gray market should involve a mixture of regulatory and criminal law enforcement. The more success a regulatory campaign achieves, the more reasonable it will be for law enforcement authorities to assume that careless sellers are not totally innocent. That is, if most hand-to-hand transfers are casual and undocumented, it will be hard to single out a seller for moral condemnation and criminal prosecution; but if general standards of care about minimum age are high, the sellers who violate those standards will be easier targets.

Reducing gun availability in black markets is principally the task of criminal law enforcement strategies and personnel. The black market dealer is in an illegal business and is therefore a hopeless candidate for regulatory exhortation. Supply reduction in black markets will resemble narcotics law enforcement, with buy-and-bust campaigns and the use of informers. This kind of criminal law enforcement is labor-intensive. Because of the high cost, the level of priority that policing authorities must assign to black market guns to produce stringent enforcement will be very high and thus will rarely be found in local police departments or in police agencies of general jurisdiction; only firearms specialists such as the Federal Bureau of Alcohol, Tobacco and Firearms and specialized police subunits (so-called gun squads) will engage in sustained black market countermeasures.

Varieties of Supply Conditions

Although gray market and black market channels are found in many urban environments, their use as a source of supply for minors will probably vary with the level of general availability in a jurisdiction. Where gun availability is high, the gray market would be a much more important source of guns for youths than the black market. With very large numbers of handguns widely distributed in the population, there are many more guns to be casually transferred. The chance that a random burglary will produce a handgun to be sold or converted to the adolescent housebreaker's personal use is much higher when 40 percent of the households in a city have handguns than when only 10 percent do. This larger supply of gray market guns would make it correspondingly easier for a 16-year-old who wanted a gun to find it. Furthermore, there is also a much greater chance that teenagers will have access to handguns taken from their own homes. Thus, it would be difficult for black marketeers to charge substantial premium prices to underage customers. The gray market, then, would be a dominant, if not exclusive, source of supply.

With low general handgun availability, however, there will be fewer gray market guns for youths to borrow, to buy, and to steal. Then the black market will be a more important channel of supply to the underage customer. In places like New York City and Boston, where the proportion of households with handguns is believed to be much smaller than in cities like Atlanta, Houston, and Miami, more resources should be devoted to black market countermeasures and fewer to policing and regulating the gray market. In high-availability areas, the gray market will require a larger fraction of enforcement effort.

The distinction between high-availability and low-availability cities should alert us to the probability that efforts to keep firearms from youths are hostage to the general condition of gun availability. As hard as it might be to reduce the black market availability of handguns in low-ownership cities like New York and Boston, it would seem to be harder still to reduce gun availability to youngsters in high-ownership cities like Atlanta, Miami, and Houston.

Prevention versus Apprehension

Two different but complementary law enforcement goals are the reduced supply of guns to youths and the removal of prohibited weapons from young persons who carry or possess them. The ultimate aim of each strategy is to reduce the level of firearm violence committed by minors. The obvious advantage of preventing youths from obtaining guns in the first place is that no risk of gun violence will be run if the youth population is never armed. To the extent that prevention programs succeed in keeping youth populations gun-free, a prohibition policy is operating at maximum efficiency. But prevention programs are far from perfect, so that a second line of defense involves generating programs that try to discover and remove firearms unlawfully in the possession of minors. The target population for a prevention program should include anybody who might be part of a supply chain of weapons to minors, including adult gun sellers and owners. The targets of apprehension programs that try to remove guns from prohibited underage owners are limited to young people under the age of eligibility for ownership.

Programs designed to apprehend illegal gun possessors and remove their guns are less effective than prevention programs in one respect but more effective in two other dimensions. The disadvantage of a removal strategy is that the high-risk population spends some time in possession of guns. An apprehension effect may come after the fact of gun violence. The advantage of apprehension strategies is that the population of guns and to a lesser extent of persons who have to be screened is smaller. To cut off market sources of supply to young persons, one has to regulate the commerce in all the weapons that are the subject of the prohibition, not just those weapons that are eventually acquired by minors. A removal strategy, in contrast, is only interested in those guns that are in fact illegally possessed. Whereas the search for illegal weapons will involve screening and inconveniencing many young people who are not carrying guns, it will inconvenience very few adults. The particular beneficiaries of the shift in emphasis from prevention to apprehension will be adult gun owners and sellers. The second efficiency of gun removal strategies is that when a minor is apprehended while carrying a loaded gun, the risk that he or she was headed for trouble is usually quite high. The proximity to social harm of an adolescent who is carrying a gun on the street means that successful apprehension leads to lower rates of gun violence in the immediate future.

The same environmental conditions limit the effectiveness of both prevention and removal strategies. If guns are freely available, preventing a teenager from acquiring one particular gun can easily be neutralized by alternative sources of supply. The salutary impact of removing a gun from a youth may also be short-lived if the confiscated weapon can be easily replaced. For this reason, both handgun prevention and removal should be easier to implement successfully in conditions of low handgun availability.

There may also be a relationship between the level of general handgun availability and the optimal mix of prevention and apprehension strategies in the enforcement of a minimum handgun age. Very high levels of handgun availability can frustrate both prevention and apprehension, but not in equal measure. Cutting off a few sources may have only a slight impact on the availability of guns to youths in a high-availability environment. High availability will also frustrate gun removal programs, but the apprehension of youths with guns will still reduce gun violence during the period immediately following the apprehension, a period when the immediate risk of adolescent gun violence may be quite high. Thus the comparative advantage may lie with programs that emphasize gun removal in high-availability environments. Furthermore, if high availability spills over to higher levels of adolescent gun carrying and use, the same number of police searches will turn up many more guns. So the unit cost of gun apprehension, ironically, is reduced by the very circumstances that frustrate the overall effectiveness of a gun removal strategy.

The foregoing analysis suggests two hypotheses. First, both prevention and apprehension will be more effective in restricting gun violence by minors in environments of low handgun availability. Second, strategies aimed at removing guns possessed by adolescents will be emphasized to the detriment of prevention programs in conditions of high availability. Neither hypothesis has been put to a rigorous test.

Other Minimum Age Requirements

Whereas preventing minors from carrying handguns was an unimportant chapter in the legal regulation of youths until quite recently, efforts to restrict the availability of other substances and privileges have been a substantial undertaking in the United States and other developed nations. Two major government efforts that have attempted to enforce relatively high minimum ages have involved alcohol (typically age 21) and tobacco (typically age 18 but going up). What does the history of these regulations teach us about the prospects of age-specific handgun prohibition?

State efforts to enforce a minimum age for tobacco and alcohol have not produced black markets in the sense of ongoing businesses devoted to illegal sales, mostly because of the ample supply of cigarettes and alcohol diverted from ordinary channels of commerce. Until quite recently, there was not even much gray market activity fueling the supply of cigarettes to middle adolescents. State and local regulation of tobacco purchases was so lax that most adolescents who wanted to obtain cigarettes could purchase them through ordinary retail outlets.

State efforts to enforce minimum age limits for alcohol were much more substantial than for cigarettes. Beverage control authorities typically issued special licenses to businesses that wished to sell alcohol for consumption on the premises or to take home. Enforcing age limits in on-site locations such as bars and restaurants is relatively easy, because the consumers are visibly present to be inspected by proprietors, and enforcement authorities can monitor the compliance of businesses by direct observation of the premises.

However, keeping alcoholic beverages sold in bulk form at liquor stores from being diverted to underage consumers is a much more difficult proposition than keeping them out of bars. The principal gray market diversions of alcoholic beverages sold at retail to qualified purchasers are: (1) theft or borrowing from home liquor supplies by minors, (2) social sharing of alcohol by those just over the legal age with their younger acquaintances and dates, and (3) planned purchase by those over the drinking age of quantities of alcohol intended for the sole or joint use of minors. Similar gray market opportunities exist for tobacco, and the recent increase in regulatory resources to reduce direct sales to minors will probably shift underage supply from over-the-counter sales to gray market channels.

The analogy between handguns and either alcohol or cigarettes is incomplete, because there are differences between the substances and in the social context of commerce. Guns are a big-ticket item, with a high purchase price, whereas typical quantities of alcohol and cigarettes are priced lower. Handguns have a reputation for danger and carry some stigma, whereas cigarettes and alcohol do not. Firearms are also durable goods. Having a gun does not generate a high frequency of resupply needs, even for ammunition.

Even allowing for such differences, the history of attempts to enforce minimum age requirements for alcohol provides important insights for those who want to reduce the gray market for guns. For alcohol, gray markets of supply depend on social patterns of interaction. Unless teenagers are raiding the liquor cabinet of their own or some other family, the age of social peers and their willingness to help are the key variables that make alcohol relatively easy or relatively hard to obtain.

Twenty-one-year-old males co-mingle with 19-year-old males at work and in school, and they date girls who are 17 and 18 years old. Thus alcohol will be easily available to those who regularly participate in social groupings with persons old enough to make retail purchases. Without rigid social boundaries between different age groups, the effective age limit for a particular behavior may be somewhat lower than the formal limit and may be significantly influenced by patterns of social interaction in late adolescence and early adulthood.

One frequent impact of this gray market phenomenon is that minimum age restrictions tend to screen out more effectively much younger adolescents (e.g., 13-, 14-, and 15-year-olds) than those who are closer to the age border. The more the prohibited good is distributed by near peers, the larger the increment of effectiveness to be expected among the very young. If alcohol is chiefly obtained from home liquor cabinets, 15-year-olds and 19-year-olds will have equal access to supplies. If the primary source of beer is friends or friends of friends, the 15-year-old will have a much harder time obtaining alcohol than the 19-year-old. If the chief source of gray market guns is social acquaintances, it will be much easier for 19-year-olds than for 15-year-olds to obtain guns when the minimum age is 21. Under such peer supply circumstances, the adult suppliers who must become the primary target of enforcement efforts are not all that different from the young persons they supply.

There is another context in which social circumstances and expectations might be critical determinants of adolescent handgun acquisition, an aspect that drug and alcohol analysts frequently call the demand side. If possession and use of alcohol or a drug have high status for social peers, the odds increase that a particular adolescent will obtain and use it. The positive status of the substance has a sort of double-whammy effect, making younger persons more anxious to obtain it and older persons more willing to supply it.

The social status and meaning of handguns in adolescent cultures should be an important determinant of the rate of handgun ownership and use. To some extent, this may be a matter of the perceived need for self-defense in some circumstances. But social status is a powerful incentive for adolescent behavior, independent of any need for lethal forms of self-defense. Those who wish to predict and explain adolescent behavior in utilitarian terms should never forget the overwhelming value of social standing among peers to most adolescents.

Negative peer attitudes can have an immediate and substantial impact on adolescent gun violence. The steep increases in gun homicide after the mid-1980s provides frightening evidence of how quickly changes in fashion can generate community consequences. The good news may be that attaching negative stigma to gun use will have immediate and substantial impact, and perhaps that is part of the explanation for the sharp drop in shootings by youth in the middle and late 1990s. The bad news is that attaching negative stigma to risk-taking behavior among adolescents is no easy task. A generation of antismoking propaganda in the United States has had its least consistent and least dramatic impact on teenage smoking trends. If the objective of a public information campaign is to give risk-taking a bad name, teenagers will be a particularly hard sell—all the more reason for the social values of adolescence to be a priority target for any public information campaign that seeks to reduce the risk of lethal violence.

Juvenile or Criminal Court?

If a campaign to reduce firearms violence is going to be an important element in the general response to youth violence, it is worth considering whether juvenile courts or criminal courts provide the best institutional setting. It will not always be possible to choose between these settings, because juvenile court jurisdiction is almost always over by age 18, whereas the existing framework of federal and most state laws tries to enforce a minimum age of 21 for handguns. The very oldest gun law violators will only fit into the jurisdiction of the criminal court, and this is also the court best suited to hear criminal charges against persons over the age of 18 who are apprehended while trying to sell guns to minors.

But which is the best court system for offenders under 18 who possess and carry loaded guns on city streets? Addressing this question has both theoretical and practical value. As a practical matter, such cases are not rare events, and an increasing emphasis on disarming juveniles can be expected to increase the volume of weapons cases whether or not teenage armaments increase. Therefore, where best to process such cases is a matter of immediate practical importance. The theoretical value of discussing the superior court setting for gun cases is that it provides a specific context in which to debate the merits of alternative processing strategies. To isolate the major law enforcement problems being generated by youth violence, to consider them one at a time, reduces the sweeping generalizations found in debates about juvenile versus criminal courts. Greater specificity in subject matter might reduce the margin of error in policy analysis.

What might be the advantages of referring 14-, 15-, 16-, and 17-year-olds, arrested for carrying loaded handguns, to the jurisdiction of the criminal courts? First, criminal courts have the power to impose longer periods of secure confinement on persons convicted of crime than are available in the juvenile courts. But the practical value of greater sanctioning power is much more important in cases of shootings and serious injuries than in cases of carrying concealed weapons and possession. Frequently the maximum punishment available for the latter charges will be less than the duration of confinement available in juvenile court. In addition, because the juvenile weapons violator is competing with older offenders and more serious crimes in criminal court, there is no a priori reason to believe that the sanctions imposed on 15-year-olds who possess guns will be even somewhat more serious than the treatment those same cases would receive in a juvenile court.

Second, armed juveniles are serious cases, and it is often argued that serious cases belong in the jurisdiction of the criminal court. Pete Wilson (1997), the governor of California, seemed to be making this argument when he asserted: "Juvenile Court was not designed to deal with youth who commit serious and violent crime . . . or kids who carry assault weapons" (1). Implicit in this view is the notion that referring young offenders to juvenile court trivializes the offense. This is really an objection to juvenile court jurisdiction for *any* serious offense, and it might apply with greater force to the tens of thousands of violent assaults and robberies referred to the juvenile courts each year. If delinquency jurisdiction is a bad idea for any serious misbehavior, it would be a bad idea for gun cases. But the empirical foundation of this point of view is not strong. Rather than imbue marginal cases with seriousness by association, mixing juvenile cases into the adult system might have the reverse effect—a possibility that was just mentioned in connection with criminal court sanctions (see Greenwood, Petersilia, and Zimring 1980).

The comparative advantages of the juvenile court for gun cases come from that court's long history of coping with status offenses. A law that denies handguns to all below a certain age and punishes those who defy it can be called a status offense, because the behavior is forbidden only because of the offender's youthful status. A large proportion of juvenile court business during the entire century of its existence has been the enforcement of age-defined status offenses, including underage drinking, smoking, and driving and violating curfews. Whereas some status offenses, like smoking, are violations of laws motivated solely by the desire to protect the minor, a substantial number of the traditional status offenses administered by the juvenile court also involve protecting the community against dangerous behavior by the immature. Certainly the enforcement of juvenile curfews and underage drinking restrictions have community protection as a justifying objective.

It thus appears that the enforcement of minimum age gun laws involves a close fit to the strategies and procedures of juvenile courts in a high volume of other types of cases. One remarkable characteristic of the current discussion is that the continuity between gun countermeasures and traditional status offense enforcement has gone unnoticed. The fit with tradition here is not a dispositive argument for the continuation of jurisdiction by juvenile courts in gun cases. It is, however, both remarkable and disturbing when public dialogue about appropriate responses in gun cases takes place without reference to a century's experience in closely related domains.

But debating whether juvenile courts or criminal courts should do the heavy lifting in adolescent gun control is also asking the wrong question in a demonstrably important way. The social context of adolescent gun markets and behavior demonstrates that significant effort will be necessary on both sides of any age boundary between juvenile and criminal courts before a coherent strategy can be executed. More important than choosing between competing court systems is a consensus on common principles and a coordination of effort that can effectively harness both institutions to a common strategy.

THIRTEEN

The Hardest of the Hard Cases
The Young Homicide Offender

The teenager accused of criminal homicide is the worst case in a system that seeks to protect young offenders and to preserve their opportunity for normal development into adulthood. Causing a death is inflicting the greatest harm that crime can cause in a developed nation, a type of loss that the economic resources and insurance mechanisms of a rich nation cannot protect against or meaningfully compensate. If death is caused by intentional infliction of a serious injury, the youth who inflicted the injury will often have intended enough harm so that his or her moral culpability would have been great even if death had been avoided. In such cases, the combination of high levels of personal culpability and the worst-case outcome puts maximum pressure on the legal system to generate extensive punishment. Dealing with homicide is an important and particularly difficult part of a comprehensive policy toward youth violence.

These most serious cases are prominent in public concern about the legitimacy and effectiveness of the legal system. They are also difficult but important tests of the general principles that are supposed to be in play throughout the system. Homicide is one important domain to explore when trying to determine the motives and principles that should be at work in other youth crime and delinquency cases. If there is a real gap between what we do and what we say, a close look at decision-making in homicide cases will probably reveal it.

This chapter discusses the substantive principles that should govern the punishment of adolescents who kill. The first section shows that the stereotypical versions of juvenile and criminal courts are not well suited to attain just results in adolescent homicides. The second section uses cases reported in the news to explore the multiple varieties of youth homicides. The third section uses the diminished responsibility and room-to-reform conceptions discussed in chapter 5 as a method of exploring punishment principles for adolescent killers. The fourth section sets out specific case studies in the meaning of diminished responsibility: (1) the ages at which homicide offenders should be considered to be partially but not fully responsible; (2) appropriate methods for determining deserved punishments for adolescent killers; (3) constructive homicide liability as a problem for the criminal law of adolescence; and (4) capital punishment for young killers.

A False Dichotomy

If the only choice available for the trial and punishment of adolescent homicide cases was between a juvenile court solely concerned with treatment and a criminal court that ignored the age and circumstances of the defendants, the task of finding appropriate responses would be an impossible one. The intentional taking of life without justification requires a punitive response in most circumstances in which the offender has even a minimal appreciation of the nature of his or her act. Thus punishment must be one of the appropriate responses of any legal authority responsible for addressing adolescent homicide.

But the proper punishment for 15-year-olds who kill must take into account their immaturity and other particular circumstances. Otherwise, the legal authority that determines guilt and punishment will not be coherent in making retributive judgments. The popular assumption that trying very young defendants in criminal court removes any necessity to consider their immaturity and other limits is mistaken but revealing. The transfer of juveniles is often described as a decision to "try this defendant as an adult." But if the defendant is 15 years old and of slightly subnormal intelligence, to try and punish him as if he were adult in all respects is a dangerously counterfactual enterprise.

The language used to describe the process of transferring defendants to criminal court is itself an invitation to what psychiatrists call "magical thinking," in which it is imagined that changing the location of a case will suddenly remove the characteristics that cause conflict and ambivalence. The physical reality of jurisdictional transfer is rather mundane—to try an accused "as an adult" in a criminal court changes only the location of the hearing; it does not change the characteristics of the defendant. If we could in fact transform adolescents into adults by an act of juridical will, the procedure would be in great demand by parents and schools in circumstances far removed from delinquency and crime. This particular branch of magical thinking was immortalized by the stand-in for a revolutionary leader in the Woody Allen film *Bananas,* who proclaims in his inaugural address: "All children under sixteen are hereby sixteen."

Some comparative statistics on waivers from juvenile to criminal courts illustrate the unique problems that are generated by adolescents accused of homicide. The proportion of juvenile homicide charges waived in Texas is six times as large as for the crime with the next highest rate of transfer petitions; and the gap between waiver rates in homicide and those for other offenses is much larger than the contrast between other classes of offenses (Dawson 1992; Eigen 1981).

The sanctioning options usually available in juvenile court fall short of the perceived need for punishment in a substantial proportion of homicide cases. Pressure for greater punishment can be accommodated either by giving more punishment power to juvenile courts or by transferring defendants to criminal courts, which already have much greater punishment powers. In either case, an appropriate judicial performance in adolescent homicides should require a particularized inquiry about the offense and the offender, a mixture of factual detail and principles that has been specifically fashioned from an analysis of homicide offenders and their crimes.

It is therefore discouraging that the processing of thousands of adolescent homicides through state criminal courts has produced very little discussion of the particular deserts of those accountable. This silence is consistent with three different possibilities:

1. The lack of particular analysis of adolescent homicides is an indication that transferred defendants are treated with equal severity as adults.
2. The sentencing discretions available in the prosecution and adjudication procedures result in leniency toward youthful defendants that is substantially without announced principle or discernible pattern.
3. There is a silent common law of unarticulated principles that could be used to both explain and predict the punishment choices.

The most likely of these patterns is probably the second. The system for deciding the punishment of immaturity is probably fundamentally lawless. If so, the lack of appropriate legal standards to explain outcomes in homicide cases would have negative consequences that reach far beyond the particular results. If the outcomes are arbitrary, the pattern of arbitrariness is quite likely to be contagious. If the high stakes in homicide cases cannot produce dialogue and analysis of the justice of particular outcomes, there is little prospect of doing better in the treatment of lesser crimes. To default in providing a principled analysis of the punishment in homicide cases is to run the substantial risk that the whole process will be unprincipled.

Immaturity and Culpability: Some Lessons from Malcolm Shabazz

A New York case that was widely publicized in the summer of 1997 is an instructive illustration of the manifold impact of youth and immaturity on the just punishment for an offense. Malcolm Shabazz was a much traveled 12-year-old when he obtained gasoline and deliberately set a fire in the apartment of his custodial grandmother, knowing that she was at home. Malcolm is the grandson of the black radical Malcolm X, and his grandmother, Betty Shabazz, was Malcolm X's widow. She died as a result of the burns she sustained in the fire.

Testimony at court hearings portrayed Malcolm as extremely troubled, with clinical indications of schizophrenia and a documented history as a chronic fire-setter. The boy's defense attorney and a clinical psychologist retained by the prosecution both denied that the defendant intended to kill his grandmother. "I do not believe he consciously meant to do harm to his grandmother," said Dr. Elizabeth Osborn, a clinical psychologist hired by the prosecution. "I believe it was an unconscious act to scare her, make her change, get her to do what he wanted" (Gross 1997).

The youth and immaturity of the offender affect a large number of factors that bear on the just punishment in this case. Data about youth and immaturity may be required to make a judgment about whether the chronic fire-setting behavior was compulsive (a condition not uncommon in this age group), whether the defendant subjectively appreciated the risk of death or of great bodily harm that was attendant on his act, and the plausibility of the defendant's fantasy of an imaginary companion in charge of his decisions (Gross 1997).

What is crystal clear in the Shabazz case is that youth and immaturity are not just factors to be added on to modify an otherwise deserved penalty for a particular course of conduct and its result. The immaturity of an actor has a pervasive influence on a large number of subjective elements of the offense, including cognition, volition, and the appreciation that behavior like setting a fire can produce results like death. The defendant's status and perceptions are relevant to a large number of issues, each of which can affect the extent of personal culpability and therefore of deserved punishment.

To use a metaphor from mathematics, immaturity is not just a single variable in the equation that determines punishment but a characteristic that may affect many different variables. It is best to think of youth and immaturity as factors that may influence every aspect of conduct, other than the character of the resulting harm, that plays a major role in determining the extent of blameworthiness. Malcolm Shabazz and a 25-year-old arsonist with no known developmental difficulties are not two different sorts of people who have committed the same crime; they are two different sorts of people who have committed different crimes, offenses that are fundamentally different because of the characteristics and perceptions of the offenders.

The fatal fire that Malcolm Shabazz set was not the typical act of homicidal youth violence for a number of reasons. He was much younger than the typical juvenile killer. The indications of mental illness are much more substantial than in the usual run of cases. The intention to injure is usually easier to infer because of the use of a gun, knife, or personal force on the deceased. But the potentially pervasive influence of youth and immaturity on the subjective factors that affect the degree of personal culpability is a standard feature of the lethal violence of adolescents.

The Malcolm Shabazz case is not a typical instance of adolescent killing for one other reason: there are no typical cases of adolescent homicide. The substantial variety encountered in adolescent homicide is apparent to any conscientious reader of the daily press. At the opposite end of the spectrum from Malcolm Shabazz is the Lam Choi case, reported in the same month:

> Lam Choi, the alleged slayer of crime boss Cuong Tran, was certified yesterday to stand trial as an adult. . . . Tran, thirty-seven, was shot to death at 1:40 A.M. on November 15 after leaving the Pierce Street Annex, a popular bar at Fillmore and Greenwich Streets. . . . Choi, who was seventeen at the time of the shootings, was allegedly in a group with three adults and another youth the night of Tran's slaying. Prosecutors said the group spoke with the victim inside the bar and four of them followed him to his car, where Choi shot Tran. (Schwartz 1997)

Yet another San Francisco Bay shooting of the same vintage, a case in which the victim survived a nearly fatal wound, overlaps very little with either the Shabazz or the Choi circumstances:

> Police said children who witnessed the late-morning incident told them that a thirteen-year-old boy deliberately shot the girl after she dared him to use the handgun he was carrying. Witnesses said the two got into a shoving match, the argument escalated and he fired one shot into her chest. (Walker and Herscher 1997)

A further case from the current season's crop of newspaper coverage concerned the sentencing of the young man who, at age 14, fired the shots that killed one British tourist and injured a second in Florida. This defendant was the youngest of the three teens who stopped the car but also the only one of the group who fired a gun (Peltier 1997).

Another adolescent homicide received sustained media coverage just as this text was being prepared for its initial publication. In West Paducah, Kentucky, a 14-year-old high school freshman broke up a high school prayer meeting by opening fire with a .22 caliber handgun. Twelve shots were fired. Two of the students died from the gunshot wounds, and six others were injured (Hoversten 1997).

The assertion that there are no typical adolescent killings is a jurisprudential argument rather than a criminological one. The statistical analysis of homicide cases involving adolescent offenders does reveal recurrent fact patterns. Overwhelmingly, the weapon used in fatal assaults is the firearm. When homicides are committed by juveniles, there is a much higher likelihood of more than one offender than when homicide is committed by adults. In addition, the rate of homicidal injuries is much higher among the two oldest age groups typically within the jurisdiction of the juvenile court: 16- and 17-year-olds.

However, blameworthiness of adolescent killers comes in many different degrees. When it is time to assess an individual defendant's conduct and circumstances to determine the degree of his or her culpability, both the number of significant variables and the distribution of factors that influence culpability are great. There is, first, the age of the accused, as well as his or her age-related judgment and experience. Second, there are the precipitating circumstances that led to the lethal assault and the extent to which these were the fault of the accused. If there was a fight, who started it? Who was responsible for the first use of lethal force? If there was group involvement, the extent to which a particular defendant's conduct was responsible for the lethal outcome must be considered. Thus the degree of culpability for homicide will be spread over a wide range, with a relatively small concentration of cases at any particular point on the continuum. If there were ever an attractive group of homicide cases for *prix fixe* penalties, juvenile killers are certainly not in that category.

The wide range and difficulty in determining the deserved punishment in juvenile killings are also arguments against guideline grids or other mechanically produced sentencing benchmarks, which tend to rely on a very few characteristics, such as age and previous criminal record, to produce modal sentencing values. More appropriate to the complexity of the task would be a common law of adolescent culpability constructed over time in the course of judicial analysis of large numbers of youth homicide cases.

Yet the existing appellate court discussion of juvenile homicide cases involves much of the judicial effort that would be necessary to construct a common law of culpability, with almost none of its benefits. Appellate courts consider the circumstances of adolescent homicide cases in the course of reviewing the propriety of judicial waiver from juvenile court jurisdiction. The best that can be expected from this process is the division of defendants into two rough categories characterized by different average levels of culpability. What cannot be addressed are the principles that should govern an appropriate response to a particular killing, whether it has been adjudicated in a juvenile or a criminal court.

The Theory Gap

Given the high volume of homicide cases and the substantial importance of each offense, the absence of a sustained analysis of culpability is both a peculiar and an important gap. There is a lack of theory concerning the principles that should govern the punishment of adolescent killers. Part of the explanation may be the fact that the issues involved do not all comfortably fit into unified categories of legal theory or court jurisdiction. In the United States, the juvenile court and the criminal court are regarded as not merely two different legal institutions but also two different subjects for analysis and theory. In the Shabazz case, the 12-year-old Malcolm appeared in family court but would have been processed in the criminal courts of

New York if he had been 13. The problems in comprehending Malcolm Shabazz's case do not change dramatically on his thirteenth birthday, but as long as we segregate the two systems, there is no coordinated way to consider their joint problems.

Another reason for the lack of a theory is the preoccupation with the jurisdictional questions that characterizes policy debates about violent adolescents. Americans conduct long dialogues about what kind of court should try juveniles accused of homicide under the mistaken impression that they are addressing substantive questions about the degree of penal responsibility for these criminal acts.

A Practice in Search of a Theory

The absence of analytic attention to the proper punishment for young homicide defendants does not mean that the present system ignores age and immaturity when deciding on sanctions in juvenile and criminal courts. There is substantial evidence that age and immaturity are powerful influences on practice. Texas prosecutors, it will be recalled, do not even request transfer to criminal court in seven out of every ten homicide charges (see chapter 10). The relatively thin evidence on the youngest offenders in criminal courts also suggests that factors associated with youth produce lesser punishments (Greenwood, Petersilia, and Zimring 1980). The current system in homicide cases seems like a classic case of what has been called "practice in search of a theory" (Vorenberg and Vorenberg 1973). But the combination of high stakes, nonexistent principles, and the low visibility of discretion is a prescription for arbitrariness and injustice. Coherent theory that is specific to adolescent homicide is an important practical need in the justice system, not merely a matter of academic nicety.

Two Principles Applied

This section uses the two broad doctrines in chapter 5 as the organizing categories for policy analysis of adolescents charged with homicide. The first surveys the issues generated by diminished responsibility as a doctrine of substantive criminal law applicable to young killers. The second discusses the ways in which government policies toward children and youths, the sorts of concerns earlier discussed under the heading of room to reform, might affect both the extent of punishment and the conditions under which it should be administered.

Diminished Responsibility and Desert

Those elements of an offender's constitution and perception that are relevant to diminished responsibility should affect the amount of punishment deserved as a consequence of conviction for a particular criminal act. Some theorists would like to have one deserved punishment for a particular offense by a particular offender, the one appropriate penal price for an offense, but I hold with Norval Morris (1974), who considers desert to be a guiding principle, one that defines a range of punishments that are consistent with the degree of blameworthiness in a particular case. Set the punishment below the minimum that is deserved, and the community will suffer, because the consequences to the defendant unduly depreciate the seriousness of the criminal act in the circumstances in which it was committed. Set the punishment above the maximum level that is deserved, and both the community and the offender will suffer, because more suffering than is justified by the particular circumstances of the offender's culpability will have been imposed. But any punishment within the deserved range would be considered retributively appropriate.

The offender's diminished responsibility should be part of the elements of the offense that define the appropriate range of deserved punishment in that particular case. The immaturity, psychological and perceptual handicaps, and inability to appreciate consequences that characterize the agreed-upon facts about Malcolm Shabazz are all important elements that establish a range of just punishments in his case; and these factors would seem to be relevant whether the sentencing court was a juvenile or a criminal tribunal. When elements of diminished responsibility are frequently encountered, they should be incorporated into the basic framework of the minimum and maximum punishments available. If such factors can be used only to guide discretion within a range of minimum punishment decided on other grounds, the calculation will come too late in the process to ensure that the objective of retributive proportionality can be achieved.

Four general observations can be made about diminished responsibility because of youth and the selection of punishment for adolescent killers. First, doctrines of diminished responsibility should be applicable throughout the full spectrum of the severity of an offense. The politically popular notion that immaturity should be allowed to mitigate deserved punishment only in relatively harmless crimes is nonsensical. If subjective culpability is relevant to deserved punishment at all, there is no principled basis on which one can impose a ceiling of seriousness beyond which an offender's lack of maturity or judgment is irrelevant.

Mitigation of punishment because of diminished responsibility may hamper the effectiveness of criminal law as an instrument of control, but if moral consistency is the appropriate standard, diminished responsibility should stand or fall as an issue of general applicability. Homicide should not be excluded from the reach of otherwise applicable doctrines of diminished responsibility.

Second, the greater the significance of subjective rather than objective elements in determining the range of appropriate punishments for a crime, the greater the impact of diminished capacity because of immaturity on deserved punishment. The more the applicable branch of the criminal law concerns itself with not simply harm inflicted but also the circumstances of advertence and intention that produced it, the larger the potential role for personal handicaps that diminish subjective culpability in mitigating the range of deserved punishment.

This emphasis on the subjective makes the criminal law of homicide an area where the potential influence of mitigation is enormous. Criminal acts that cause death are variously classified in the United States as involuntary manslaughter, manslaughter, second-degree murder, first-degree murder, and (in three-quarters of the states) capital murder. From manslaughter to first-degree murder, the range of minimum punishment is from probation to life imprisonment, and the elements that differentiate these crimes are almost exclusively the subjective features of intent, advertence, and motivation that highlight the importance of doctrines of diminished responsibility. When the difference between premeditation (first-degree murder) and malice (second-degree murder) can mean 15 years more imprisonment (Zimring, Eigen, and O'Malley 1976) and when equally lethal acts can be punished by probation (if negligent) or long imprisonment (if grossly reckless), a defendant's youth and immaturity should have a very large influence on the level of deserved punishment.

There are also branches of the substantive criminal law where individual guilt and punishment are determined almost solely by an individual's intent, rather than physical participation in criminal acts, through such doctrines as the liability of conspirators for the criminal acts committed by their coconspirators and the penal liability of an accessory for the crimes of the principal (Kadish 1985). The greater the weight that the law places on the solely subjective dimensions of behavior in a particular case, the greater the mitigational potential of diminished responsibility because of immaturity. When the only basis for punishment is the agreement and intention of the defendant, the defendant's immaturity should have a major impact on the deserved punishment.

The greater leverage of diminished responsibility as an accessory is of tremendous practical significance for adolescent homicide because so many violent acts committed by teenagers are committed in groups. I showed in chapter 6 that the majority of all family court charges for serious crimes in New York involved cooffenders. In the last section of this chapter, I show that half of all offenders under 18 who were arrested for homicide were arrested with at least one other person. When the circumstances that generate a homicide charge involve only the offender's presence or knowledge, rather than physical participation in the infliction of injuries that cause death, the reduction in the range of deserved punishment for the passive, or tag-along, accessories can and should be quite substantial. I return to this point when discussing constructive liability for unintended outcomes.

The high volume of accessorial charges is one important reason why a relatively small proportion of juvenile homicide charges result in prosecutorial requests for judicial waiver. The evidence of antisocial intention of a triggerman in a fatal gun assault are far more substantial than those of the 14-year-old associate standing next to the shooter or the 16-year-old waiting in the car. In addition, the link between the defendant's act and the harm inflicted is much closer for the triggerman.

Third, it is important to recognize the substantial number of different blameworthiness issues where the defendant's overall immaturity, inexperience in understanding the link between risk-taking and causing harm, and incapacity to control or deflect peer pressure should be taken into account in setting punishment for homicides. In addition to the standard questions regarding *mens rea* and mistake, the immaturity of an accused might also be relevant to the application of the standard presumptions of Anglo-American law. Recall the prosecution psychologist who believed that Malcolm Shabazz did not intend the death of his grandmother when he started a fire in her apartment. The standard slogan in criminal law is that "a man intends the natural and probable consequences of his actions." Should we be quick to assume that a boy intends the natural and probable consequences of his actions when that boy is 12, or 14, or 16 years of age? A number of standard criminal law doctrines, including strict liability, may not fit the circumstances and psychology of immature defendants as well as they are believed to suit moral judgments about competent adults.

The large number of issues in which an offender's age and immaturity can be relevant to the range of deserved punishment suggests a procedural consequence that is contrary to the current trend in processing juvenile homicide cases. Case-by-case determinations of culpability by a judge would seem to be as important in homicide cases as in any other type of criminal case. Both waiver hearings and individualized sentencing determinations may be necessary to meet the complex challenge of justice in adolescent homicide cases, but the legislative trend is in exactly the opposite direction. The approved mode for murder charges is transfer at the discretion of the prosecution, and the substantive law that governs sentencing in criminal courts is utterly silent on immaturity and its implications. The last section of this chapter concerns some of the many questions of culpability that need to be addressed by criminal courts.

Homicide Sentencing and Youth Policy

One important standard for a justice system is the extent to which it can adjudicate young offenders without compromising the objectives of government policy toward young people in general. I argue in chapter 5 that youths who violate the law are nonetheless the young people who must be considered subjects of a government youth policy. The slogan for this conclusion is that the kid is a criminal but the criminal is still a kid (Greenwood and Zimring 1985). The principal objective of policy in the adjudication and sentencing of minors is to avoid damaging a young person's development into an adulthood of full potential and free choice; thus the label for this type of policy is "room to reform."

In an ideal world, the punishment of all young people who violate the law would avoid disfiguring stigma, debilitating penal confinement, and other permanent developmental handicaps. In an ideal world, of course, 15-year-olds would not commit intentional homicide. Whenever a community's retributive demands are legitimate and substantial, there may be a conflict between maximizing the developmental opportunities of young offenders and meeting the retributive necessities of homicide.

One important distinction between concerns of youth policy and diminished responsibility is that room-to-reform considerations are outside the range of deserved punishment for a particular individual's participation in a specific criminal act. Every circumstance that is material to the determination of diminished capacity helps to establish the minimum and maximum deserved punishment. There can thus be no real conflict between diminished capacity and the range of deserved punishments, because the former has helped to determine the latter.

But government policy toward youths should not be a part of any kind of equation that determines penal desert. The fact that we want all our teenagers to develop into healthy and realized adults has no direct bearing on the minimum level of punishment felt necessary for an offense or on the maximum beyond which punishment would exceed desert and is therefore unjustified. In addition, because the interests of a youth policy are not a part of the determination of desert, the two may be in direct conflict. The smallest punishment appropriate to desert for a terrible crime may inflict exactly the kind of damage that government youth policy seeks to avoid.

When there is unavoidable conflict between the objectives of youth policy and the minimum demands for deserved punishment, the latter should carry the day. This will not be an unjust result if youth and immaturity have been fully accommodated in the calculation of diminished responsibility, but the outcome in such cases will be a disservice to socially important interests by not allowing young people to fully recover from their adolescent mistakes. However, when desert and youth support conflict, electing the minimum deserved punishment becomes the sad necessity of the sentencing court.

Still, youth policy can be much better accommodated, even in the treatment of adolescent killers, than is evident in current practice. The value of promoting normal adolescent development can properly influence the amount of punishment selected within the confines of an already established desert range, and the nature and conditions of adolescent punishment can be designed in ways that will serve the interests of government youth policy vastly better than the current system.

To say that a government policy that favors youth development will not affect the range of punishments deserved by particular young offenders is far from saying that the policy should have no influence on the penalty selected in particular cases. First, the range of deserved penalties for serious crimes is frequently substantial, and the influence of youth policy within that range can make a big difference. To oversimplify, assume that the range of deserved punishment for a particular type of involvement in homicide is two and one-half years at the minimum and nine years at the maximum. Even youth policies that do not have an impact on those minimum and maximum values can be powerful determinants of the actual sentence.

Second, youth policy can influence the form of a criminal punishment within a range that is established by other considerations. A recurrent example is the greater use of indeterminacy in the sentencing of young offenders convicted of very serious offenses. The presumed malleability of young offenders and the likelihood that fundamental changes in character and maturity will occur in the course of penal confinement have resulted in an emphasis on indeterminacy in the sentencing of older youths in criminal courts. Both the Federal Youth Corrections Act, which was a sentencing option in the United States until 1984, and parallel provisions in Great Britain and on the continent of Europe reflected this emphasis. All of these provisions were established for the criminal court sentencing of young offenders. In that sort of system, the effective minimum for the young offender will be the bottom of the range of deserved punishment, but the substantive concerns of a youth policy might produce the offender's release "at the pleasure of Her Majesty" shortly after that minimum has been met.

The other way in which policy toward children and youths should influence the treatment of young homicide offenders is atrociously ignored in much American practice. No matter how serious the crime committed by a 14-year-old, there is no reason short of magical thinking for concluding that the young offender has become an adult in matters such as the need for education and vulnerability to adult predation; I would argue that whenever a young offender's need for protection, education, and skill development can be accommodated without frustrating community security, there is a government obligation to do so.

One of two sentiments seems to underlie the frequent assertion that young persons who commit serious crimes do not require the services and schooling usually appropriate to their age. The first notion is that truly serious crime is a mark of maturity, a benchmark that indicates that legal emancipation is appropriate. This inference has never been backed by any empirical data. It seems instead to follow as the obverse of an assumption that the truly immature are incapable of committing homicide. The second sentiment is that withdrawal of all special projections is an appropriate punishment for crime. Some proponents of adult penalties would extend treating youths as if they were adults to denial of special conditions of confinement such as age segregation and protection from older prisoners, educational programs, counseling, and special mental health services. The implicit argument is that young offenders do not deserve anything that might benefit them, as youth-oriented protections might.

But as long as the security of confinement is not compromised, it is difficult to see a genuine conflict between providing youth services and punishing even the most serious offenses. On utilitarian grounds, the education and training of the young is a positive value even if long-term confinement is its context. From a retributive perspective, the provision of age-appropriate conditions of confinement would seem analogous to providing needed medical care for all prisoners, a continuing obligation that does not compromise the punitive bite of confinement. Education and security from predatory assault are not privileges conferred on young persons and revokable as a consequence of misbehavior.

To summarize: the interaction of youth policy with the retributive necessity of punishment is a contingent one. When the community's minimum level of required punishment is too high to accommodate full protection of the development of the young offender, there will be a direct conflict between what is desirable for all adolescents and what can be provided for the most serious adolescent offenders. For such true conflicts, the need for minimum deserved punishment will control.

Often, however, there will be opportunities to find punishment within the desert range that allows the offender's growth and development into nearly normal adulthood, and it will always be possible to provide education and age-appropriate security and conditions of confinement to even the most culpable of adolescent killers. In these cases, there is no good reason to terminate special policies toward youths that do not conflict with the demands of penal justice.

Case Studies in Diminished Culpability

This section is a modest down payment on the substantial work that will be necessary if the implications and limits of responsibility in youth violence are appropriately developed. I discuss here four substantive issues that range from age boundaries for diminished capacity to potential eligibility for capital punishment.

The Age Span of Diminished Responsibility

A substantial number of practical questions stand between the principles discussed earlier and an operating system of adjudication and disposition of adolescent homicide. One question concerns the age boundaries of diminished responsibility. At the lower extreme, when should we declare the transition from incapacity to minimum states of capacity not inconsistent with some punishment for serious crime? The common law had a conclusive presumption of incapacity below age 7, and presumed capacity after age 14.

Figure 13.1 shows the distribution of all homicide arrests for

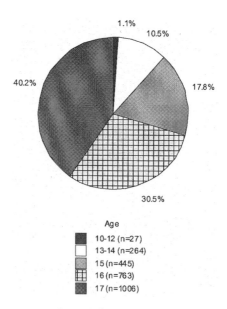

Figure 13.1. Percentage of juvenile arrests for murder and nonneglient manslaughter, ages 10–17, 1995. *Source:* U.S. Department of Justice, Federal Bureau of Investigation, 1995.

offenders under the age of 18 for 1995. Homicide arrests are rare events under age 13 and infrequent under age 15. More 15-year-olds are arrested for homicide than the total of all ages under 15, and more 16-year-olds are arrested for homicide than the total of all ages under 16.

Figure 13.2 shows estimated rates of homicide charges in juvenile court by the age at referral. Age 13 has a very low rate of prosecution referral. Significant homicide-charging activity begins at age 14 and increases steadily thereafter. By age 17, the charging rate is 19 times as large as at age 13. In practice, the significant beginning ages for homicide prosecution are 12 through 14. It is not clear whether discretionary arrest and charging play a major role in the near zero rates below age 14. The border between incapacity and capacity is usually regarded as a matter of case-by-case determination, in the first instance by prosecutors and in the second by juvenile court judges.

After the age of minimum culpability is attained, how long should diminished capacity playa role in determining deserved punishment, and how great a role should it play? The correct policy answer to this question depends on the range of capacities that are believed relevant to culpability and the ages at which they are typically attained. If all the characteristics of diminished responsibility outlined in chapter 5 are relevant to punishment, inquiry about such matters could extend up to and, not infrequently, beyond age 18 in homicide cases. If the lack of experience in learning to deflect peer pressure

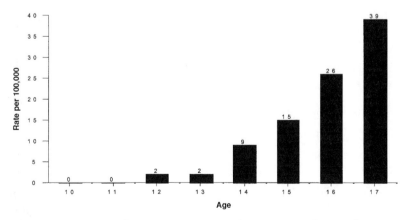

Figure 13.2. Estimated rates per 100,000 of prosecution for youth, 1992, homicide cases. *Source:* Snyder and Sickmund, 1995.

and in dealing with provocation are regarded as mitigating elements, most adolescent offenders will be operating at far from trivial deficits. In contrast, most of the basic capacities for moral judgments are achieved earlier, normally by age 14 or 15. The greater the emphasis on experience and social skills, the larger the degree of social and experiential development that must occur before criminal acts can be said to deserve the full measure of punishment.

These general observations fall far short of a specific schedule of degrees of responsibility linked to age or other attributes of the offender. One reason for this is the absence of good data on the social skills and social experience of adolescent offenders. The important elements of penal maturity have yet to be agreed upon, let alone assessed in large numbers of cases. There is reason to believe that concentrated efforts will tell us much more than we now know about the social psychology of adolescent violence, and this knowledge about general patterns of development will be helpful to some extent in developing policy.

But I doubt whether even advanced knowledge of adolescent development and the particular characteristics of young violent offenders will produce a satisfactory schedule of punishments normed to age or prior offenses. The range of individual variation among youths of the same age is notoriously large. The relationship of a particular young offender to the criminal harm is another important dimension, and this will interact with different ages in different ways. The significant variables in determining the proper punishment for a teen killer will not fit comfortably into a two-dimensional sentencing grid. For such cases, I know of no superior alternative to the combination of wide potential sentencing frames, individual judicial judgments with reasons, and appellate review.

This lack of fit with price-list sentencing is a special characteristic of adolescent homicide cases for two related reasons. First, the degree to which subjective elements influence deserved punishment is great in homicide cases of all kinds, so a wide range of punishments should be available even before immaturity complicates the matter. Second, price-list sentencing works best when the major influence in the appropriate sentence is the type of offense committed rather than variations in the offender's subjective state or capacity to control behavior. If most burglaries are punished within a relatively narrow range for offenders with equivalent criminal records, the sentencing guideline can be relatively specific and not unjust. The less important the particular offense is in defining the specific sentence, the less useful the sentencing guideline system that selects offense as the basic organizing category.

The Calculus of Juvenile Desert

Once the substantive decision is made to recognize immaturity as a mitigation of culpability and thus an influence on the range of deserved punishment, two different approaches can determine appropriate sanctions for particular young offenders: discounting and independent determination. In a discounting strategy, the starting point for a calculation of the deserved punishment for a youth would be the deserved punishment of an adult for the same type of offense. If adult burglars with particular criminal histories typically get four years of penal confinement at sentencing, the way to calculate the appropriate penalty for a 15-year-old burglar is to determine a discount from that sentence. If, on the average, conditions of diminished responsibility for 15-year-olds should produce a 50 percent punishment reduction, one calculates the punishment for the youth by multiplying the adult sentence times 1.0 minus the discount, or in this case, 4 years x (1.0 - 0.5) = 2 years. Variations on this discounting strategy, which is directly dependant on the adult penalty for the type of punishment and its duration, have been suggested for juveniles in criminal courts (Feld 1998) and in juvenile courts (Institute for Judicial Administration 1977).

Little has been written about how the wide variety of different characteristics of adolescent offenders might be translated into a schedule of discounts. Barry Feld (1998), who advocates discounting for young offenders in criminal court as an alternative to the current juvenile court system, describes the process:

> This categorical approach might take the form of an explicit "youth discount" at sentencing. A fourteen-year-old offender would receive, for example, 25 percent of the adult penalty, a sixteen-year-old defendant, 50 percent, and an eighteen-year-old adult the full penalty, as is presently the case. The "deeper discounts" for younger offenders correspond to the developmental continuum of responsibility.

The notion is evidently for the same age-based discounts across all categories of offense types and liability.

A contrasting approach might take its hierarchy of offense seriousness from the adult system, so that burglary would be regarded as less serious than robbery but more serious than theft, but would not use the average penal sanctions imposed on adults as the basis for computing the penalties for adolescents. For a number of reasons, I believe that such independent determinations of sanctions for young offenders are more appropriate in both juvenile and criminal courts.

The independent calculation of sanctions for young homicide offenders more accurately reflects both the nonquantifiable nature of criminal punishments and the large variation in levels of culpability that characterize adolescent offenders. The average term of penal confinement for adult killers is generally an aggregate of many different grades of offenses and degrees of criminal culpability. Time served for voluntary manslaughter may be not much longer than time served for nonfatal violent crimes. Second-degree murder sentences are much longer in many jurisdictions. Aggregating the two groups of sentences and taking a group mean would provide a rather arbitrary measure of desert for adult killers. Providing separate averages for the two offense categories assumes that the types of homicides reflected in the adult distribution are also found among juveniles and that the relationship of blameworthiness in the two classes is the same for juveniles as it is for adults. This does not seem to me a plausible set of assumptions.

There is also no reason to suppose that terms of penal confinement proportionally express different levels of deserved condemnation. Is the community condemnation expressed in a ten-year sentence twice as much as in a five-year sentence, and is five years five times one year? If not, discounting should not be based on a fixed proportion of a term of confinement. If adult punishments are inexact, even crude measures of blameworthiness and variations in terms of confinement are only roughly correlated with levels of culpability, providing a specified fraction of an adult penalty as a youth penalty or creating a schedule of different fractions treats a crude and multiply determined average of prison time served as if it were a much more sensitive and accurate measure of the community's sense of deserved punishment. No matter how carefully the fractions are measured and reported, the enormous margin of error to be found cannot be reduced. Indeed, it turns out that any system of discounting fractions for young offenders may exacerbate the problems that result from the problematic nature of adult penalties as a currency of culpability.

First, age is an incomplete proxy for levels of maturity during the years from age 12 to 18. The variation among individuals of the same age is great, and individualized determinations of immaturity are thus superior to averages based on aggregate patterns (see chapter 3). Second, the vulnerabilities associated with early and middle adolescence play a more important part in explaining some patterns of homicide than others. The passive accomplice who acquiesces in a robbery that turns lethal, rather than be called chicken by his peers, is a more attractive candidate for extensive mitigation of punishment than one of the same age who instigated the robbery, even though that more active role was also motivated by the need to make a positive social impression. Some types of provocation in group conflicts may also lead to extensive mitigation, as when the 13-year-old in Oakland was accused of being "too chicken" to shoot by his victim. Those situations that put extreme pressure on particular vulnerabilities characteristic of adolescents make them strong candidates for sharply reduced punishment when a fatality results. Moreover, the large variation in the level of achieved maturity interacts with the differential vulnerabilities found in different circumstances to present a complicated landscape, one much too complex for an age-determined series of presumed discounts from a standing price list of penalties.

My own view is that measuring mitigated penalties as a percentage of usual time served would be an inappropriate strategy in both juvenile and criminal courts. In juvenile courts, the expected sentence for an adult guilty of a similar offense may be only remotely related to the proper disposition of the youthful offender. The type of confinement to be served is different, the adolescent and the adult have different senses of time, and the mix of purposes behind sanctioning decisions is also not the same as in the criminal court.

The case for fixed discounts might seem stronger for young offenders being sentenced in criminal courts but is still far from compelling. The criminal law has extensive experience in creating offense categories to allow mitigated punishment for homicides. Second-degree murder was invented as one such mitigation strategy; voluntary manslaughter is another. It is worth noting that nowhere was the penalty for manslaughter derived as a fraction of the penalty for first-degree murder. Each step down the ladder of culpability for homicide has its own penalty range, which has never, in my experience, been derived as a fraction of the going rate for particular grades of murder.

The traditional method of special sentences for youths in criminal courts also avoided deriving punishments by using a particular fraction of adult penalties in the United States or in Europe. Instead, indeterminate terms with relatively short minimum sentences is a typical pattern. The fact that fixed discounts have never been adopted as the mechanism to implement diminished responsibility should inspire caution.

Constructive Doctrine and Adolescent Homicide Liability

A cluster of related doctrines imposes criminal liability on adults for the lethal acts of others and for deaths that they might cause, even if a particular defendant did not have a specific intent to injure. These include the felony murder rules, the doctrine of accessorial liability, and rules stating that accessories are guilty of the criminal acts committed by those they have aided or agreed to aid in the commission of a crime. A standard example of the web of constructive liability begins when A, B, and C agree to rob a convenience store. A provides the plans but stays home; B drives C to the store but waits in the car; C pulls a gun on the salesclerk, who resists. The gun goes off during the struggle, and the salesclerk is mortally wounded. A, B, and C are all guilty of first-degree murder in most U.S. states. The rules of accessorial liability make A and B liable for C's acts in furtherance of their common design. The felony murder rules make the intention to further the robbery a sufficient mental state to generate liability for first-degree murder if the robbery causes a death. The intention to commit the robbery is the legal equivalent of malice, and murder statutes typically impose first-degree liability on all parties accountable for the forcible felony that caused the death (Zimring and Zuehl 1986).

Rules relating to accessorial liability are of great importance to adolescent offenders, because group involvement is greater in teen violence than at any other age. An analysis of Federal Bureau of Investigation homicide data shows that just over half of all persons arrested for homicide under the age of 18 were involved in an offense for which at least one other homicide arrest was made. That is more than twice the proportion of multiple arrest defendants in over-18 homicide arrests, or 51 percent versus 23 percent (U.S. Department of Justice, Federal Bureau of Investigation 1994). Felony murder doctrine is also important—about one-fifth of all homicide arrests of persons under 18 are for police-nominated felony killings.

Accessorial liability can interact with the vulnerability of adolescents to group pressure to create very marginal conditions for extensive criminal sanctions. This is not to deny that some juvenile accomplices may have played dominant roles in particular deaths. Rather, I would argue that the range of culpability is very great and that the culpability at the low end of the distribution should be rather small. A case can be made for allowing the waiver of a youth to criminal court on solely accessorial responsibility for a killing only if there is evidence that the particular defendant knew of and encouraged the use of lethal force. In a justice system in which only homicide leads to transfer in large proportions, requiring more than constructive liability for homicide would seem to make sense.

I know of no extensive analysis of felony murders and accessorial liability for adolescent offenders. But perhaps large numbers of accused accessories transferred into the criminal courts might lead to the first sustained dialogue about deserved punishment and adolescent accessories in the history of Anglo-American criminal law.

The case for substantial mitigation from accessorial responsibility for a killing is based on the greater emphasis on subjective culpability for the accomplice. The felony murder rule might be distinguishable from other accessory situations. Because it imposes strict liability, no subjective mental state beyond the intention to commit a forcible felony is required, and even 16-year-olds can intend to rob. It might be argued, however, that the law assumes maturity and capacity beyond ordinary adolescent attainments as the foundation on which strict liability for the outcome of forcible felonies is based. The question is not one that has received any sustained attention during a period when most adolescent homicides were disposed of in low-stakes and informal juvenile court hearings, but it would be possible for a court to find that the imposition of strict liability depends on more than minimal capacity for criminal liability in general.

As a practical matter, if transfer to criminal court is to be restricted to cases that are the moral equivalent of intentional homicide, it should not be based solely on liability for the homicidal acts of another under the felony murder rules. This type of restriction would not eliminate criminal court processing of felony killings, but it would restrict the defendants to those whose active support and participation in the killing can be established. The system's most serious sanctions should be reserved for those young offenders whose participation in homicide was not solely as a nonaggressive accomplice. Strict liability to murder prosecution, if retained for any cases, should be reserved for more experienced felons.

Capital Punishment and the Adolescent Killer

The only legal issue concerning the diminished capacity of adolescent killers that has received sustained attention in the United States is the constitutional question of whether the Eighth Amendment's prohibition of cruel and unusual punishment implies that very young killers cannot be executed. Defense attorneys had sought a per se exclusion of persons under 18 at the time an offense was committed from eligibility for the death penalty, arguing from minimum ages that are observed in other nations and in several U.S. states. The U.S. Supreme Court first declined that invitation in 1989 but has excluded since 1988 the eventual execution of offenders under 16 at the time the crime was committed on Eighth Amendment grounds, even if they are otherwise competent and culpable (*Thompson v. Oklahoma*, 1988). Then in 2005, the Court extended the ban to all offenders under 18 in *Roper v. Simmons.*

The reasoning of the justices in cases like *Roper v. Simmons* and the earlier *Thompson v. Oklahoma* does not provide clear exposition on questions of diminished responsibility for adolescent killers, for three reasons. First, the issue comes up in a death penalty context, and strong categorical sentiments about capital punishment dominate the responses of many observers to detailed questions about death penalty policy. To put great weight on the importance of a defendant's youth after *Thompson* and *Roper,* it is first necessary to remove the principles to be found in the cases from the death penalty context. This has not yet been done.

Second, the Eighth Amendment cases have a limited basis for constitutional review. It is not the self-appointed duty of the Supreme Court to state a minimum age for execution that would be appropriate on policy grounds. Instead, the Court will only limit state power when clear violations of contemporary standards of decency would otherwise occur. Thus the standards the Court has established may well be far short of the appropriate policy on minimum age that many of the justices might choose as policy.

Third, the Supreme Court emphasized the practices in various punishment systems rather than the reasons behind them. *Thompson v. Oklahoma,* for example, debates how many states have implicit or explicit minimum ages for the death penalty instead of why minimum ages might be regarded as necessary to a morally coherent death penalty. The illumination this provides on basic issues about adolescent capacity and culpability is indirect at best. Diminished responsibility may be the reason for minimum age standards in states and nations that observe age limits for the death penalty, but it is the age limits rather than the rationale for them that have center stage in the constitutional debate.

With these considerable limits, the death penalty case law still has value as a precedent in any discussion of a defendant's youth as a mitigating factor, The four-judge plurality in *Thompson v. Oklahoma* endorsed a prohibition on death for all offenders under the age of 16, and Sandra Day O'Connor's concurrence supported that result in the circumstances of the Oklahoma statute. If the constitution forbids executing anyone for any crime committed before age 16, this must be because a presumption of diminished capacity requires such minimum age standards under the Eighth Amendment. When age at the time of the offense is the standard, the substantive context being enforced must be a notion of diminished culpability for the crime rather than incapacity to comprehend the punishment.

If one reads the later case of *Roper v. Simmons* as suggesting a ban on executions for crimes committed under the age of 18, the use of that limit for the Eighth Amendment rule should not be regarded as an endorsement for the execution of 19- and 20-year-olds who commit murder. The Court has clearly indicated that juries must be instructed that youth can be taken into account in the penalty trial. In addition, *Thompson* and *Roper* are the only instances in death penalty jurisprudence, along with *Atkins v. Virginia* on mental retardation, in which a defendant responsible for a capital murder cannot be executed because of diminished capacity at the time of the crime.

The struggle in the Supreme Court over death as a sanction for young killers has its broadest impact by establishing general principles to govern the sentencing of young offenders in criminal court. Cases like *Roper* and *Thompson* involve defendants already waived from juvenile court and convicted of aggravated murder in criminal courts. By restricting the availability of the death sentence, the Court has already recognized that the defendant's youthful status follows him or her into criminal court and precludes the treatment of any young person in criminal court jurisdiction as fully adult for all purposes. The view that young persons are no longer young when transferred to criminal court is not only irrational but also against the weight of U.S. Supreme Court authority. The principle was invoked in Eighth Amendment jurisprudence because of the special status of the death penalty. But the Court's emphasis on the fact of youth rather than on the form of the court is a principle of general applicability.

Conclusion

The search for appropriate legal standards for adolescent homicides is important in its own right and also as an example of the type of analysis that is necessary to determine just punishments for other types of adolescent offenders in criminal courts. Very little legal analysis or argument currently addresses the punishment of serious adolescent offenses in criminal court. This chapter demonstrates the variety and complexity of the issues when the substantive criminal law of homicide is measured against the circumstances arid developmental limits usually found in adolescent homicide cases.

The conventional belief about punishment for young killers is that the important decisions have been made once the issue of transfer to criminal court has been decided. Not so. Rather than being the end of difficult decisions, the transfer determination should be regarded as requiring a series of factual and legal inquiries that are as subtle, problematic, and controversial as can be found in the modern criminal law of personal violence.

Building principle into the punishment of adolescent homicides in criminal courts has been, for some time, an unmet challenge for American criminal law. The increase in automatic transfers and the high priority of youth violence in penal policy remind us that a void in principles at the heart of the legal response to homicide becomes a greater embarrassment with each passing day.

Notes and References

Notes to Chapter One

1. Juvenile Justice and Delinquency Prevention Act of 1974, 42 U.S.C. § 3723(10)(H) (1974).

2. See Sanford Fox, "Juvenile Justice Reform: An Historical Perspective," 22 *Stanford Law Review* 1187–1239 (1970); Douglas Rendleman, "Parens Patriae: From Chancery to the Juvenile Court," 23 *South Carolina Law Review* 205–259 (1971); and Neil Cogan, "Juvenile Law, before and after the Entrance of 'Parens Patriae,'" 22 *South Carolina Law Review* 147–151 (1970).

3. *Youth: Transition to Adulthood,* Report of the Panel on Youth of the President's Science Advisory Committee (Washington, D.C.: Government Printing Office, 1973) (hereafter Panel on Youth) at 26.

4. Panel on Youth, at 26; and U.S. Bureau of the Census, *Historical Statistics of the United States, Colonial Times to 1970* (Washington, D.C.: Government Printing Office, 1975) at 379.

5. Illinois Juvenile Court Act, § 21 [1899] Illinois Laws 137.

6. David S. Tanenhaus, "The Evolution of Juvenile Courts in the Early Twentieth Century," in Margaret K. Rosenheim, Franklin E. Zimring, david S. Tanenhaus and Bernardine Dohrn, eds., *A Century of Juvenile Justice* (Chicago: University of Chicago Press, 2002).

7. See Stephen L. Schlossman, *Love and the American Delinquent: The Theory and Practice of "Progressive" Juvenile Justice, 1825–1920* (Chicago: University of Chicago Press, 1977).

8. John H. Ralph and Richard Rubinson, "Immigration and the Expansion of Schooling in the United States, 1890–1970," 45 *American Sociological Review* 943–954 (1980); Samuel Bowles and Herbert Gintis, *Schooling in Capitalist America* (New York: Basic Books, 1976); and bibliographies therein.

9. Robert A. Burt, "Developing Constitutional Rights of, in, and for Children," in *Pursuing Justice for the Child,* Margaret K. Rosenheim, ed. (Chicago: University of Chicago Press, 1976) at 225–245.

10. Anthony M. Platt, *The Child Savers: The Invention of Delinquency* (Chicago: University of Chicago Press, 1969) at 100.

11. Charles Larsen, *The Good Fight: The Life and Times of Ben B. Lindsey* (Chicago: Quadrangle Books, 1972) at 7.

12. Larsen, *The Good Fight, supra* note 11, especially chaps. 2–4.

13. Judge Julian Mack, "The Juvenile Court," 23 *Harvard Law Review*, 104–122 (1909) at 107.

14. Juvenile Court of Cook County, *Annual Report* (1907) at 123.

15. Larsen, *supra* note 11, at 34.

16. Denver Juvenile Court, *Annual Report* (1903) at 151. The peak age of referral may have been 14, rather than 12, because of internal inconsistency in the addition of one column. But from other tables in the report (at 150) it seems most likely that 12 is the correct age.

17. See U.S. Bureau of the Census, *Historical Statistics of the U.S.: Colonial Times to 1970* (Washington, D.C.: Government Printing Office, 1975); and Panel on Youth, at 76.

18. For a discussion of the phrase "adolescent society" see chap. 1 of James Coleman, *The Adolescent Society: The Social Life of the Teenager and Its Impact on Education* (New York: Free Press of Glencoe, 1961).

19. In the mid-1920s, for example, there were approximately two cars for every three families in the Lynd's Middletown. Even then, the right to use the family car was regarded by adolescents as a major source of disagreements with parents. Adults saw the automobile as a contribution to adolescent independence, juvenile delinquency, sexual promiscuity, and religious decline in the community. See Robert S. Lynd and Helen M. Lynd, *Middletown: A Study in American Culture* (New York: Harcourt, Brace and World, 1929) at 251–263.

20. Coleman, *The Adolescent Society, supra* note 18, at 7.

References to Chapter One

Bowles, Samuel, and Herbert Gintis. *Schooling in Capitalist America.* New York: Basic Books, 1976.

Burt, Robert A. "Developing Constitutional Rights of, in, and for Children." In *Pursuing Justice for the Child*, edited by Margaret K. Rosenheim. Chicago: University of Chicago Press, 1976.

Cogan, Neil. 1970. "Juvenile Law, before and after the Entrance of 'Parens Patriae.'" *South Carolina Law Review* 22: 147–151.

Coleman, James. *The Adolescent Society: The Social Life of the Teenager and Its Impact on Education.* New York: Free Press of Glencoe, 1961.

Denver Juvenile Court. 1903. *Annual Report.*

Fox, Sanford. 1970. "Juvenile Justice Reform: An Historical Perspective." *Stanford Law Review* 22: 1187–1239.

Illinois Juvenile Court Act, § 21 [1899] Illinois Laws 137.

Juvenile Court of Cook County. 1907. *Annual Report.*

Juvenile Justice and Delinquency Prevention Act of 1974, 42 U.S.C. § 3723(10)(H) (1974).

Larsen, Charles. *The Good Fight: The Life and Times of Ben B. Lindsey.* Chicago: Quadrangle Books, 1972.

Lynd, Robert S., and Helen M. Lynd. *Middletown: A Study in American Culture.* New York: Harcourt, Brace, and World, 1929.

Mack, Judge Julian. 1909. "The Juvenile Court." *Harvard Law Review* 23: 104–122.

Platt, Anthony M. *The Child Savers: The Invention of Delinquency.* Chicago: University of Chicago Press, 1969.

Ralph, John H., and Richard Rubison. 1980. "Immigration and the Expansion of Schooling in the United States, 1890–1970." *American Sociological Review* 45: 943–954.

Rendleman, Douglas. 1971. "Parens Patriae: From Chancery to the Juvenile Court." *South Carolina Law Review* 23: 205–259.

Schlossman, Stephen L. *Love and the American Delinquent: The Theory and Practice of "Progressive" Juvenile Justice, 1825–1920.* Chicago: University of Chicago Press, 1977.

Tanenhaus, David S. "The Evolution of Juvenile Courts in the Early Twentieth Century." In *A Century of Juvenile Justice,* edited by Margaret K. Rosenheim, Franklin E. Zimring, David S. Tanenhaus, and Bernardine Dohrn. Chicago: University of Chicago Press, 2002.

U.S. Bureau of the Census. *Historical Statistics of the United States, Colonial Times to 1970.* Washington, D.C.: Government Printing Office, 1975.

Youth: Transition to Adulthood. Report of the Panel on Youth of the President's Science Advisory Committee. Washington, D.C.: Government Printing Office, 1973.

Notes to Chapter Two

1. The classic anthropological treatment of this subject is Margaret Mead, *Coming of Age in Samoa* (New York: Morrow, 1928); see also Margaret Mead, *Growing Up in New Guinea* (New York: Morrow, 1930); John Whiting, *Becoming a Kwoma* (New Haven: Yale University Press, 1941); Margaret Mead and Martha Wolfenstein, eds., *Childhood in Contemporary Culture* (Chicago: University of Chicago Press, 1955); William N. Stephens, *The Family in Cross-Cultural Perspective* (New York: Holt, Rinehart and Winston, 1963); and Margaret Mead, *Culture and Commitment,* 2nd ed. (New York: Columbia University Press, 1978).

2. Anthropologists have studied this phenomenon in situations of rapid cultural change where role models become much less uniform and have a wider range. See, for example, Melville J. Herskovits, *Acculturation: The Study of Culture Contact* (Gloucester, Mass.: P. Smith, 1958); Edward Spicer, ed., *Perspectives on American Indian Culture Change* (Chicago: University of Chicago Press, 1961); and Louise S. Spindler, *Culture Change and Modernization* (New York: Holt, Rinehart and Winston, 1977). A classic sociological account of the historical development and outcome of this process is Emile Durkheim, *The Division of Labor in Society,* George Simpson, trans. (New York: Macmillan, 1933).

3. See Lawrence A. Cremin, *The Transformation of the School* (New York: Knopf, 1961); and Robert A. Carlson, *The Quest for Conformity: Americanization through Education* (New York: Wiley, 1975).

4. The Chinese and Cuban experiences are two obvious examples, al-

though even there, keeping a consistent agenda has been and remains a problem. For China, see Hsi-en Ch'en, *The Maoist Educational Revolution* (New York: Praeger, 1974); William Kessen, ed., *Childhood in China* (New Haven: Yale University Press, 1975); and R. F. Price, *Education in Communist China,* 2nd ed. (New York: Praeger, 1979). For Cuba see Hugh S. Thomas, *Cuba; Or Pursuit of Freedom* (London: Eyre and Spottswood, 1971); and Arthur A. Gillette, *Cuba's Educational Revolution* (London: Fabian Society, 1972).

5. See *Youth: Transition to Adulthood,* Report of the Panel on Youth of the President's Science Advisory Committee (Washington, D.C.: Government Printing Office, 1973). Note that the use of "adolescence" was deliberately eschewed in this book to avoid its manifold connotations.

6. Leon S. Robertson, "Patterns of Teenaged Driver Involvement in Fatal Motor Vehicle Crashes: Implications for Policy Options," *Journal of Health Politics, Policy and Law* 6 (1982), 303–314.

7. See Arlene Skolnick, "Children's Rights, Children's Development," in *The Future of Childhood and Juvenile Justice,* Lamar T. Empey, ed. (Charlottesville: University Press of Virginia, 1979); and F. Raymond Marks, "Detours on the Road to Maturity: A View of the Legal Conception of Growing Up and Letting Go," 39 *Law and Contemporary Problems* 78 (1975).

8. Skolnick, "Children's Rights, Children's Development," *supra* note 7, at 163.

9. Richard H. Kuh, "Dissent," in Franklin E. Zimring, *Confronting Youth Crime: Report of the Twentieth-Century Task Force on Sentencing Policy toward Young Offenders* (New York: Holmes and Meier, 1978) at 21.

10. Kuh, "Dissent," *supra* note 9, at 21.

References to Chapter Two

Carlson, Robert A. *The Quest for Conformity: Americanization through Education.* New York: Wiley, 1975.

Ch'en, Hsi-en. *The Maoist Educational Revolution.* New York: Praeger, 1974.

Cremin, Lawrence A. *The Transformation of the School.* New York: Knopf, 1961.

Durkheim, Emile. *The Division of Labor in Society,* George Simpson, trans. New York: Macmillan, 1933.

Gillette, Arthur A. *Cuba's Educational Revolution.* London: Fabian Society, 1972.

Herskovitz, Melville J. *Acculturation: The Study of Culture Contact.* Gloucester, Mass.: P. Smith, 1958.

Kessen, William, ed. *Childhood in China.* New Haven: Yale University Press, 1975.

Kuh, Richard H. "Dissent." In *Confronting Youth Crime: Report of the Twentieth-Century Task Force on Sentencing Policy toward Young*

Offenders, edited by Franklin E. Zimring. New York: Holmes and Meier, 1978.

Marks, F. Raymond. 1975. Detours on the Road to Maturity: A View of the Legal Conception of Growing Up and Letting Go." *Law and Contemporary Problems* 39: 78.

Mead, Margaret. *Coming of Age in Samoa.* New York: Morrow, 1928.

———. *Culture and Commitment,* 2nd ed. New York: Columbia University Press, 1978.

———. *Growing Up in New Guinea.* New York: Morrow, 1930.

Mead, Margaret, and Martha Wolfenstein, eds. *Childhood in Contemporary Culture.* Chicago: University of Chicago Press, 1955.

Price, R. F. *Education in Communist China,* 2nd ed. New York: Praeger, 1979.

Robertson, Leon S. 1982. "Patterns of Teenaged Driver Involvement in Fatal Motor Vehicle Crashes: Implications for Policy Options." *Journal of Health Politics, Policy and Law* 6: 303–314.

Skolnick, Arlene. "Children's Rights, Children's Development." In *The Future of Childhood and Juvenile Justice,* edited by Lamar T. Empey. Charlottesville: University Press of Virginia, 1979.

Spicer, Edward, ed. *Perspectives on American Indian Culture Change.* Chicago: University of Chicago Press, 1961.

Spindler, Louise S. *Culture Change and Modernization.* New York: Holt, Reinhart and Winston, 1977.

Stephens, William N. *The Family in Cross-Cultural Perspective.* New York: Holt, Reinhart and Winston, 1963.

Thomas, Hugh S. *Cuba; Or Pursuit of Freedom.* London: Eyre and Spottswood, 1971.

Whiting, John. *Becoming a Kwoma.* New Haven: Yale University Press, 1941.

Youth: Transition to Adulthood. Report of the Panel on Youth of the President's Science Advisory Committee. Washington, D.C.: Government Printing Office, 1973.

Notes to Chapter Three

1. Institute of Judicial Administration/American Bar Association, Juvenile Justice Standards Project, *Rights of Minors, Tentative Draft* (Cambridge, Mass.: Ballinger, 1977) at 17–32, 119–123; and Alan N. Sussman, *The Rights of Young People* (New York: Avon Books, 1977) at 15–23, 173–192, 220–250.

2. Francis J. Allen, "The Law as a Path to the World," 77 *Michigan Law Review* 157 (1978) at 169.

3. See Sussman, *The Rights of Young People, supra* note 1, at 245–246.

4. Sussman, *The Rights of Young People, supra* note 1, at 245–246.

5. See Robert Mnookin, *Child, Family, and State: Problems and Materials on Children and the Law* (Boston: Little, Brown, 1978) at 668–682.

6. See *Vital Statistics of the United States,* various years from 1946 through 1976, tables on mortality by selected causes of death and age groups.

7. *Vital Statistics of the United States,* 1976, vol. 2, pt. A, table 4-2.

References to Chapter Three

Allen, Francis J. 1978. "The Law as a Path to the World." *Michigan Law Review* 77: 157.

Institute of Judicial Administration/American Bar Association, Juvenile Justice Standards Project. *Rights of Minors, Tentative Draft.* Cambridge, Mass.: Ballinger 1977.

Mnookin, Robert. *Child, Family, and State: Problems and Materials on Children and the Law.* Boston: Little, Brown, 1978.

Sussman, Alan N. *The Rights of Young People.* New York: Avon Books, 1977.

Vital Statistics of the United States, 1946–1976.

Notes to Chapter Four

1. See Anthony Platt, *The Child Savers: The Invention of Delinquency* (Chicago: University of Chicago Press, 1969), chap. 1.

2. Francis Allen, "The Juvenile Court and the Limits on Juvenile Justice," in *The Borderland of Criminal Justice* (Chicago: University of Chicago Press, 1964), 42, 50–54.

3. *In re Gault,* 387 U.S. 1 (1987); *In re Winship,* 397 U.S. 358 (1970).

4. Richard S. Tuthill, "History of the Children's Court in Chicago," in *Children's Courts in the U.S.: Their Origin, Development, and results,* ed. Jane Addams (1904; reprint, Chicago: AMS Press, 1973).

5. Ben B. Lindsey, "Colorado's Contribution to the Juvenile Court," in *The Child, the Clinic, and the Court,* ed. Jane Addams (New York: New Republic, 1925), 217.

6. William T. Stead, *If Christ Came to Chicago* (1894; reprint, Chicago: Chicago Historical Bookworks, 1990).

7. See, for example, Julian Mack, "The Juvenile Court," *Harvard Law Review* 23 (1909): 104.

8. Compare Adams, *The Child, the Clinic, and the Court* with Platt, *Child Savers,* and Steven Schlossman, *Love and the American Delinquent: The Theory and Practice of "Progressive Juvenile Justice"* (Chicago: University of Chicago Press, 1977).

9. Schlossman, *Love and the American Delinquent,* 55–57.

10. See, especially, Platt, *Child Savers.*

11. Julia Lathrop, "The Background of the Juvenile Court in Illinois," in Addams, *The Child, the Clinic, and the Court,* 290.

12. Schlossman, *Love and the American Delinquent*, 64–66.

13. Lindsey, "Colorado's Contribution," 274.

14. Jane Addams, introduction to Addams, *The Child, the Clinic, and the Court*, 1, 2.

15. Schlossman, *Love and the American Delinquent*, app. 2, table 2, 202.

16. Robert M. Mennell, *Thorn and Thistles: Juvenile Delinquents in the United States, 1825–1940* (Hanover, N.H.: University Press of New England, 1973), 106–107.

17. Franklin E. Zimring, *The Changing Legal World of Adolescence* (New York: Free Press, 1982), 35–40.

18. *In re Gault*, 387 U.S. at 25–26.

19. Ibid., 75 (Harlan, J., dissenting).

20. Ibid., 27.

21. *In re Winship*, 397 U.S. at 360.

22. Ibid., 368.

23. *Gault*, 387 U.S. at 22.

24. Zimring, *Changing Legal World*, chs. 3 and 7.

25. Juvenile Justice and Delinquency Prevention Act of 1974 § 223(a), 42 U.S.C. § 5633(a) (1994).

26. Ibid., § 102, 42 U.S.C. § 5602.

27. Ibid., at § 311, 42 U.S.C. § 5711(a).

28. Zimring, *Changing Legal World*, 32–40.

29. Ibid., chap. 5.

30. See S.10, 105th Cong. (1997); H.R. 3, 105th Cong. (1997).

31. See, for example, S. Rep. No. 105–108 (1997); H.R. Rep. No. 105–86 (1997).

32. See Peter Greenwood, Joan Petersilia, and Franklin E. Zimring, *Age, Crime, and Sanctions: The Transition from Juvenile to Criminal Court* (Santa Monica, Calif.: Rand, 1980).

33. Franklin E. Zimring and Gordon Hawkins, *The Scale of Imprisonment* (Chicago: University of Chicago Press, 1991), chap. 5.

34. Franklin E. Zimring, *American Youth Violence* (New York: Oxford University Press, 1998), chap. 1.

35. Addams, introduction, 2.

36. Miriam Van Waters, "The Juvenile Court from the Child's Viewpoint," in Addams, *The Child, the Clinic, and the Court*, 217.

References to Chapter Four

Addams, Jane, ed. *The Child, the Clinic, and the Court*. New York: New Republic, 1925.

Allen, Francis. "The Juvenile Court and the Limits on Juvenile Justice." In *The Borderland of Criminal Justice*. Chicago: University of Chicago Press, 1964.

Greenwood, Peter, Joan Petersilia, and Franklin E. Zimring. *Age, Crime, and Sanctions: The Transition from Juvenile to Criminal Court* (Santa Monica, Calif.: Rand, 1980).

In re Gault, 387 U.S. 1 (1967).

In re Winship, 397 U.S. 358 (1970).

Juvenile Justice and Delinquency Prevention Act of 1974 §§ 102, 223(A), 311; 42 U.S.C. § 5602, § 5633(a), 5711(a) (1994).

Lathrop, Julia. "The Background of the Juvenile Court in Illinois." In *The Child, the Clinic, and the Court*, ed. Jane Addams. New York: New Republic, 1925.

Lindsey, Ben B. "Colorado's Contribution to the Juvenile Court." In *The Child, the Clinic, and the Court*, ed. Jane Addams. New York: New Republic, 1925.

Mack, Julian. "The Juvenile Court," *Harvard Law Review* 23 (1909): 104–122.

Mennel, Robert M. *Thorn and Thistles: Juvenile Delinquents in the United States, 1825–1940*. Hanover, N.H.: University Press of New England, 1973.

Platt, Anthony. *The Child Savers: The Invention of Delinquency*. Chicago: University of Chicago Press, 1969.

Schlossman, Steven. *Love and the American Delinquent: The Theory and Practice of "Progressive" Juvenile Justice*. Chicago: University of Chicago Press, 1977.

S.10, 105th Cong. (1997); H.R. 3, 105th Cong. (1997).

S. Rep. No. 105–108 (1997); H.R. Rep. No. 105–86 (1997).

Stead, William T. *If Christ Came to Chicago*. 1894; reprint, Chicago: Chicago Historical Bookworks, 1990.

Tuthill, Richard S. "History of the Children's Court in Chicago." In *Children's Courts in the U.S.: Their Origin, Development, and results*, ed. Jane Addams. 1904; reprint, Chicago: AMS Press, 1973.

Van Waters, Miriam. "The Juvenile Court from the Child's Viewpoint." In *The Child, the Clinic, and the Court*. ed. Jane Addams. New York: New Republic, 1925.

Zimring, Franklin E. *American Youth Violence*. New York: Oxford University Press, 1998.

Zimring, Franklin E. *The Changing Legal World of Adolescence*. New York: Free Press, 1982.

Zimring, Franklin E., and Gordon Hawkins. *The Scale of Imprisonment*. Chicago: University of Chicago Press, 1991.

References to Chapter Five

Elliott, Delbert. 1994. "Serious Violent Offenders: Onset, Developmental Course, and Termination: The American Society of Criminology 1993 Presidential Address." *Criminology* 32:1.

Elliott, Delbert, and Scott Menard. 1996. "Delinquent Friends and Delinquent Behavior: Temporal and Developmental Patterns." In *Delinquency and Crime: Current Theories,* edited by J. David Hawkins. New York: Cambridge University Press.

Howell, James C., and David Hawkins. 1998. "Prevention of Youth Violence." In *Crime and Justice: An Annual Review of Research,* edited by Michael Tonry and Mark Moore. Chicago: University of Chicago Press.

In re Gault. 387 U.S. 1, 87 S.Ct. 1428 (1967).

LaFave, Wayne R., and Austin W. Scott, Jr. 1972. *Criminal Law.* 2nd ed. St. Paul, Minn.: West.

Morris, Norval. 1982. *Madness and the Criminal Law.* Chicago: University of Chicago Press.

Roper v. Simmons, U.S. (2005).

Stanford v. Kentucky, 492 U.S. 361, 109 S.Ct. 2969 (1989).

Steinberg, Laurence, and Elizabeth Cauffman. 1996. "Maturity of Judgment in Adolescence: Psychosocial Factors in Adolescent Decision Making." *Law and Human Behavior* 20: 249–272.

Zimring, Franklin E. 1981. "Kids, Groups, and Crime: Some Implications of a Well-Known Secret." *Journal of Criminal Law and Criminology* 72: 867–885.

———. 1982. *The Changing Legal World of Adolescence.* New York: Free Press.

———. 1998. *American Youth Violence.* New York: Oxford University Press.

Zimring, Franklin, Joel Eigen, and Sheila O'Malley. 1976. "Punishing Homicide in Philadelphia: Perspectives on the Death Penalty." *University of Chicago Law Review* 43: 227–252.

Notes to Chapter Six

1. C. SHAW & H. MCKAY, *Male Juvenile Delinquency as Group Behavior,* in *Report on the Causes of Crime,* 191–199 [II WICKERSHAM COMM'N REP., NO. 13 (1931)], reprinted as chapter 17 in THE SOCIAL FABRIC OF THE METROPOLIS (J. Short ed. 1971) [hereinafter cited as THE SOCIAL FABRIC].

2. *See* THE SOCIAL FABRIC, at 256, n. 2.

3. D. TAFT & R. ENGLAND, CRIMINOLOGY 180 (4th ed. 1964).

4. VERA INSTITUTE OF JUSTICE, FAMILY COURT DISPOSITION STUDY (1981) (unpublished draft).

5. The Vera study dichotomized juvenile court cases into individual and group events. A case represented an individual charged. *Id.*

6. For general reviews of the literature on this subject *see:* R. HOOD & R. SPARKS, *Subcultural and Gang Delinquency,* in KEY ISSUES IN CRIMINOLOGY 80–109 (1970) (includes data on British and Scandanavian group behavior by age); K. SVERI, *Group Activity,* in 1 SCANDINAVIAN STUDIES IN CRIMINOLOGY 173–185 (C. Christiansen ed. 1965); PRESIDENT'S COMM. ON

JUVENILE DELINQUENCY AND YOUTH CRIME, JUVENILE GANGS (Report of G. Geis 1965).

7. The number of unambiguously serious, particularly violent, offenses in the typical self-report study is quite small. The Philadelphia cohort data apparently include larger numbers of homicide arrests, and rape arrests (14 and 44, respectively). *See* M. WOLFGANG, R. FIGLIO, & T. SELLIN, DELINQUENCY IN A BIRTH COHORT 68–99 (1972). As the authors note, the method of scoring used in this study does not provide information on how many events these arrests represent. *Id.* at 23–24. A separate accounting of armed robbery or assault with deadly weapons was not published. The 193 robbery arrests in the Philadelphia cohort were not classified by event or seriousness, other than in seriousness scores. By contrast, the Rand juvenile court study reported 253 armed robbery arrests that resulted in the 104 case sample that is the basis for figure 4.

8. Juvenile Justice and Delinquency Prevention Act of 1974, Pub. L. No. 93–415, 88 Stat. 1109 (codified at scattered sections of 5, 18, 42 U.S.C.) [hereinafter cited as Juvenile Justice Act].

9. *Id.*

10. *See, e.g.,* F. E. ZIMRING, *American Youth Violence: Issues and Trends,* 1 CRIME & JUST. ANNUAL REV. RESEARCH 67 (1979).

11. Juvenile Justice Act, *supra* note 8, UNIFORM CRIME REPORTS (1974).

12. *See, e.g.,* NATIONAL ACADEMY OF SCIENCE PANEL ON RESEARCH IN DETERRENCE AND INCAPACITATION (FINAL REPORT 1978), for a summary of deterrence literature and methods.

13. *See id.* At 99-103 for a list of more than a dozen studies that use the risk variables displayed in figure 6.6.

14. A particular fear with respect to statistics that generate "artificial deterrence" is that "junk crimes" and "junk arrests," defined as crimes and arrests that are not likely to receive serious sanctions in the adult system, are the major share of variations between cities and over time. If this is the case, variations in juvenile arrests rates could thoroughly confound efforts to assess the general deterrent impact of criminal sanctions over time or in comparative studies.

15. The alternative to this approach, however, is attractive. Given the difference between juvenile and adult criminal sanctions for similar behavior, deterrence theory can exploit wide variations in the age of jurisdiction, and variations in patterns for similar crime, to discover whether individuals respond to differences in risks when they cross over the borderline between juvenile and criminal justice at varying points in their criminal careers.

16. *See, e.g.,* R. SHINNAR & S. SHINNAR, *The Effects of the Criminal Justice System on the Control of Crime: A Quantitative Approach,* 9 LAW & SOC'Y REV. 581 (1975). *See also* J. Q. WILSON, THINKING ABOUT CRIME 198–291 (1975).

17. *See, e.g.,* Shinnar & Shinnar, *supra* note 16; J. PETERSILIA & P. GREENWOOD, CRIMINAL CAREERS OF HABITUAL FELONS (1979). The only mention of the problem of incapacitating one of the group is found in the PANEL ON RESEARCH, *supra* note 12, at 65 *(see* especially n. 63 and the

text accompanying n. 64). In contrast, Albert Reiss has recently demonstrated the impact of group offending on incapacitation effects. A. REISS, *Understanding Changes in Crime Rates,* in CRIME RATES AND VICTIMIZATION 13–14 (A. Reiss & A. Biderman eds. 1980).

18. J. CONKLIN, ROBBERY AND THE CRIMINAL JUSTICE SYSTEM 108 (1972); *see also* the table at 106.

19. P. COOK, *A Strategic Choice Analysis of Robbery,* in SAMPLE SURVEYS OF THE VICTIMS OF CRIME 180 (W. Skogan ed. 1976).

20. The comparison between gun robbers and other robbers charged (see fig. 4.3: 90 percent versus 87 percent multiple offenders) lends further support to this interpretation.

21. *See* F. E. ZIMRING, CONFRONTING YOUTH CRIME: A REPORT OF THE TWENTIETH-CENTURY TASK FORCE ON SENTENCING POLICY TOWARD YOUTH OFFENDERS (1978).

22. *See, e.g.,* S. GLUECK & E. T. GLUECK, FIVE HUNDRED CRIMINAL CAREERS (1930); S. GLUECK & E. T. GLUECK, LATER CRIMINAL CAREERS (1937); S. GLUECK & E. T. GLUECK, CRIMINAL CAREERS IN RETROSPECT (1943) (3 vols. of followup studies on the postrelease careers of 510 inmates of the Massachusetts State Reformatory released in 1921–22).

23. *See, e.g.,* B. BOLAND & J. WILSON, *Age, Crime, and Punishment,* PUBLIC INTEREST, Spring 1978, at 22; J. Q. WILSON, *supra* note 16.

24. For this discussion of the implications of the Wolfgang data (Wolfgang, Figlio, and Sellin, *supra* note 7) on the concentration and predictability of youth violence, *see* F. E. ZIMRING, *supra* note 10, at 94–98.

25. For a preliminary report of the Philadelphia followup study, *see* M. WOLFGANG, *From Boy to Man,* in THE SERIOUS JUVENILE OFFENDER 101 (Hudson & Mack eds. 1978) (proceedings of a National Symposium, Government Printing Office).

26. J. PETERSILIA & P. GREENWOOD, *supra* note 17; a second Rand report, DOING CRIME, utilizes a weighted sample of all prison inmates who retrospectively study preprison careers for currently incarcerated inmates. RAND CORP., DOING CRIME (Apr. 1980).

27. For age specific arrest estimates (with insufficient warnings about this difficulty), *see* F. E. ZIMRING, *supra* note 21, table 1-2, at 37.

28. *See* M. WOLFGANG, R. FIGLIO, & T. SELLIN, *supra* note 7.

29. Office of Children's Services, N.Y. Division of Criminal Justice Services, *cited in* B. BOLAND & J. WILSON, *supra* note 23, at 28 (table 1).

30. *Id.* at 27–28.

31. This estimate was derived by Peter W. Greenwood, in P. Greenwood, J. Petersilia, & F. E. Zimring, Age, Crime, and Sanctions: The Transition from Juvenile to Adult Court (1980), from K. S. Teilmann & M. W. Klein, *Assessment of the Impact of California's 1977 Juvenile Justice Legislation* (1977) (Draft, Social Science Research Institute, University of Southern California).

32. P. GREENWOOD, J. PETERSILIA, & F. E. ZIMRING, *supra* note 31.

33. *See* J. COFFEE, *Privacy versus Parens Patriae: The Role of Police Records in the Sentencing and Surveillance of Juveniles,* 57 CORNELL L. REV. 571, 579–594 (1972), for a discussion of arrests as a means of build-

ing a dossier on juveniles and for discussion of analogous procedures in New York City.

34. F. E. ZIMRING, *supra* note 21, at 65–82.

35. *Id.* at 35–44, 65–82.

36. A first effort to control for offense seriousness by age in Los Angeles is discussed in P. GREENWOOD, J. PETERSILIA, & F. E. ZIMRING, *supra* note 31.

37. M. WOLFGANG, R. FIGLIO, & T. SELLIN, *supra* note 7, at 23–24.

38. *Id.* at 24.

39. My discussion in the text assumes a "modern" definition of delinquency, that is, a status conferred when a minor is found to have committed an act that would have been criminal if performed by an adult. Broader definition of delinquency, including standards such as "in danger of leading an immoral life," or "associating with bad companions," would obviate the necessity for determining the nature of the 12-year-old's participation. *See* INSTITUTE OF JUDICIAL ADMINISTRATION, AMERICAN BAR ASS'N STANDARDS RELATING TO JUVENILE DELINQUENCY AND SANCTIONS (tentative draft 1977) at 17–27 [hereinafter cited as JUVENILE DELINQUENCY AND SANCTIONS].

40. *See*, e.g., Criminal Code of 1961, ILL. REV. STAT. ch. 38, § 5–2 (1980); *see also* F. B. SAYRE, *Criminal/ Responsibility for the Acts if Another,* 43 HARV. L. REV. 689 (1930).

41. This weakness characterizes any research procedure that converts events into seriousness scores and gives the total score to each offender, as well as studies that use offense and arrest. *See*, e.g., M. WOLFGANG, R. FIGLIO, & T. SELLIN, *supra* note 7; P. STRASBURG, VIOLENT DELINQUENTS (1978) (A Report to the Ford Foundation from the Vera Institute of Justice).

42. For example, two of the juvenile justice Standards volumes are closely related to juvenile court policy toward youth crime, but they contain no substantive analysis of the appropriate role of doctrines of accessorial liability, or conspiracy. JUVENILE DELINQUENCY AND SANCTIONS, *supra* note 39, INSTITUTE OF JUDICIAL ADMINISTRATION, AMERICAN BAR ASS'N, STANDARDS RELATING TO DISPOSITION (tentative draft 1977). While the role of peer pressure is not discussed, standard 3.4 argues against delinquency jurisdiction if a parent or guardian coerced a juvenile's participation in a criminal act, JUVENILE DELINQUENCY AND SANCTIONS, *supra* note 39, at 33, commentary. Further, the commentaries in these volumes contain no analysis of patterns of youth crime, the magnitude of the problem, or typologies of youth crime.

Note to Chapter Seven

1. The recent historical pattern turns out, however, to be one where youth adult rates (ages 18–24) paralleled the age 14–17 rates through the initial increase (Cook and Laub 1998, 45).

References to Chapter Seven

Cook, P. J., and John Laub. 1998. "The Unprecedented Epidemic in Youth Violence." *Crime and Justice* 24: 24–64.

Fagan, Jeffrey, Franklin E. Zimring, and June Kim. 1998. "Declining Homicide in New York City: A Tale of Two Trends." *Journal of Criminal Law and Criminology* 88: 1277–1323.

Greenberg, David. 1985. "Age, Crime and Social Explanation." *American Journal of Sociology* 91: 1–21.

Hirschi, Travis, and Michael Gottfredson. 1983. "Age and the Explanation of Crime." *American Journal of Sociology* 89: 552–584.

Steffensmeier, Darrell J., Emilie Allan, Miles Harer, and Cathy Streifel. 1987. "Age and the Distribution of Crime." *American Journal of Sociology* 94: 803–831.

U.S. Bureau of the Census. 1998. *Statistical Abstract of the United States.* Washington, D.C.: Government Printing Office.

U.S. Federal Bureau of Investigation. 1997. *Uniform Crime Reports.* Washington, D.C.: Government Printing Office.

Zimring, Franklin E. 1981. "Kids, Groups, and Crime: Some Implications of a Well-Known Secret." *Journal of Criminal Law and Criminology* 72: 867.

———. 1982. *The Changing Legal World of Adolescence.* New York: Free Press.

———. 1998. *American Youth Violence.* New York: Oxford University Press.

Zimring, Franklin E., and Gordon Hawkins. 1997. *Crime Is Not the Problem: Lethal Violence in America.* New York: Oxford University Press.

References to Chapter Eight

Blumstein, Alfred, and Richard Rosenfeld. 1998. "Explaining Recent Trends in U.S. Homicide Rates." *Journal of Criminal Law and Criminology* 88: 1175–1216.

Council on Crime in America. 1996. *The State of Violent Crime in America: A First Report of the Council on Crime in America.* Washington, D.C.: New Citizenship Project.

Dilulio, John. 1995, November 27. "The Coming of the Super-Predators." *Weekly Standard,* p. 23.

———. 1996. *How to Stop the Coming Crime Wave.* New York: Manhattan Institute.

Fox, James A. 1996. *Trends in Juvenile Violence: A Report to the United States Attorney General on Current and Future Rates of Juvenile Offending.* Boston: Northeastern University Press.

Shannon, Lyle, Judith L. McKim, Kathleen R. Anderson, and William E. Murph. 1991. *Changing Patterns of Delinquency and Crime: A Longitudinal Study in Racine.* Boulder, Colo.: Westview Press.

Snyder, Howard, and Melissa Sickmund. 1995. *Juvenile Offenders and Victims: A National Report.* Washington, D.C.: U.S. Government Printing Office.

U.S. Department of Commerce, Bureau of the Census. 1960–94, 1995. *Current Population Reports: Estimates of the Population of the United States by Age, Sex, and Race.* Washington, D.C.: U.S. Government Printing Office.

U.S. Department of Justice, Federal Bureau of Investigation. 1976–93, 1994, 1995–96. *Crime in the United States.* Washington, D.C.: U.S. Government Printing Office.

Wilson, James Q. 1974. *Thinking about Crime.* New York: Basic Books.

———. 1995. "Crime and Public Policy." In *Crime,* edited by James Q. Wilson and Joan Petersilia. San Francisco: Institute for Contemporary Studies Press.

Wilson, James Q., and Joan Petersilia, eds. 1995. *Crime.* San Francisco: Institute for Contemporary Studies Press.

Wolfgang, Marvin, Robert Figlio, and Thorsten Sellin. 1972. *Delinquency in a Birth Cohort.* Chicago: University of Chicago Press.

Zimring, Franklin E. 1975. "Firearms and Federal Law: The Gun Control Act of 1968." *Journal of Legal Studies* 4: 133–198.

———. 1998. *American Youth Violence.* New York: Oxford University Press.

Zimring, Franklin E., and Gordon Hawkins. 1997. *Crime Is Not the Problem: Lethal Violence in America.* New York: Oxford University Press.

References to Chapter Nine

Friedman, Lee. 2002. "Status Offenders." *A Century of Juvenile Justice.* Chicago: University of Chicago Press.

Furstenberg, F. F., Jr., J. Brooks-Gunn, and S. P. Morgan. 1987. *Adolescent Mothers in Later Life.* Cambridge: Cambridge University Press.

Hamburg, B., and S. L. Dixon, 1992. "Adolescent Pregnancy and Parenthood." In *Early Parenthood and Coming of Age in the 1990s,* edited by Margaret K. Rosenheim and Mark F. Testa. New Brunswick, N.J.: Rutgers University Press.

Hayes, C. D., ed. 1987.*Riding the Future: Adolescent Sexuality, Pregnancy, and Childbearing.* Vol. 1. Washington: National Academy Press.

Luker, K. 1995. *Dubious Conceptions: The Politics of the Teen Pregnancy Crisis.* Cambridge: Harvard University Press.

Schlossman, S. L. *Love and the American Delinquent: The Theory and Practice of Progressive Juvenile Justice, 1825–1920.* Chicago: University of Chicago Press, 1977.

U.S. Bureau of the Census. *U.S. Census of the Population: 1950.* Vol. 2. *Characteristics of the Population.* Pt. 1. *United States Summary.* Washington, D.C.: Government Printing Office, 1953.

Weeks, J. R. 1976. *Teenage Marriages: A Demographic Analysis.* Westport, Conn.: Greenwood Press.

Zimring, F. E. 1982. *The Changing Legal World of Adolescence.* New York: Free Press.

References to Chapter Ten

Allen, Francis A. 1964. *The Borderland of Criminal Justice.* Chicago: University of Chicago Press.

Clauson, Lynda E., and Richard J. Bonnie. 2000. "Juvenile Justice on Appeal." In *The Changing Borders of Juvenile Justice,* edited by Jeffery Fagan and Franklin E. Zimring. Chicago: University of Chicago Press.

Feld, Barry. 1987. "Juvenile Court Meets the Principle of the Offense: Legislative Changes in Juvenile Waiver Statutes." *Journal of Criminal Law and Criminology* 78: 471.

Ferguson, Bruce, and Allan C. Douglas. 1970. "A Study of Juvenile Waiver." *San Diego Law Review* 7: 39–54.

In re Gault, 387 U.S. 1, 87 S. Ct 1428, 18 L. Ed. 2d 527 (1967).

Mack, Julian. 1909. "The Juvenile Court." *Harvard Law Review* 23: 104–122.

Platt, Anthony. 1969. *The Child Savers.* Chicago: University of Chicago Press.

Redding, Richard, and James C. howell. 2000. "Blended Sentenciing in American Julvenile Justice." In *The Changing Borders of Juvenile Justice,* edited by Jeffrey Fagan and Franklin E. Zimring. Chicago: University of Chicago Press.

Schlossman, Steven. 1977. *Love and the American Delinquent: The Theory and Practice of "Progressive" Juvenile Justice, 1825–1920.* Chicago: University of Chicago Press.

Singer, Simon. 1996. *Recriminalizing Delinquency.* New York: Cambridge University Press.

Tonry, Michael. 1996. *Sentencing Matters.* New York: Oxford University Press.

Twentieth Century Fund Task Force on Sentencing Policy toward Young Offenders. 1978. *Confronting Youth Crime.* New York: Twentieth Century Fund.

U. S. Department of Justice. 1998. *Uniform Crime Reports 1977.* Washington: Government Printing Office.

Zeisel, Hans, and Shari Diamond. 1977. "The Search for Sentencing Equity: Sentencing Review in Massachusetts and Connecticut." *American Bar Foundation Journal* 2: 883–940.

Zimring, Franklin E. 1981. "Notes toward a Jurisprudence of Waiver." In *Issues in Juvenile Justice Information and Training,* edited by John Hall, Donna Hamparian, John Pettibone, and Joseph White. Columbus, Ohio: Academy for Contemporary Problems.

———. 1982. *The Changing Legal World of Adolescence.* New York: Free Press.

———. 1991. "The Treatment of Hard Cases in American Juvenile Justice: In Defense of Discretionary Waiver." *Notre Dame Journal of Law, Ethics, and Public Policy* 5: 267–280.

———. 1998. *American Youth Violence.* New York: Oxford University-Press.

———. 2000. "Penal Proportionality for the Young Offender." In *Youth on Trial,* edited by Thomas Grisso and Robert Schwartz. Chicago: University of Chicago Press.

References to Chapter Eleven

Bortner, M.A., Marjorie S. Zatz, and Darnell F. Hawkins. 2000. "Race and Transfer: Empirical Research and Social Context." In *The Changing Borders of Juvenile Justice,* edited by Jeffery Fagan and Franklin E. Zimring. Chicago: University of Chicago Press.

Clauson, Lynda E. Frost, and Richard J. Bonnie. 2000. "Juvenile Justice on Appeal." In *The Changing Borders of Juvenile Justice,* edited by Jeffery Fagan and Franklin E. Zimring. Chicago: University of Chicago Press.

Dawson, Robert O. 2000. "Judicial Waiver in Theory and Practice." In *The Changing Borders of Juvenile Justice,* edited by Jeffery Fagan and Franklin E. Zimring. Chicago: University of Chicago Press.

Empey, LaMar T. 1979. *The Future of Childhood and Juvenile Justice.* Charlottesville: University Press of Virginia.

Fagan, Jeffrey, and Franklin E. Zimring, eds. 2000. *The Changing Borders of Juvenile Justice.* Chicago: University of Chicago Press.

Feld, Barry C. 2000. "Legislative Exclusion of Offenses from Juvenile Court Jurisdiction: A History and Critique." In *The Changing Borders of Juvenile Justice,* edited by Jeffery Fagan and Franklin E. Zimring. Chicago: University of Chicago Press.

Moone, Joseph. 1993. *Children in Custody 1991: Private Facilities. Prevention Fact Sheet 2, 5.* Washington, D.C.: Office of Juvenile Justice and Delinquency Prevention.

National Criminal Justice Information and Statistics Service. 1974. *Children in Custody.* Washington, D.C.: National Criminal Justice Information and Statistics Service.

Titlebaum, Lee. 2002. "Status Offenders." In *A Century of Juvenile Justice,* edited by Margaret Rosenheim, Franklin E. Zimring, David S. Tanenhaus, and Bernardine Dohrn. Chicago: University of Chicago Press.

U.S. Department of Justice, Bureau of the Census. 1997. *Current Population Reports: Estimates of the Population of the United States by Age, Sex, and Race.* Washington, D.C.: U.S. Government Printing Office.

U.S. Department of Justice, Bureau of Justice Statistics. 1974, 1997. *Correctional Populations in the United States.* Washington, D.C.: U.S. Government Printing Office.

U.S. Department of Justice, Bureau of Justice Statistics. 1997. *Children in Custody*. Washington, D.C.: U.S. Government Printing Office.

Zeisel, Hans. 1981. "Race Bias in the Administration of the Death Penalty: The Florida Experience." *Harvard Law Review* 95: 456–468.

Zimring, Franklin E., Gordon Hawkins and Sam Kamin. 2001. *Punishment and Democracy: Three Strikes and You're Out in California*. New York: Oxford University Press.

Washington, D.C.: National Criminal Justice Information and Statistics Service.

References to Chapter Twelve

Gardner, Martin. 1997. *Understanding Juvenile Law*. New York: Matthew Bender.

Greenwood, Peter, Joan Petersilia, and Franklin E. Zimring. 1980. *Age, Crime, and Sanctions: The Transition from Juvenile to Criminal Court*. Santa Monica, Calif.: Rand Corporation.

Hawkins, Gordon, and Franklin E. Zimring. 1989. *Pornography in a Free Society*. New York: Cambridge University Press.

Lott, John, and David Mustard. 1997. "Crime, Deterrence and Right-to-Carry Concealed Handguns." *Journal of Legal Studies* 26: 1–68.

Newton, George, and Franklin E. Zimring. 1969. *Firearms and Violence in American Life*. Task Force Report to the National Commission on the Causes and Prevention of Violence. Washington, D.C.: U.S. Government Printing Office.

Podger, Pamela. 1995, October 18. "Latest Reynolds Effort Will Target Gun Crimes." *Fresno Bee,* p. AI.

Wilson, Pete. 1977, August 25. Letter to the California Senate (returning Senate Bill 669 without signature).

Zimring, Franklin E. 1975. "Firearms and Federal Law: The Gun Control Act of 1968." *Journal of Legal Studies* 4: 133–198.

———. 1982. *The Changing Legal World of Adolescence*. New York: Free Press.

———. 1996. "Kids, Guns, and Homicides: Policy on an Age-Specific Epidemic." *Law and Contemporary Problems* 59: 25–37.

Zimring, Franklin E., and Gordon Hawkins. 1987. *The Citizen's Guide to Gun Control*. New York: Macmillan.

References to Chapter Thirteen

Atkins v. Virginia (2002), 536 U.S. 304.

Dawson, Robert. 1992. "An Empirical Study of Kent Style Juvenile Transfers to Criminal Court." *St. Mary's Journal* 23: 975.

Eigen, Joel. 1981. "The Determinants and Impact of Jurisdictional Transfer in Philadelphia." In *Readings in Public Policy,* edited by John Hall and Donna Hamparian. Columbus, Ohio: Academy for Contemporary Problems.

Feld, Barry. 1998. "Juvenile and Criminal Justice Systems' Responses to Youth Violence." In *Crime and Justice: An Annual Review of Research,* edited by Michael Tonry and Mark Moore. Chicago: University of Chicago Press.

Greenwood, Peter, Joan Petersilia, and Franklin E. Zimring. 1980. *Age, Crime, and Sanctions: The Transition from Juvenile to Criminal Court.* Santa Monica, Calif.: Rand Corporation.

Greenwood, Peter, and Franklin E. Zimring. 1985. *One More Chance: The Pursuit of Promising Intervention Strategies for Chronic Juvenile Offenders.* Santa Monica, Calif.: Rand Corporation.

Gross, Jane. 1997, July 30. "Experts Testify Shabazz Boy Is Psychotic." *New York Times,* p. B1.

Hoversten, Paul. 1997, December 2. "In Kentucky, 'Blood Was Everywhere.'" *USA Today,* p. 3.

Institute for Judicial Administration. 1977. *Standards for Juvenile Justice.* Vols. 1–2. New York: Institute for Judicial Administration.

Kadish, Sanford. 1985. "Complicity, Cause, and Blame." *California Law Review* 73: 323–404.

Morris, Norval. 1974. *The Future of Imprisonment.* Chicago: University of Chicago Press.

Peltier, Michael. 1997, August 29. "Florida Teen Guilty in British Tourist Shooting." *Reuters.*

Roper v. Simmons, 125 S.Ct. 1183 (2005).

Schwartz, Stephen. 1997, June 28. "Accused Killer Will Be Tried as an Adult." *San Francisco Chronicle,* p. A17.

Snyder, Howard, and Melissa Sickmund. 1995. *Juvenile Offenders and Victims: A National Report.* Washington, D.C.: U.S. Government Printing Office.

Thompson v. Oklahoma, 487 U.S. 815 (1988).

U.S. Department of Justice, Federal Bureau of Investigation. 1976–96. *Crime in the United States.* Washington, D.C.: U.S. Government Printing Office.

Vorenberg, James, and Elizabeth Vorenberg. 1973. "Early Diversion from the Criminal Justice System: A Practice in Search of a Theory." In *Prisoners in America,* edited by Lloyd Owin. Englewood Cliffs, N.J.: Prentice Hall.

Walker, Thaai, and Elaine Herscher. 1997, March 12. "Oakland Girl Shot by Schoolmate." *San Francisco Chronicle,* p. A17.

Zimring, Franklin E. 1982. *The Changing Legal World of Adolescence.* New York: Free Press.

Zimring, Franklin E., Joel Eigen, and Sheila O'Malley. 1976. "Punishing Homicide in Philadelphia: Perspectives on the Death Penalty." *University of Chicago Law Review* 43: 227–252.

Zimring, Franklin E., and James Zuehl. 1986. "Victim Injury and Death in Urban Robbery: A Chicago Study." *Journal of Legal Studies* 15: 1–40.

Index

Abbott, Grace, 42
accessorial liability, 89, 90, 203, 214–15
accomplices, 88–90, 124, 214–15
accountability, 21, 44, 54, 68, 140
Addams, Jane, 9, 38, 39, 42
adolescence
  changes in social meaning of, 5–15, 29
  decision-making skills and, 3, 17, 18, 21, 29, 58, 59, 63, 126, 127–28, 130
  as developmental period, 3, 17–22
  individual developmental variants in, 3, 23–27
  "learner's permit" view of, 17–22, 29, 32, 62, 68, 126
  legal conceptions of, 65–68, 69, 126
  modern teenagers and, 12–15, 126–27
  pregnancy and parenting during, 123, 125–37
  See also crime, adolescent
"adolescence-limited" offending, 63
"adolescent society, the," 12, 14
adulthood, skill acquisition for, 17–21, 29, 63, 126
advertence, homicide and, 202
African Americans, 111–14, 120, 160, 162, 169, 171, 172–73
age, 19, 55
  capacity and, 54, 56–57
  capital punishment prohibitions and, 67, 216–17
  as crime pattern factor, 71, 91–103
  demographic change projections and, 106–16, 120
  diminished responsibility and, 61–62, 68, 194, 204, 208–11
  driving privileges and, 24–26, 68
  as group crime factor, 76, 77, 83–84
  gun control initiatives and, 176, 177–83, 186, 187–90

of homicide offenders, 145, 194, 200, 209
for juvenile court jurisdiction, 11, 42, 80, 139, 145–47
legal punishment and, 65–68, 69
of majority, 65–66, 68
of maturity, 20, 51
motion picture rating system and, 26
teen pregnancy/parenting concerns and, 131
transfers to criminal court and, 53
See also minimum age restrictions
age-grading, 23–27, 29
age segregation
  modern adolescence and, 12, 14
  penal facilities and, 156, 207
alcohol consumption, 9, 178, 179, 187–88, 191
Allen, Woody, 195
Amish culture, 17
antismoking campaigns, 134–35, 189
appellate courts, 154, 199, 210
apprehension, risk of, 81
apprehension programs, gun control and, 185–87
arbitrariness, homicide punishments and, 196, 200
arrests
  age distribution of, 82, 86, 91–103
  juvenile homicides and, 112–14, 208–9, 214
  long-term projections of, 106, 118
  recent decline in, 101–2, 121–22
  statistics concerning, 77–78, 79, 86, 88, 90
arson, 71, 91–97, 100, 101, 103
assault, 93, 96, 151, 175, 191
Atkins v. Virginia (2002), 217
Atlanta, Ga., 185
at-risk children
  juvenile court and, 6, 33
  parens patriae doctrine and, 6
  teen pregnancy/parenting and, 132–33, 136–37

parents (*continued*)
  parens patriae doctrine and, 5–6
  in single-parent households, 110,
    115
  teenage, 123, 124, 125–37
  See also family
paternalism, 15
  age-related prohibitions and, 180
  female offenders and, 161, 171
  teen pregnancy/parenting and, 128,
    131–33
pathologies, teen pregnancy/parenting
    and, 128–29
"peer group," origination of term,
    15
peer-management skills, 61
peer orientation, 19
peer pressure, 60–62, 68, 71, 203,
    209–10, 213
penal capacity, 52, 54, 55, 66–67, 68
penal proportionality, 49–69, 156
penal responsibility, 3, 21
personal handicaps, 50–51, 201, 202
phase-specific criminality, 71, 91, 94,
    95, 97, 101, 103
Philadelphia, Pa., 85, 116
philanthropic agencies, 6
physical mobility, 14, 19, 29
Poe, Edgar Allan, 73
pornography, 178, 179
poverty, 110–11
power
  autonomy and, 15
  parental, 8
premeditation, homicide and, 202
prenatal care, 131
preponderance of the evidence, 41
prevention programs
  gun control and, 185–87
  teen pregnancy and, 125–26, 129,
    130, 131–32, 134–37
prisons, 35-36, 42, 43, 173. *See also*
    incarceration
privileges, 3, 21, 68
  strategies for granting, 24–27, 29
probation, 9, 37, 38–39, 202
probation officers, 7
Progressive era, 6–9, 18
Prohibition, 179
proof, standards of, 40–41
property crimes, 71, 91–97, 103
prosecutorial discretion, 89, 140, 150,
    151–53, 169–70, 204

protective programs, teen pregnancy,
    132–34, 137
public policy, 123
  child welfare and, 5–8
  guns, adolescents, and, 176, 177–78,
    181–84
  teen pregnancy/parenting and, 125,
    130–37
  youth crime and, 71, 105, 106
public schools, 3, 6, 8, 11, 12, 18
punishment
  adolescence legal construction and,
    65–68, 69
  age-related prohibitions and, 180
  appropriate determination of, 87–90
  capital. *See* death penalty
  crime categories as determinant of,
    153
  as deterrence factor, 80–82, 142
  for gun law violations, 181, 190–91
  for homicide offenders, 193–202,
    206, 210–12, 216–18
  juvenile court and, 41–42, 50, 55,
    68, 140, 141–49, 170, 213
  mandatory penalties and sentences,
    153, 177
  mitigating conditions for. *See* miti-
    gating conditions
  penal proportionality concerns and,
    49–69, 156
  protection from, 44–47
  punitive theory of transfer and,
    155–56
  reforms for minority offenders and,
    166–68
  Republican legislative initiatives
    and, 44
  risk of, 81
  "room to reform" and, 64, 142,
    193–94, 201, 204–5
  teen pregnancy and, 125
  youth policy as factor, 204–7
  See also criminal sentencing; dimin-
    ished responsibility

race. *See* minority overrepresentation
Racine, Wis., 116
racism, 159
"radical nonintervention" theory, 64
railroad regulation, family regulation
    vs., 7–8
Rand Corporation, 77, 89
rape, 93, 96, 169